Policing
the Wild North-West

Policing
the Wild North-West

A Sociological Study of
the Provincial Police in
Alberta and Saskatchewan
1905–32

ZHIQIU LIN

© 2007 Zhiqiu Lin

Published by the University of Calgary Press

2500 University Drive NW

Calgary, Alberta, Canada T2N 1N4

www.uofcpress.com

No part of this publication may be reproduced, stored in a retrieval system or transmitted, in any form or by any means, without the prior written consent of the publisher or a licence from The Canadian Copyright Licensing Agency (Access Copyright). For an Access Copyright licence, visit www.accesscopyright.ca or call toll free to 1-800-893-5777.

Library and Archives Canada Cataloguing in Publication

Lin, Zhiqiu, 1959-

Policing the wild North-West : a sociological study of the provincial police in Alberta and Saskatchewan, 1905-32 / Zhiqiu Lin.

Includes bibliographical references and index.

ISBN 978-1-55238-171-7

1. Alberta Provincial Police—History. 2. Saskatchewan Provincial Police—History. 3. Police—Alberta—History. 4. Police—Saskatchewan—History. 5. Royal Canadian Mounted Police—History—20th century.

I. Title.

HV8157.L55 2007   363.2097123   C2006-906988-3

We acknowledge the financial support of the Government of Canada, through the Book Publishing Industry Development Program (BPIDP), and the Alberta Foundation for the Arts for our publishing activities. We acknowledge the support of the Canada Council for the Arts for our publishing program. We thank the Alberta Historical Resources Foundation for its support of this project.

Printed and bound in Canada by AGMV Marquis

∞ This book is printed on 60 lb. Rolland Enviro 100 natural text

Cover design, page design and typesetting by Mieka West

Cover photo: Murder Scene, Edmonton, Alberta, October 1929. Glenbow Archives, NC-6-12636g.

For Allisha and Ting

TABLE OF CONTENTS

Acknowledgments   ix

Introduction   1
   The Evolution of Modern Professional Police
   Police and the Evolution of the Objects of Control
   The Effect of Modern Police on Crime Trends
   Conclusion

1 The Creation of the Provincial Police in Alberta and Saskatchewan, 1905–17   25
   The Legal Foundation of Policing in Alberta and Saskatchewan
   The Role of the Royal North-West Mounted Police in the Prairie Provinces, 1905–16
   Explanations for the Creation of the Provincial Police: The Prohibition Thesis versus the War Thesis
   The Creation of the Provincial Police
   Conclusion

2 The Organizational Structures and Operation of the Provincial Police in Alberta and Saskatchewan, 1917–32   47
   The Board of Commissioners of the Alberta Provincial Police
   The Quasi-Military Organizations of the Provincial Police Forces
   The Adoption of Technical Innovations by the APP and the SPP
   Police Independence from Communities and Politics
   Conclusion

3 The Shift in the Objects of Police Control in the Prairie Provinces   67
   The Objects of Provincial Police Control
   The Policing Policy Thesis
   Changes in Criminal Behaviour
   Conclusion

4 Provincial Police Activities in Controlling the "Dangerous Classes" and Serious Crime, 1917–32   85
   The Influx of Foreign Immigrants
   Policing Strikers, Vagrants, and Radicals
   "Canadianizing" Foreign Immigrants

Policing Serious Crime
Empirical Examination of the Correlation
  between Immigration and Crime
Conclusion

5 The Police Enforcement of Prohibition Laws, 1917–24:
  Legitimation Crisis 119
    The Prohibition Legislation
    Police Enforcement of the Prohibition Laws
    Sources of Illegal Liquor: Liquor Export Warehouses
      and Illicit Stills
    Physicians and Druggists as Bootleggers
    Public Discontent and Police Unpopularity
    Conclusion

  Conclusion: The Return of the RCMP 145
    The Federal-Provincial Agreements
    Continuity in Personnel and Equipment
    The Legacy of the SPP
    Farewells to the APP: Popular Reaction
    Continuity in Transition
    Conclusion

  Appendices 171
    Appendix A
      Interrupted Time-Series Analysis for the
      Arrest Rates in Public Order Offences
    Appendix B
      Time Series Regression Methods: Co-integration
      and Error-Correction Models
    Appendix C
      Modelling the Relationship between Crime
      Rates and Police Strength
    Appendix D
      Statistical Examination of the Relationship
      between Immigration and Crimes

  References 195

  Notes 203

  Index 227

ACKNOWLEDGMENTS

Many thanks to those who have helped me in the course of writing this book. I would like to express my wholehearted appreciation to my dissertation supervisor, Dr. Augustine Brannigan, for his support and guidance. His advice and suggestions have immeasurably improved my doctoral dissertation on which this book is based. I want to especially to thank Dr. Frank Atkins for introducing me to co-integration and error-correction methods, as well as Dr. R. Wanner for his advice on various statistical issues and for his constant support and encouragement.

I also wish to acknowledge the assistance I received by the staff of the Provincial Archives of Alberta, the Provincial Archives of Saskatchewan, and the Glenbow Museum, where I did the research for this book. The Provincial Archives of Saskatchewan and the Glenbow Museum also kindly granted me permission to use their collections of photographs of the Provincial Police for this book. This research was made possible by a research grant from the Social Sciences and Humanities Research Council of Canada (SSHRCC). The author also gratefully acknowledges the financial support of the Alberta Historical Resources Foundation, which made the publication of this book possible.

I am grateful to Elaine Grandin and Mark Baron for their friendship and encouragement while I was in Calgary and for their assistance in proofreading drafts of this book. In the preparation of this book, I have also benefited from excellent suggestions by two anonymous reviewers to whom I would like to express my gratitude. I would also like to thank Tiffany Neil for her excellent assistance in editing the bibliography and charts, and in creating the index. Finally I must express my appreciation to my editors at the University of Calgary Press, John King and Peter Enman, for their patience in answering my various questions and for their many valuable editorial suggestions.

INTRODUCTION

"... the notion of the regulation and reconciliation of conflicts through the rule of law ... seems to me a cultural achievement of universal significance."
– E. P. Thompson[1]

The North-West Mounted Police (NWMP) were the first public police, created by Sir John A. Macdonald in 1873 as a temporary measure to enforce law and order in the newly formed North-Western Territories. Macdonald's objective was to "effectively occupy the west for Canada until the growth of population established Canadian ownership beyond any doubt."[2] However, the NWMP, later called the Royal Canadian Mounted Police (RCMP), did more than what Macdonald planned for them; they played an extremely active role in the settlement of western Canada in the latter part of nineteenth century. As a result, the history and image of the NWMP are so tightly woven into the fabric of Western identity that few have realized that for many years, every province of western Canada had its own police force. British Columbia had its provincial police during 1858–1950; Manitoba during 1870–1932; Alberta during 1917–32 and Saskatchewan during 1917–28.[3] This book is about the rise and fall of the provincial police in Alberta (1917–32) and Saskatchewan (1917–28). It investigates the transitions between federal and provincial responsibilities for policing in the two provinces during the period 1905–32 and examines the relationships between police development and the major changes in western Canada associated with immigration and settlement, World War I, prohibition, and the Great Depression.

The 1867 British North American (BNA) Act, following the British legal tradition that law enforcement should be in the hands of local governments, explicitly endowed the provinces with policing power in Canada. In addition to Manitoba and British Columbia, Quebec also created its own police as early as 1870, and Ontario followed suit in 1896. In 1905, when Alberta and Saskatchewan became provinces, the new governments attempted to establish their own police forces. Due to their financial difficulties, however, instead of creating their own police forces, the new governments rented policing services from the Royal North-West Mounted Police (RNWMP).[4]

After the outbreak of World War I, the RNWMP suddenly withdrew from their civil policing duties in the provinces due to the force's serious shortage of experienced officers and increased demand to protect the nation's security. Only then were the provincial governments compelled to establish their own provincial police forces. Due to serious financial crises faced by the provinces about a decade later, however, the Alberta and Saskatchewan governments disbanded their provincial police forces in 1932 and 1928, respectively. Since then, the RCMP have been maintaining law and order in both provinces.

Although the Alberta and Saskatchewan provincial police forces existed only for a relatively short period of time, and little was known about them after their disbandment, they played an important role in the enforcement of law and order and social and economic development in these provinces in their formative years. The provincial police witnessed one of the most fascinating periods of history in western Canada. They experienced World War I, prohibition, the western settlement, the Great Depression, the increasing prevalence of serious crimes, as well as many technical innovations in policing. At the same time, unlike the history of the Manitoba provincial police, about which virtually no documentation was preserved, there exist rich archival materials about the activities of the Alberta and Saskatchewan provincial police forces, including various historical documents and records, as well as statistical data derived from police annual reports.[5] In spite of their fascinating experience and the surviving data, surprisingly, there is virtually no serious research about the forces and their significance in the context of the development of modern police and the settlement of western Canada. This book, based on the rich archival materials, not only recounts the rise and fall of the provincial police forces in Alberta and Saskatchewan, but also investigates a number of questions that have emerged from recent historical studies of policing and the development of modern police forces. These include: what was the relationship between the provincial police development in Alberta and Saskatchewan and the patterns and trends in modern police development elsewhere? How did development of the police interplay with diverse social and political factors? Did the development of policing affect the trends in crime, and if so, how? How did police enforcement of moralist laws affect police popularity and legitimacy? And what was the relationship between police activities and politics in the early part of the twentieth century?[6]

Since the 1960s, a large amount of literature on the evolution of modern police forces has been published. It comprises studies concerned mainly with the history of specific police forces in various social and political contexts, with police behaviour, police reform movements, and the effect of the police on society. The scope and scholarship of these studies varied significantly, as did the intended audiences. Many accounts were the work of retired police chiefs; other contributions were from historians, criminologists, and sociologists. At the theoretical level, the literature has tended to be descriptive and lacks overall analytical and theoretical integrity. Based on the narratives of the development of the provincial police in the two provinces, this book examines various theories and arguments in the studies of modern police. It proposes that the development of the provincial police coincides with a professionalization process over time, although this process is not a linear one.[7]

The exploration of the professionalization process of the provincial forces in this study will be organized around the following three general themes: (1) the professionalization of police forces; (2) the evolution in the objects of police control from the dangerous classes to serious crimes; and (3) the effect of the presence of police on the crime rates. These themes suggest that police institutions in modern societies have adopted the structure of bureaucratic administration; that is, policing has been increasingly conducted according to legal rules and procedures with reference to standards of universality and equity, regardless of ideological and political considerations and ethnic or moral preference. This professionalization process helped police, through the enforcement of the rule of law, to cultivate their legitimation by fostering the belief that they served the interests of a whole community.

THE EVOLUTION OF MODERN PROFESSIONAL POLICE

In the early nineteenth century, professional policing institutions were created to replace the ancient parish watch and constable systems because the latter had proven unable to cope with ever-increasing and widespread lawlessness and social disorder. The emergence of the new police bureaucracies signifies the beginning of the process of professionalization.

Before the establishment of modern professional police, policing was conducted mainly by part-time, amateur parish watchmen and constables. The watchmen and constables acted to prevent all disturbances and disorders, as well as to provide various services, including lighting and repairing street lamps, cleaning streets, and maintaining the towns' sewage systems. They were often armed with rattles for summoning help. The payments for their work did not come from a regular salary, but from the collection of fees resulting from arrests and the other civil actions they performed. From the beginning of the nineteenth century, this system was increasingly incapable of maintaining order. The deteriorating social order was a by-product of the dramatic and profound social and economic changes prompted by the industrial development in manufacturing and the commercialization of agriculture. The birth of full-time, uniformed police was represented by the creation of the London Metropolitan Police (L.M.P.) and the Irish Constabulary (I.C.). These signified the emergence of a new kind of civil power characterized by its location "in a social space midway between an outside military force and the group of people to be controlled."[8]

There are three competing, but not mutually exclusive, arguments concerning the origins of the professional police in modern society. Police historians, including Lane, Palmer, and Silver, argue that the creation of the professional police was primarily a response to the widespread riots and collective violence in the early nineteenth century. This argument is buttressed with evidence from many countries, including the United States, England, Ireland, and Canada. In England the "dangerous classes" (composed of the poor, the transient, the unemployed, and the working class) were identified as a key source of increasing crime and violence.[9] Robert Storch argues that the serious threat of the "dangerous classes" to the existing social order was much imagined by the middle and upper classes. Their apprehension of serious social disorder was generated mainly by a deep rupture in class relations during rapid social changes.[10]

In Ireland the development of the Irish Constabulary was a direct result of the extensive and persistent collective violence in the seventy years after 1780.[11] Roger Lane describes the period when professional police were created in American cities as "the most riotous" in American history. A series of major riots occurred in many large cities, including Boston, New York, and Philadelphia.[12] The creation of the North-West Mounted Police in Canada can also be explained if not by riots, then by the perceived disorder of the Riel Rebellion (1869–70) and crime committed primarily by the native population, frontier settlers, American whisky traders, and rebellious Metis.[13]

However, in Carson's analysis of the development of rural Scottish police, the greatest threat to civil order arose from the vagrancy – new classes of the wandering poor – created by industrial development and the commercialization of agriculture. The problem of vagrancy became so serious that it represented "almost an alternative lifestyle in early nineteenth century Scotland."[14] The fact that the uniformed police were created to suppress vagrancy had less to do with the universal trends in imposing the new social order upon the previously unregulated than with locally pragmatic concerns.

Because of the perceived connection between vagrancy and crime in the places where vagrants congregated, the land depreciated in value. Reducing vagrancy and crime for the protection of the value of property in local communities was a critical factor in the rise of police in rural Scotland during the first half of the nineteenth century. Financial burden was another important reason to suppress vagrancy. According to the Scottish Poor Law prior to 1845, the parishes had responsibility for supporting the "legal poor" in rural Scotland.[15] The poor were supported using money collected through the parish landholders and the inhabitants. When vagrancy expanded at an unprecedented rate, it became cheaper to use police to remove them from their communities than to support them on charity.

The validity of the riot and vagrancy theses does not preclude the contribution of other factors. J.J. Tobias views the spread of the police in nineteenth-century England in connection with the rapid urban growth that characterized this period.[16] This framework has been fruitfully employed by Monkkonen to explain the development of American city police in the nineteenth century. According to Monkkonen, the adoption of a professional police model evolved hand in hand with the establishment of new towns and cities in the United States. City officials usually looked at the municipal operations of larger cities for practical suggestions to manage their own communities. Once the professional model appeared, it spread by diffusion.[17]

Although historians like Lane, Silver, and Monkkonen identify the broad social context in which the police were created, they fail to offer mechanisms that can account for the actual process of the formation of the police in specific communities. Based on the San Francisco record, P.J. Ethington demonstrates that it was political factors, specifically the vigilance movements in 1856 and 1877, that "provide us with the crucial mediation needed to bridge the gap between trends in law enforcement, class conflicts – indeed any such generality – and the specific implementation of a specific set of institutional characteristics."[18] Helen Boritch makes similar points. The police reform movement in nineteenth-century Toronto was prompted directly by the expansion of the "dangerous classes." But a more local process had a decisive impact upon the evolution of policing. This process involved "the dynamic interplay between bureaucratic concern with legitimation, self-maintenance and self-determination on the one hand and the competing demands imposed by local politicians and middle-class reformers on the other."[19] Ethington and Boritch's analyses suggest that patterns in the development of the police can be understood only by recognizing how the local forces were formed in context of the larger social movements. In San Francisco the change was initiated by middle-class vigilance groups. In Toronto the reform was spurred by a more constitutional change engineered by middle-class interests. However, there was a move toward professional policing throughout the English-speaking world.

These three different theses – riots, vagrancy, and diffusion – are not mutually exclusive. The initial creation of the professional police in different societies was related in various degrees to the efficient control of the dangerous classes, including vagrants. However, this function was performed by the police in the name of the rule of law and, as such, it entailed the imposition of universalistic values on the lower orders of society. A nominally impartial bureaucratic organization was the ideal structure to perform such a function.

The London Metropolitan Police and the Irish Constabulary are considered the two prototypes of the modern professional police. The former was created by the Home Secretary, Robert Peel, in 1829; and the latter was established by several English politicians, including Robert Peel, in 1822. Compared with the ancient parish watching system, the distinctive features of these police organizations were their greater emphases on police legitimation and efficiency.

The London Metropolitan Police were an unarmed, civilian police force. The major task of the police was to control crime and various offences against laws as well as to maintain order. In contrast, the Irish Constabulary (I.C.) were a quasi-military police force designed to replace the British Army in suppressing a series of rebellions against British rule in Ireland. The repressive nature of the I.C. was characterized by the fact that they were armed heavily with rifles and carbines and that the members of the force were trained, distributed, and disciplined according to military rule. Unlike the Metropolitan Police, the Irish Constabulary were also designed to cope with a wide range of problems. Richard Hawkins lists about twenty routine duties performed by the Constabulary, such as enforcement of varied local regulations (including Spirits Acts, Town Improvement Acts, Acts for the Protection of Children and Animals), collecting and compiling agricultural statistics, executing warrants, preventing the spread of farm animal diseases, and conducting a host of investigations for various departments.[20]

Both police forces were uniformed. The London Metropolitan Police adopted dark blue uniforms. The members of the Irish Constabulary wore military-style khaki dress. The Commissioners of the London Metropolitan Police believed that by wearing uniforms, the force could avoid the charges of "an army of spies," deter criminals, and aid in the control of crowds.[21] The Irish Constabulary were controlled by the Dublin Parliament; and the London Metropolitan Police by the Home Office. The fact that the police forces were controlled by the central governments marked a departure from the English traditions in which borough and county police had always been in the hands of local authorities. Both forces were organized along military lines with ranks of officers (superintendents and inspectors), non-commissioned officers (sergeants), and "men" (constables). The police district consisted of divisions. Nevertheless, contrary to the practice in the British Imperial Army, an officer class was created solely on promotion by merit. The London Metropolitan Police had no restriction on marriage in their recruitment standards because the Commissioners believed that married constables were "steadier" than bachelors.[22]

Both the London Metropolitan Police and the Irish Constabulary emphasized moral cooperation with civil society and attended to legitimacy in order to improve their efficiency. In theory, the functions of the police can be efficiently realized only with the moral cooperation of civil society. Silver writes that "the police ... rely not only on a technique of graduated discretionary, and ubiquitous coercion but also on a new and unprecedentedly extensive form of moral consensus."[23] In other words, the ability of police to supervise daily life requires a pervasive moral assent from the governed. Miller goes even further to say that "the police have an active role in creating their own public image, and in fact many people's perception of the government derives from their contact with its lowest level of authority, the policeman."[24]

Traditionally, sociologists have emphasized the importance of the moral consensus of the population. Durkheim argues that crime is "an act which is criminal when it offends the strong, well-defined states of the collective consciousness."[25] However, as societies modernized the moral consensus of societies with mechanical solidarity fragmented. Historians, like Walker and Lane, argue that in modern society there was little moral consensus from the population on the issues of what laws should be enforced, what order should be maintained, and who should enforce it and how.[26]

Silver believes that the police could "evoke, establish, and sustain that assent."[27] Miller also writes that

> ... in societies with representative governments, the police must obtain and then utilize voluntary compliance with their authority. Effective law enforcement requires general agreement that the power of the police is legitimate.... Public sympathy and support are by no means automatic; the police must work to achieve and maintain legitimacy.[28]

For Weber, legitimation is the process by which authority obtains consensus from the population.[29] Legitimation of police power is a complex process influenced by the ideological, political, and economic contexts in which the police operate. Because the early populations reacted to the police according to their social positions and political beliefs, different police forces had to find their own ways to establish consensus. The London Metropolitan Police emphasized impartiality in discharging their duties. They presented themselves as representatives of the government, the impersonal authority. The power of the police was itself restrained by the rule of law.

In comparison, the Irish Constabulary adopted a different strategy to promote legitimacy. From the perspective of the I.C., personal connections of its members with the communities they served were a primary source of *biased* law enforcement. The force was explicitly separated from the community. Police constables were stationed in detached barracks rather than at home in the communities. The officers were not allowed to serve in a community in which they had family connections or businesses. They were subject to periodic changes of district. To avoid involvement in local politics, the officers could not vote in local elections. By contrast, the Commissioners of the London Metropolitan Police adopted a policy assigning constables to the divisions where their homes were, since they had the "advantage of knowing the inhabitants."[30]

There are several reasons for the disparities between the two forces. The creation of the quasi-military model of the I.C. by the Chief Secretaries (who were British politicians) in Ireland, but not in England, was because Ireland was treated and occupied to some extent as a British colony and because the mobility of the I.C. appeared more appropriate for rural conditions in Ireland. In addition, rural communities in Ireland were more fractiously rebellious than urban communities in England. Palmer provides statistics supporting this argument.[31] In rural Ireland, crime tended to be collective, chronic, community-supported, and violent. It was at times difficult to distinguish from political protest. These social conditions in Ireland led the British politicians to create a military-style police force, the I.C. which could be repressive. Such a force was politically unacceptable in the mother country, England, not only because of the hostile social attitude of the population to such a force, but also because a mobile force was inappropriate in the urban environment of London. In addition, in England, crime was mainly property related and there were lower levels of interpersonal violence.

The military-style policing in Ireland was also consistent with public familiarities with military presence in Irish communities. There had long been a standing army in Ireland prior to the establishment of the Irish Constabulary, to suppress a succession of Irish rebellions, agrarian crime, and to protect England's western islands from French and Spanish invasions. But, this was not so in England. By not militarizing the London Metropolitan Police, Robert Peel allayed Englishmen's resistance to the introduction of the "new police." And by devising a military style force in Ireland, the social control function merely devolved from a formal army to a paramilitary bureaucracy.

The influence of the L.M.P. and the I.C. on colonial policing was profound. In many colonial states, the police were established not only as an agency to police the population, but also as the first institution that represented colonial governments. Sir Charles Jeffries and later Stanley Palmer asserted that the London Metropolitan Police served as the "model" for urban police and the Irish Constabulary for rural forces in the British

Empire. They emphasized the impact of the Irish Constabulary.[32] Jeffries explains that

> ... the really effective influence upon the development of colonial police forces during the nineteenth century was not that of the police of Great Britain but that of the Royal Irish Constabulary.... Into the merits or demerits of this system, as applied to Ireland, it is not for me to enter; but it is clear enough that from the point of view of the colonies there was much attraction in an arrangement which provided what we should now call a *para-military* organization or gendarmerie, armed, and trained to operate as an agent of the central government in a country where the population was predominantly rural, communications were poor, social conditions were largely primitive, and the recourse to violence by members of the public who were *agin the government* was not infrequent. It was natural that such a force, rather than one organized on the lines of the purely civilian and localised forces of Great Britain, should have been taken as a suitable model for adoption to Colonial conditions.[33]

The colonial police were mainly modelled after the I.C. not only because the I.C. were appropriate to the primitive or rural conditions in the British colonies, but also because a military-style police force was more effective in helping the colonial states to govern the population, i.e., to impose the rule of law on the colonial population. However, the colonial police were also profoundly shaped by the colonial reality. Anderson and Killingray point out that, like other hybrid legal and administrative systems in the colonies, the colonial police came "to acquire certain distinctive features," which not only made their evolution different from the Irish Constabulary, but also different from one another.[34]

The existing research on modern police forces, especially in the English world, suggests that the evolution of the police was a professionalization process. Weber suggests that "bureaucracy is the means of transforming social action into rationally organized action."[35] It is the most efficient form of organization in the performance of routinized tasks. Weber points out that

> ... the decisive reason for the advance of bureaucratic organization has always been its purely *technical* superiority over any other form of organization. The fully developed bureaucratic apparatus compares with other organisations exactly as does the machine with the non-mechanical modes of production. Precision, speed, unambiguity, knowledge of the files, continuity, discretion, unity, strict subordination, reduction of friction and of material and personal

costs – these are raised to the optimum point in the strictly bureaucratic administration.[36]

The replacement of the part-time, amateur parish watchmen with the full-time, uniformed police signified the birth of the modern professional police. Both the L.M.P. and I.C. adopted the structure of bureaucratic organization in a Weberian sense. These forces emphasized the discharge of police duties according to rules and procedures in order to eliminate personal biases and political interference. The advance of bureaucratic organization in modern society is the explicit manifestation of the process of professionalization.

However, the adoption of the bureaucratic organization does not mean that the police automatically obtain their legitimacy. The Irish Constabulary was a case in point. The military style of the police reflected the repressive status of the force in Ireland. The primary activities of the I.C. were to impose English imperial law and moral order on the Irish, if necessary, by force. Although the I.C. adopted bureaucratic administration and other measures to promote impartiality, the police force never won the confidence of the Irish population. This raises an important point: the attainment of legitimation does not derive solely from bureaucratic organization, but also depends on police activities and the way in which they define the objects of laws and social control.

POLICE AND THE EVOLUTION OF
THE OBJECTS OF CONTROL

The second grand theme in police studies concerns the evolution of the focus of police control, particularly the shift from a focus on the dangerous classes (i.e., class control) to a more universalistic process of crime control. Since their creation, the professional police have performed many duties, such as enforcing laws, maintaining order, preventing crime, issuing various permits and licences, and conducting prosecutions. In the colonial state, the police also tended to act as representatives of the political authority of the state.[37] Although police priorities varied in place and time, the control of the "dangerous classes" and later the prevention of crime were the most common police activities in police history. The transition in police focus from the dangerous classes to crime control is a further manifestation of the professionalization of police function.

As we discussed earlier, the police were frequently thought to have evolved into a professional bureaucracy because of the real and imagined threat from the urban dangerous classes and the rural vagrants. This implies that the main role of the police was social control of the margins on the behalf of the elites. From this perspective, society consisted fundamentally of two groups: the ruling elites and the subordinate groups of society. In this social context, policing activities were highly class-oriented and social control was directed primarily against the threatening conduct, not all of which consisted of serious crime. There were a variety of ways to control the dangerous classes in police history. Ironically, as police evolved, the dangerous classes came to include not only traditional vagrants, rioters, thieves, and immigrants, but also radical workers.

Based on an analysis of U.S. cities from 1865 to 1915, Sidney L. Harring argues that the primary function of the police in the last century was to suppress strikes during industrial disputes and to regulate workers' recreational behaviour, such as drinking, dancing, and gambling.[38] The police, as a capitalist institution, played a central role in the making of a class society. Bruce C. Johnson rejects such a one-dimensional picture. Johnson points out that the police role during industrial conflicts was not determined solely by the interests of local capitalists. In ordinary small American towns, the local police actually supported workers' strikes, while in company towns, the police frequently suppressed the strikes. The police role varied according to "the political and cultural setting."[39]

Although police work was determined by the nineteenth-century social structures within which social inequalities thrived, Monkkonen believes that there was at least an element of value neutrality in police work. This was because the police controlled the dangerous classes not only in a punitive fashion, but in humane ways. The humane aspect of police work derived from the fact that the police provided a broad range of welfare services such as lodging for tramps and food to the indigent.[40] At the same time, the police frequently exercised the repressive power of arrest over the dangerous classes. The primary purpose of the police was to protect stability and the social order through the enforcement of laws. However, the population formed the notion that they had an equal right to be protected from the distress of urban industrial life and from its crime and violence. The police in fact provided such protection for the population. This was an unexpected consequence of the organizational structure and physical presence of the police. Muraskin interprets the police activities of helping the poor as an explicit objective of members of the propertied class to promote progress and human betterment.[41]

The idea that police exclusively served the class struggle between the bourgeoisie and working class oversimplifies reality. This working class was extremely varied, especially in the new world populated with immigrants of tremendous ethnic diversity. The relationship between the police and the public varied considerably in different communities. All studies agree upon one point: the subordinate groups were not only the subject of the police control, but also the beneficiary of the services provided by the police. The humane dimension of the police services had the ability to neutralize the punitive aspects of police work and cultivated the sense that the police acted for interests of the whole community.

An important way of controlling the "dangerous classes" was to impose a new moral order over those classes. Silver writes that "the power of the police over mass disorder, stems not only from superior organization and the rational application of force but also from its presence as the official representative of the moral order in daily life."[42] In nineteenth-century England, it was argued that social regulations would help to "civilize" the dangerous classes. In Canada, Macleod shows that the function of the North-West Mounted Police was to "Canadianize" the "dangerous classes" – the natives and the immigrants from central Europe and the United States.[43] Storch characterized the role of imposition of moral order as "an all-purpose lever of urban discipline." He writes:

... a great deal of the bitterness against the new police was a consequence of the fact that they were placed among the working class to monitor all phases of working-class life – trade-union activities, drinking, gambling, sports as well as political activity. The overall mission of the police was to place working-class neighbourhoods under a constant and multifaceted surveillance.[44]

In this sense, Storch calls the policeman a "domestic missionary." Silver suggests that "in a broader sense, [the police] represented the penetration and continual presence of central political authority through daily life."[45] The police were established to fill the social control vacuum created by industrial development which "separated class from class and eroded away older, more personal mechanisms of social control."[46] Police surveillance signified a deep penetration of the political authority of the state into daily life. The professionalization of control which evolved with the police role also entailed *moralization* of working-class life.[47]

However, control of the dangerous classes was not constant. Police work shifted in response to the conditions transforming society during the late nineteenth century. Monkkonen writes that "the police changed from an agency controlling a class of people through both positive and coercive means to an agency controlling a specific class of behaviour."[48] This change in focus varied to some extent in both locations and times. In some cities, the police focused more on serious criminal behaviour and on crime prevention. In others, assisting the vulnerable classes became a major concern.

Monkkonen first suggests the occurrence of the transition in police function in his study of police activities in twenty-three American cities during the period 1860–1920.[49] Especially after the 1890s, the "dangerous classes" increasingly became the mandate of the newly established social welfare and social service departments of the municipalities. The poor and the marginal were no longer viewed as hazards to order but as vulnerable to privation. For police, crime control increasingly replaced social control and class control.

This transition was suggested by the decline in arrest rates for public order offences and the increase in homicide arrest rates. Monkkonen argues that the transformation was completed by the 1920s and that it represented the second major transformation in the role of professional policing.[50]

Based on the data collected from Toronto in the period 1859–1955, Boritch and Hagan examined Monkkonen's transformation thesis.[51] The findings suggest the occurrence of a similar pattern in Toronto. The transition was prompted by two major interrelated factors: (1) technological innovations concerning communication and information systems in the late nineteenth century; and (2) the creation of various government welfare and service bureaucracies. However, the timing of the transformation in Toronto was much later than that suggested by Monkkonen. Boritch and Hagan argue that the variation on the timing of the change is due to Monkkonen's questionable definition of public order offences. Public order offences used in Monkkonen's research include drunkenness, disorderly conduct, and vagrancy. This definition does not take into account historical changes in the concept of public order. Boritch and Hagan write:

... our most important finding is that the focus of the police varied across different kinds of public order offences depending on the specific historical context. As one type of problem behaviour and one part of the *dangerous classes* receded from police attention, another type of public order offence replaced it.[52]

While the arrest rates for drunkenness, disorderly conduct, and vagrancy dropped, the arrest rates for other public order offences, such as prostitution, gambling, and city bylaw violations, might increase. By ignoring such historical shifts in definition, Monkkonen oversimplifies the transition.[53] Weinberger and Reinke's study dismisses the applicability of Monkkonen's theory of the changing model of policing in some European cities. Strong evidence from Manchester in England and Wuppertal in Germany shows that both crime control and class control were major tasks of the police in the early twentieth century.[54]

Weinberger and Reinke's discussions of the reasons why the transformation did not occur point to the importance of ideological and political contexts in shaping the police roles in society. In the beginning of the establishment of the police in Manchester, in order to obtain the moral assent of the community, the police took a range of administrative tasks as their duties to cultivate a cooperative relationship with welfare organizations. Those services provided by the police played an important role in legitimating police power. Even after the turn of the twentieth century, such social service functions were held to be valuable for both the police and the community and earned the respect of the public. In Wuppertal, a similar multi-dimensional definition of police work was maintained.

Since the creation of modern professional police, political battles over control of the police have always existed. The purpose of the long-lasting reform movement toward professional police in the U.S. cities in the late nineteenth century was mainly to remove political interference from the management of police work. Macleod points out that police activities must be responsive to the changing demands of political systems as well as to the elected representatives of the people. It seems that political influence is unavoidable. The central issue here is how much political influence on the police is proper. Macleod explains that "to give politicians in power too much control over the police is to risk having them use law enforcement as an excuse to stifle opposition."[55]

In the case of the NWMP, the I.C., and the L.M.P., the police were controlled by national politicians. The most frequent contacts between the police and politics were primarily through patronage appointments, promotions, and in some cases, placement of officers, noncommissioned officers, and constables. The direct intervention of politicians in police work was kept to a minimum. However, for many police forces, the influence of local politics was detrimental. This was because the police always had to respond to local politicians through enforcing the laws enacted by those politicians – whether popular or unpopular. In the early nineteenth century, typically, unpopular laws comprised moralistic legislation containing middle-class values and norms. The liquor laws in the prohibition movement in the nineteenth and early twentieth century in North America are a case in point. The prohibition movement was a product of ethnocultural differences. Gusfield treats the prohibition movement as "a reflection of clashes and conflicts between rival social systems, cultures, and status groups."[56] It has also been "both a protest against a changing status system and a mechanism for reflecting the distributions of prestige."[57] Following Gusfield, Lane also argues that for politicians the results of those battles over the sale of liquor had both symbolic and material consequences. The right to grant or deny liquor sales was measured "in dollars as well as other power."[58]

Walker points out that the problem of enforcing unpopular law constantly troubled the police because the source of unpopular law was always political.[59] Both in Canada and the United States, there were different policies in different provinces or states regarding liquor sales, ranging from absolute prohibition to free licence. However, the responsibility for enforcing these policies fell to the police. As a result of the laws, police work became very controversial. The NWMP's experience with the enforcement of liquor law illustrates this point.

The NWMP experienced a great deal of difficulty in enforcing the liquor law in the Northwest Territories. After 1885, the new settlers from Europe and the United States fiercely resented prohibition. The resentment was directed at the NWMP who were responsible for enforcing the law. The police found themselves in a very difficult situation in which they could not properly perform their other routine duties because of their unpopularity. Macleod notes that "the situation for the force was much more serious than the discomfort caused by unpopularity. The police knew that their success in controlling more serious crime was directly proportional to the amount of co-operation they received from the public."[60]

The shift of police focus from the dangerous classes to crime symbolized a further professionalization of modern police. This transition suggests that policing moved away from a value-oriented approach to social control.[61] Unlike police control of the dangerous classes, police activities in the prevention of crime and apprehension of criminals had universal significance as police activities were clearly directed by unambiguous laws and the police and the public had a similar perception of crime, particularly serious crime.

The distinction between control of dangerous classes and control of serious crime has special significance in the context of discussion of the legitimation of police. The proportion of class control to crime control in policing has a direct bearing on the extent of legitimation of police authority. A greater extent of crime control allows police to gain a greater amount of legitimation among the policed population; the same is not true for class control. This is because crime control emphasizes unambiguous rules and procedures rather than ambiguous ideological, moral, and political values and preference. It is easier for the police to cultivate consensus with the public in the process of crime control. In comparison, class control could be divisive and arbitrary and calls into question the impartiality of justice and of the police.

However, social services rendered by the police directed towards the vulnerable classes and the poor appear to be beneficial to maintaining police legitimacy. This suggests that the professionalization of police work and the specialization on crime control will not mean that all "community-based" policing will be made irrelevant. Redefining the dangerous classes as vulnerable classes permits a moral agenda to persist, especially when conceptualized in a utilitarian fashion.

THE EFFECT OF MODERN POLICE ON CRIME TRENDS

The third grand theme in police studies is the impact of modern professional police on crime rates. Compared with the ancient parish watches, modern policing institutions seemed to have more impact on society. However, the assessment of actual effect of the police in an overall sense is a difficult task. In the last decades, historians and sociologists have begun to measure the impact of the police upon the trends in crime and violence in the past 150 years. In this section, we will discuss historical trends in crime and violence and the association between policing and crime trends, as well as the impact of other social and economic factors on crime rates.

Lane describes the crime trends in the last 150 years as a U-shaped curve. This curve suggests that there was a gradual decline in serious crime through the nineteenth century, followed by a rise in the last decades of the nineteenth century. However, the pattern seems to be a much simplified description of a complex reality.[62] Gurr examines the U-shaped curve hypothesis by surveying more than one hundred publications on crime. British crime history indicates that incidence in assault, murder, and manslaughter in London and all parts of England have declined for the most part of the last two centuries, but increased after 1950. New Zealand also experienced a similar trend in various violent crimes.[63]

In the United States as a whole, the central feature of crime trends is the occurrence of three great surges of interpersonal violence circa 1860, 1900, and 1960. These waves make it difficult to conclude whether the crime rate tended to decline in the long run. The long-term tendency in homicide rates has been downward until recent years in America. This trend can also be found in most other Western countries and some Eastern European states and Japan. The trends in assault and robbery are consistent with the trend in homicide in most Western countries, except France, Germany, and some states in the United States. Therefore, Gurr correctly points out that

> ... the thesis that rates of serious crime in Western societies have traced a reversing U-shaped curve is a simplification of a much more complex reality. It characterizes some but not all offences. The evidence for it is substantial in some societies, especially the English-speaking and Scandinavian countries, but either lacking or contradictory in others.[64]

Some students of crime history have attempted to discover explanations for the long-term trends in the Western crime. A variety of factors have been studied including various social institutions and social movements. As police gradually shifted their focus to crime control at the end of the last century, policing began to be thought of as an important factor explaining the trends in crime. Monkkonen argues that there is a close relationship between the strength of police forces and the level of crime. He proposes that "an increase in policing represses crime."[65]

Gurr's findings, based on the data from London, Stockholm, and New South Wales in the period 1829–1970 suggest that increased policing had an effect upon crime rates relating to interpersonal violence.[66] Gillis's study on the national police in France during the period 1865–1913 suggests that an increase in policing would immediately produce more arrests but would deter crime in the longer term. Gillis writes that "the initial effect of policing on crime may be positive and subsequent ones negative. If this eventual deterrence outweighs the initial inflationary effect, crime rates will decline with increased policing."[67]

Various studies also attempt to explain a long-term decline in public order offences.[68] Monkkonen believes that a decline in the offences was not because of the behavioural change of the offenders, but because of the changes in policing policies.[69] He argues that "the measure of police behaviour is, of course, variation in arrests." The changes in the arrest rates in American cities during the period 1860–1920 are an indication of changes in the role of policing and in the structure and behaviour of the police bureaucracies, rather than the variations in actual offences.

For Watts, the police always give serious crime the top priority in their work. Watts argues that in the period when the police focused on serious crime fighting they devoted relatively less time and effort to public order offences. Changes in police policies and practice associated with an alarming increase in serious crime provide a plausible explanation of the decline in public disorder arrests.[70]

In addition to the long-term crime trend, studies of crime history also suggest that there are numerous factors that affect short-term crime trends. These include wars, economic recessions, ethnocultural and class conflict, changing standards and demands for control, the use of urban spaces, urbanization, the rise and decline of Victorianism, legal change, and levels of alcohol consumption and public drunkenness.

Urbanization has been widely accepted by historians and sociologists as a significant correlate of the growth of crime. However, Lane's study of the data from Massachusetts in the nineteenth century provides little evidence for such a theory. He argues that the growth of cities has civilized people's social behaviour.[71] Ferdinand's study shows that the level of economic activity has an inverse correlation with rates of robbery, burglary, larcenies, and assaults and seems to have had little effect on murder and manslaughter.[72] Major wars appear to have depressed major crime, while forcible rape changed directly with economic prosperity. Fairburn and Haslett's study suggests that there was a different level of violent crime in New Zealand and England during the period 1853–1940 related to different levels of social organization and Englishmen at home versus in the colonial state.[73]

The research by Monkkonen, Gillis, and Gurr suggests that policing has had a deterrent effect on some serious crimes in the long term. However, it is difficult to control for other factors, including short-term factors. Concerning the trends in public order offences, the central issue is how to interpret the decline in the rates of these offences: as a real decline or as a change in patterns of control? It is very difficult to find precise answers for these questions.

CONCLUSION

The development of the modern police is a professionalization process. This process manifested itself in three interrelated developments: the emergence and development of professional police, the shift of the police focus of control, and the impact of modern policing on crime rates. These grand narratives suggest that police institutions in modern societies have adopted the structure of bureaucratic administration. Policing has been increasingly conducted according to legal rules and procedures with reference to standards of universality and equity, regardless of ideological and political considerations, and ethnic or moral preference. This professionalization process assisted police in cultivating their legitimation – a belief that the police served the interests of a whole community.

The professionalization of policing is reflected first in the creation of a modern uniformed professional police. There was not a universal reason for the creation of the police in all places and times. The control of the dangerous classes was a common activity that the new police performed initially after their creation. At first, these police activities were highly class-biased. The most important characteristics of modern professional police are their bureaucratic organizations. The merits of such organizations are their capacity to eliminate political and ideological influence on police activities by emphasizing the autonomy of the rule of law. This bureaucratic administration presented police institutions as an independent and impartial authority enforcing law and order in society. Therefore, the professional police were able to carry out the activities of controlling the dangerous classes in the name of service to the interests of the whole community.

The second major development in modern policing was the shift of police function from class control to crime control. The original police function of controlling the dangerous classes was structured by class-bound rules and procedures. Subsequently, by shifting to the control of serious crime, police activities were conducted increasingly by reference to the rule of law and procedures of conduct containing standards of universality and equity. Police became increasingly independent of political and ideological influence. Police increased their ability to create "a sense of the justice of existing arrangements ... thereby fostering a sense of community and consent in a society of conflicting [social groups]."[74] Consequently, policing institutions were more capable of legitimizing themselves among the policed population as neutral managerial institutions. This professionalization process of policing is consistent with E.P. Thompson's argument that "the notion of the regulation and reconciliation of conflict through the rule of law ... seems to me a cultural achievement of universal significance."[75]

However, the legitimation of the police was a complex, interactive, and ongoing negotiation process. This process required the police to use their judgment and creativity. Police legitimation was concerned not only with professionalized police organization and police activities, but also with the needs of communities in which police were active. Police were required constantly to adjust their activities to meet the demands of the communities. Although few police acts stipulated that police were to provide social services to the policed population, many police forces in different societies continued to assist the "vulnerable classes" as successors to the "dangerous classes" early in the nineteenth century. This is the reason why many police forces continued to provide social services long after the force had shifted their focus from repressive class control to crime control.

As a result of the professionalization of policing, the police were concerned increasingly with crime. Although several studies suggest that there were clear deterrent effects on crime, the correlation between policing and crime rates over a long period of time is a complex issue. In theory, replacement of the old parish watch system with the bureaucratic police should have had a significant impact on crime rates. But it is almost impossible to examine this argument since there are few systematic crime statistics available before the formation of modern professional police. At the same time, crime rates were related not only to policing, but also with many other social factors. Because the social factors cannot always be measured completely, a confident isolation of the effect of policing on crime trends from the effect of other factors is never easy. Compared to the impact of the other measures of modern discipline, it is not clear how much the police can account for the declining trends in crime. Even so, in this book we explore the impact of changes in police forces, police strength, and alternative police policies on different trends of crime in the period 1905–50. This period allows some comparisons to be drawn between the Northwest Mounted Police, the provincial police, and the RCMP on crime in Alberta and Saskatchewan.

Although we attempt to apply the concept of professionalization to examine police history, it does not follow that we can dismiss the huge complexities of history as highlighted by E.P. Thompson.[76] The argument of police development as a professionalization process is merely an analytical vehicle and a theoretical perspective. We will make no attempt to treat the theory as a doctrine in which every event in police history fits the professionalization theme. On the contrary, we simply argue that there were possibilities that police development followed general professionalization trends as these trends have already been recognized in other spheres of social life in modern society. The development of the police was a very complex social process. The police were not only agencies transforming societies, but were themselves subject to the influence of many social and political factors. Because of such complexities, the professionalization process cannot be linear. Politicians often attempted to transform police into part of their political machines. At the same time, police frequently had to respond to government policies as well as community needs. This meant that police development had its own dynamics in the short run, in additional to this general trend toward professionalization in the long run.

Following this general conceptual framework, in this book, we will inquire into a number of interrelated key issues under the three general themes outlined in this chapter, including (1) the formation and organization of the police in each province, (2) the effect of the different police forces on the changes in the objects of control (immigrants and serious criminals), (3) the problem of controlling morality during prohibition and the implication of this for legitimacy, and (4) the impact of the police on crime and, particularly, the effect of shifting agendas of control associated with changes from the RNWMP, to the "provos," to the RCMP as each force enjoyed hegemony in the two provinces.

1   THE CREATION OF THE PROVINCIAL POLICE IN ALBERTA AND SASKATCHEWAN, 1905–17

The North-West Mounted Police (NWMP) were the first police force responsible for maintenance of law and order in western Canada. They were a quasi-military, uniformed professional police force. In 1917, the Government of Canada withdrew the Royal North-West Mounted Police (RNWMP) from civil police duties in Alberta and Saskatchewan.[1] The provincial governments were compelled to establish their own police forces. Both the RNWMP and the provincial police forces were modern professional police. The formation of the provincial police in Alberta and Saskatchewan and the transfer of civil police duties from the RNWMP to the provincial police did not signify the transformation of the policing system from the old to the new. Rather, they were part of the overall professionalization process of policing in the prairie provinces. The various causal relations and theoretical approaches specified in studies of the development of policing are highly relevant to this study.

THE LEGAL FOUNDATION OF POLICING
IN ALBERTA AND SASKATCHEWAN

The idea of provincial police was initially brought into being by the 1856 County and Borough Police Act in England, which aimed at modernizing and centralizing policing in rural England. The Act required local governments to establish police forces and to use policemen for a wide range of administrative functions within local communities. The establishment of provincial police forces in mid-nineteenth-century England actually strengthened local authorities during the centralization of policing.[2] The British government, through the 1867 British North American (BNA) Act, introduced the idea of provincial police into Canada. The BNA Act expressly empowered provincial governments to enact laws in areas of "the administration of justice in the provinces, including the constitution, maintenance, and organization of provincial courts, both of civil and of criminal jurisdiction, and including procedure in civil matters in those courts."[3] At the same time, the BNA Act also conferred upon the federal government the power to make law regarding criminal law and procedures. Hogg interprets this provision as an explicit authorization of "provincial policing and prosecution of offenses under the Criminal Code although there is ... concurrent federal power as well on the basis that federal legislative power over the criminal law ... carries with it the matching power of enforcement."[4]

In practice, both the federal and provincial governments exercised their policing power. The provinces of Manitoba and Quebec in 1870, British Columbia in 1880, and Ontario in 1896 enacted their police or constable acts and established provincial police forces.[5] Concomitantly, the federal Parliament passed the Police Act of Canada in 1868. This act authorized the establishment of the Dominion Police force to enforce federal legislation in the provinces.[6] The North-West Mounted Police (NWMP) were created by the North-West Territories Act (1873) to establish the federal administration of justice in the territories.[7] The establishment of the Dominion Police and the NWMP marked a departure of policing in Canada from the British tradition, according to which the enforcement of law had been the responsibility of local governments. According to Macleod, the reason for Sir John A. Macdonald's departure from the British tradition was that "he intended the Mounted Police to be a temporary organization which would be phased out once the West passed through the frontier stage."[8]

However, in reality, the NWMP played a critical role in developing the North-West Territories and later the provinces of Alberta and Saskatchewan. The North-West Territories were created by the federal government under the 1873 North-West Territories Act; and the territorial government had financial difficulties from the time of its creation. After 1888, the influx of immigrants from eastern Canada, the United States, and European countries further aggravated the financial difficulties. To achieve financial self-sufficiency, the politicians from western Canada requested provincial autonomy.[9] Only after almost eighteen years of such requests did Laurier's Liberal government finally decide to grant provincial autonomy.[10] The provinces of Alberta and Saskatchewan were created by the Saskatchewan Act and the Alberta Act in September 1905.[11] According to these Acts, the new provinces enjoyed full provincial status as stipulated under the BNA Act. Thus, they had the power to administer justice within their jurisdictions. The RNWMP Commissioner, A. Bowen Perry, anticipated the possibility of the creation of the provincial police forces in the foreseeable future. Perry reported in the 1905 Annual Report that:

Since inauguration of the provinces, we have continued to carry on our duties as hitherto, pending the organization of the new governments. Even should either government not desire the assistance of the force in carrying out the administration of justice, one or two years must elapse before we can be entirely relieved.[12]

According to the plan of Prime Minister Sir Wilfrid Laurier, the federal government would continue to control the public land and school legislation that would allow a tax-supported separate Roman Catholic school system in the provinces. In return, he would offer the services of the RNWMP to new provinces. But the RNWMP never became a subject of negotiation. After the inauguration of the provinces, the federal government attempted to persuade Alberta and Saskatchewan to use their powers to establish their own police forces as the other western provinces had already done.[13] However, it was recognized that the practical solution to the issues of policing in the provinces for both the federal and the provincial governments was that the RNWMP would continue to provide services in the provinces. Section 33 of the 1894 Mounted Police Act provided a legal basis for such a federal arrangement. Section 33 allowed the Governor-in-Council to "enter into arrangements with the government of any province of Canada for the use or employment of the force, and to agree upon the amount of money which shall be paid by each province for such services."[14] Based on this legal provision, Laurier instructed the comptroller of the RNWMP to negotiate with the new provinces. The provincial and the federal governments reached agreements about policing services that covered the next five years (April 1906–April 1911). According to the agreements, a strength of five hundred policemen in the two provinces would be maintained and each provincial government would contribute the sum of $75,000 annually for the service and the federal government would cover the rest of the expense. In addition, all the money collected for fines under provincial legislation and the Criminal Code of Canada would be forwarded to the provincial attorney general departments. The execution of duties relating to the administration of justice in the provinces would be subject to the orders of the attorneys general of the provinces.[15] However, the federal government would remain in control of the force.

The rationale for Alberta and Saskatchewan to contract police services appears to have been largely financial. The annual payment of $75,000 was a relatively small amount of money. The value of fines that was forwarded to the provinces could be expected to cover a substantive part of the $75,000 fee. These financial arrangements were attractive to the provinces. This became evident when each provincial government had to pay nearly half a million dollars annually for keeping their own provincial police after 1917.[16] At the same time, other considerations might also suggest reasons for the provincial use of the Mounties. Commissioner Perry in the 1906 Annual Report remarked that "the present arrangement is an advantageous one for the provinces, as well as for the Dominion. The immediate withdrawal of the force, in the height of the rapid settlement, would have caused a feeling of unrest and disquiet, prejudicial to all interests."[17] This suggestion was a proper estimate of the influence of the RNWMP among the prairie settlers. When the federal government decided to withdraw the RNWMP's services from Alberta in 1917, the fanatic protests by various associations proved that Perry's view of the situation was correct.[18]

The employment of the RNWMP in the provinces did not imply that the provincial governments were unable to exercise their constitutional power of policing in other ways. Shortly after the creation of the provinces, Alberta and Saskatchewan enacted laws to institute provincial policing, as well as policing in cities, towns, and villages. In Saskatchewan, the Provincial Legislative Assembly passed the first Constables Act of the province in 1906.[19] The Act authorized the Lieutenant-Governor-in-Council to create and to control a police force that had province-wide jurisdiction. Justices of the peace were also empowered to appoint provincial constables. However, such appointments were allowed only for a specific purpose or occasion and for a period of one month. According to Stenning, the Saskatchewan Constables Act was almost identical to the Manitoba Constables Act of 1870.[20]

In fact, the Saskatchewan Constables Act was employed eagerly by the new government. Provincial constables were appointed shortly after the proclamation of the Act. Some historians believe that both the Constables Act and the appointment of the provincial constables were for the purpose of administrating regulations concerning liquor sales.[21] This argument is consistent with the later development of policing in Saskatchewan; in 1911 the Saskatchewan government also employed the Constables Act to create the Saskatchewan Secret Service. The primary tasks of the Service were to enforce the provisions of the Liquor Licence Act. Charles Augustus Mahoney was appointed as the Chief Constable and the Chief of the Secret Service on December 7, 1911. Inspectors and detectives of the Secret Service also often acted as agents for the provincial Liberal Party. They gave advice on political conditions, such as local organizational matters; and frequently acted as a party apparatus.[22] This political involvement was continued later by the Saskatchewan Provincial Police established in 1917.

Similar to the government of Saskatchewan, the Alberta Legislative Assembly also enacted the province's first Constables Act in 1908.[23] The Act allowed justices of the peace to appoint constables whose power could be extended to the whole province. One year later, the Constables Act was revised to extend the power of appointing constables to the judges of the Provincial Supreme Court and of the District Courts in the province, in addition to the Lieutenant-Governor-in-Council. The Lieutenant-Governor-in-Council had exclusive power to control the constables.

While this Act provided the legal foundations for the province to establish its own police force, it was generally never used for that purpose because of the employment of the RNWMP in Alberta. It was employed only to appoint individual provincial constables and special constables for various purposes by justices of the peace and police magistrates, and later by the Board of the Commissioners of the Alberta Provincial Police. Some private companies, such as the Pacific Railway Company, frequently asked to have special constables appointed to enforce the Railway Act for their own interests. However, some private companies abused this special constable system by using the constables to protect their business interests from other competitors rather than to enforce laws. According to Inspector Dennis Ryan, for instance, Brewster Transport Company employed two special constables at the Banff Springs and Lake Louise Hotels for the purpose of preventing other transport companies or individuals from seeking business at the hotels.[24]

The Legislative Assemblies in Alberta and Saskatchewan also provided a legal basis for cities, towns, and villages to appoint constables who had judicial power within the communities. The Saskatchewan City Act empowered city councils to appoint policemen.[25] The Alberta Municipal Districts Act authorized district councils to appoint constables.[26] However, there was no provision regarding the organization and control of municipal police forces. The Town Acts of Saskatchewan and Alberta had the same stipulations conferring on town councils the power to appoint town policemen.[27] The councils of villages in both Saskatchewan and Alberta could appoint one or more village constables.[28] In order to save expenses, few towns or villages had actually appointed their own constables. The 1919 Alberta Police Act granted the Attorney General the authority to compel cities, towns, and other rural municipalities to appoint their own police constables and to enforce their bylaws.[29]

THE ROLE OF THE ROYAL NORTH-WEST MOUNTED POLICE IN THE PRAIRIE PROVINCES, 1905–16

Although the legal foundations for creating the provincial police forces were established in the very beginning of the creation of the provinces, no such forces were created due to the financial difficulties faced by the provinces. According to the agreements about police services between the federal government and the provincial governments, the RNWMP policed Alberta and Saskatchewan from 1905 to 1917. During the period, the RNWMP undertook various tasks of policing the provinces. One of the important factors prompting the development of policing in the prairies was western settlement. The influx of immigrants not only contributed to ever-increasing crime, but also fomented the prohibition movement. The prohibition movement was a result of the ethnic conflict between the settlers from the United States and eastern Canada and the immigrants from central Europe and other countries. The ethnic conflicts manifested themselves in the ambiguous provincial legislation concerning the consumption and sale of liquor. The flood of immigrants was associated with the completion of the transcontinental railway. The railway also brought in a large floating population of railway labourers and harvesters. During that period, the RNWMP in the two provinces experienced enormous pressure from the settlement and related social problems. The police not only took care of those newcomers by providing various services, but also fought serious crime and "social evils" associated with them.

According to the agreement between the federal and provincial governments, the RNWMP were empowered to enforce provincial liquor regulations. The police explicitly showed their distaste for this. This attitude was certainly related to the experience of the enforcement of liquor laws in the North-West Territories before 1905. The early administration of liquor laws had a devastating effect on the RNWMP's reputation and its services among the population.[30] In fact, the Commissioner of the RNWMP in 1913 had tried unsuccessfully to exclude the enforcement of provincial liquor laws from the Mounties' duties. The Commissioner, Major Perry, remarked that "[the RNWMP's] duties in the provinces are altogether connected with criminal matters."[31] The offences under the liquor regulations were certainly not criminal in their nature. Criminal matters were regarded as more important tasks than others. The increase in serious crime associated with the growth of the immigrant population provided a legitimate reason for the RNWMP to view the enforcement of the liquor law as trivial. Some divisional officers complained that the enforcement of the provincial statutes or local bylaws, including liquor regulations, entailed a great deal of work on the posts and various detachments. The enforcement constantly interrupted more important work.[32]

The Mounties' difficulties in enforcement of liquor regulations were aggravated by a deficiency in strength of the force. According to the agreements with the provinces, each province would have 250 officers including noncommissioned officers and constables. The arrangement was made based on the strength of the RNWMP in the ten years after Sir Wilfrid Laurier's Liberal government took power in 1896.

The RNWMP consisted of nine divisions in the provinces, five in Alberta and four in Saskatchewan. A division was made up of various detachments spread out over various settlements located on the main highways. They were usually at the main routes of travel. The force was primarily responsible for policing in rural areas of the provinces. The incorporated cities, towns, and villages, which were legally required to conduct their own policing (although few did), stretched the resources of the RNWMP even more thinly.[33]

Several years after assuming police duties in the new provinces, Commissioner Perry recognized that the force was insufficient for the vast territories of the provinces. The strength of the RNWMP might be sufficient to provide services for the provinces at the time when the agreements were reached, but the agreements did not project the dramatic increase of police work because of the huge increases in immigration and the rapid expansion of the railway in the new provinces. In 1912 the Commissioner described the rapid development of the provinces when he reported that

… the provinces have nearly doubled in population since they were constituted; settlers have penetrated into all portions except the most northerly parts; thousands of miles of railway have been constructed; hundreds of thriving towns and villages are now to be formed where a few years ago none existed; production has increased ten-fold. These great changes have been wrought by an army of people drawn from nearly every civilized country.[34]

This development generated an enormous amount of work that taxed the police to the limits. The responsibilities imposed on individual members of the force were greater than ever. Many detachments consisted of only one noncommissioned officer or constable who performed the duties that previously were conducted by three or four people. The police officers were afraid that the force was no longer sufficient to provide the quality services that had been received by the population in the past; this could be detrimental to the force's distinguished reputation cultivated over several decades. However, the uncertainty of the long-term fate of the force due to the provisional agreements between the federal and the provincial governments precluded the expansion of the force substantially until the outbreak of World War I in 1914.

By 1904, the total population in Alberta was 142,000, while that of Saskatchewan was 194,000. However, over the period 1904–14, the population in Alberta increased threefold. In Saskatchewan the population also tripled. This was because over the ten-year period, 308,042 immigrants settled in Alberta and 278,179 in Saskatchewan. The influx of immigration had not only overtaxed the services of the force, but also changed the nature of their duties permanently. Within the first several years of policing the provinces, the RNWMP mainly enforced federal legislation, such as the Criminal Code, the Indian Act, the Railway Act, and some North-West Territories Ordinances, which were accepted as provincial regulations (as not many provincial statutes had been enacted at that time). The police still regarded the enforcement of the Indian Act as an important duty because controlling the native population was one of the reasons for establishing the force in the first place. They continued to keep the natives on the reserves and prevent them from accessing illicit liquor and performing "sun" dances. Many officers believed that the natives had become "law-abiding people" due to the constant police surveillance.[35]

However, the centrality of the police duties had begun to shift from controlling the native population and providing a peaceful environment for incoming settlers, to maintaining law and order and furnishing various services to new settlers. In the first dozen years after the establishment of the police force, the police were mainly concerned with assimilating the natives under Canadian legal and cultural control. In the second period of the development of the force, the police developed techniques for dealing with various crimes associated with settlements and the beginning of urbanization.

From the beginning of the twentieth century, because of the great influx of settlers from the United States and Europe, a major task of the police was to help settlers assimilate into Canadian society. At the same time, the police had begun to devote a substantial proportion of their strength to dealing with increasing crime that was proportionate to the growth of the population. Immigrants, particularly from central European countries, were assumed to be primarily responsible for the increases in crime.

For example, inspector of Regina District reported that "the foreign elements are responsible for at least seventy-five per cent of crime."[36] In 1912 the Commissioner noted that "the names of the accused indicate an undue proportion of our alien population responsible for these crimes of violence. The West is paying the penalty for drawing a large immigration from central Europe."[37]

The Commissioner's report also recorded that most of the cases handled by the police under the Canadian Criminal Code were assault, theft, and drunkenness. They were committed primarily by immigrants and the large transient population composed of railway labourers, teamsters, and harvesters. The police treated homicide and property-related crime, such as horse and cattle stealing, as the most serious crimes.[38] These crimes were given top priority, although services continued to be an essential part of police duties.

The force also had judicial responsibilities.[39] The police officers had powers of justices of the peace. They tried summary cases and conducted preliminary hearings on indictable cases except those offences committed in cities where offenders were tried by local justices of the peace.[40] The police also were authorized to maintain common jails, to escort all prisoners to trial, and to attend all criminal courts.

The force also played an essential role in the government administration. Much time and energy were consumed in assisting various departments, including the Department of Immigration, the Department of the Interior, the Department of Agriculture, and the Department of Customs. Tasks included the collection of duties, inspection of imported animals at custom posts, patrolling the international boundaries to prevent smuggling, acting as fire and game guardians, and providing a variety of services for new settlers. Occasionally, the police distributed relief to settlers during the severe and bitterly cold winters. In addition, they delivered grain seeds and mail for settlers in remote settlements.[41]

EXPLANATIONS FOR THE CREATION OF THE PROVINCIAL POLICE: THE PROHIBITION THESIS VERSUS THE WAR THESIS

One of the central issues in the history of the provincial police in Alberta and Saskatchewan involves the factors that precipitated the provinces into the situation in which they had to create their own police forces under short notice. The official reason for the transition was World War I. However, contrary to this argument, some historians, like Robertson, Palmer and Palmer, and Moir, contend that it was the enforcement of prohibition that frightened the RNWMP and forced the provincial governments to create their own police forces.[42] We propose that the transition was a result of an interplay between several factors, although the war was probably decisive.

The prohibition thesis is stated by Palmer and Palmer as follows:

> The N.W.M.P. had attempted to enforce prohibition from 1875 to 1891 during the territorial period, and had primarily been rewarded by public hostility. In order to avoid having to enforce prohibition again, Mounted Police officials recommended cancelling their policing contract with the provincial government, which was then forced to establish its own police force.[43]

Although the formation of the Saskatchewan Secret Service in 1911 seemingly resolved the problem of the liquor law enforcement in Saskatchewan, Robertson also insists that the prohibition enforcement played an important role in determining the withdrawal of the RNWMP in 1917. How valid is this view?

During 1905–16, when the force assumed total responsibilities of policing the provinces, the RNWMP officers showed great reluctance to police the liquor trade and consciously avoided proactive strategies to do so. In 1911, Commissioner Perry explicitly noted that the force was unable to carry on an effective patrol system partly because of the other multifarious obligations of the police and partly because of the deficiency in strength. The force adopted a reactive strategy of policing. Since most cases under the provincial liquor ordinances and other regulations were "offences without victims," it was nearly impossible for the force to police those regulations without an active patrol system. The enforcement of the provincial liquor regulations was effectively excluded from their duties. Nevertheless, occasionally, they did investigate and prosecute offences in cases where citizens complained about the gross and open violations of the liquor laws. During the period of 1905–16, a small number of cases were recorded in the annual reports of police work each year.[44] This enforcement of liquor legislation by the RNWMP was definitely not as vigorous or effective as expected by some provincial politicians, particularly by the temperance groups in Saskatchewan.

In some cases, the RNWMP simply refused to enforce the liquor law. The 1909 Saskatchewan Liquor License Act probably created more problems for enforcement than any other liquor legislation. The Act provided for the sale of liquor in the province with a complicated licensing system. It granted the Board of Liquor Commissioners, a Chief License Inspector and other Inspectors, the power to enforce the Act. The Act contained a local option article permitting the Act to apply only in the towns and cities where most of the population supported it.[45] The RNWMP refused to enforce this complicated legislation. They argued that the Act did not stipulate that the RNWMP had the responsibility for enforcement. This forced some local members of the Saskatchewan Legislative Assembly from the constituencies supporting the regulation of the sale of liquor to urge the Attorney General, W.F.A. Turgeon, to request the RNWMP to enforce it. They complained that the failure to enforce the Act was detrimental to them politically.[46]

Because of the RNWMP's reluctant and inadequate enforcement of liquor legislation, the Saskatchewan government finally formed the Secret Service exclusively to administer the provincial liquor regulations in 1911. The establishment of the Secret Service was an attempt by the government to resolve the problem permanently. The Secret Service relieved the RNWMP from administering the liquor laws. The force was asked to report complaints under breaches of the Liquor License Act to the Deputy Attorney General's office and to forward all cases relating to the laws to the Liquor Department for investigation and prosecution.[47] Consequently, in 1911, the Commissioner once again recommended to the Prime Minister renewal of the agreements regarding the police services for another five years.

The creation of the Saskatchewan Secret Service illuminates the friction between the provincial governments and the RNWMP in enforcing provincial liquor ordinances. But the difficulties were not serious enough for either party to terminate the contract. In fact, from the beginning of 1915, the prohibition movement gained ground steadily. In Alberta, on July 21, 1915, 61 per cent of the voters approved total prohibition of liquor consumption. Concomitantly, the government declared that prohibition would come into effect on July 1, 1916. In Saskatchewan, in 1915, the prohibition force achieved a major victory on the Banish-the-Bar issue. On April 1, 1915, all bar and club licences were abolished. On December 31, 1916, following the results from a referendum, the province also adopted a total prohibition policy regarding the retail sale of liquor. Knowing that prohibition would definitely come into effect in Alberta in 1916 and that the Saskatchewan Secret Service had already taken responsibility for enforcing the liquor law in Saskatchewan, in 1915, the federal government renewed the agreement concerning the police services for an indefinite period rather than a five-year period as before![48] This renewal of the agreement was consistent with the recommendation made by Commissioner Perry in 1914 that "it would be in the interests of the force and the country, if the question of the continuance of our service could be definitely settled."[49] This renewal suggests that the federal government had no reason to be surprised by the prohibition vote in 1916 and 1917 and so daunted by the consequences as to pull out of the federal contracts. From this perspective, the prohibition thesis appears to be without substantiation. World War I was a more plausible factor.

According to the explanation given by the federal government, the sudden withdrawal of the RNWMP from civil police duties in the prairie provinces was due to the war. Before the withdrawal, the police force had experienced several changes in reacting to the war overseas during 1914–16. These changes, in fact, help us to explain the role of the war in the consequent transformation of policing in western Canada. Right after the outbreak of World War I, the RNWMP in the provinces were expanded by five hundred men under the recommendation of the Commissioner. The five hundred new recruits were composed mainly of ex-members of the RNWMP and were only hired for one year.[50] The development was primarily due to a large number of the so-called "enemy nationality" among the population in the western provinces. In the 1915 report, Commissioner Perry added that

When the war broke out, some natural apprehension was felt for the peace and good order of the Western Provinces, owing to a large percentage of the population being of enemy nationality, and it was therefore decided that the strength of the Mounted Police should be increased.[51]

The "enemy nationality" in the report referred to Germans and Austrians. According to the 1911 census in Canada, there were 173,568 Germans and Austrians; many of them had already become British subjects. They made up almost 20 per cent of the total population of 866,000 in the two provinces.[52]

For the Commissioner, another reason for the expansion of the strength of the force was to prevent a disorder that might grow out of the antagonism between different nationalities. A report by Inspector T.A. Wroughton in "G" Division warned that "every nationality is represented in this district and amongst this cosmopolitan population there are certain to be some thirsting to show their patriotism by crushing their opponents' skull."[53] Commissioner Perry said that

> An increase of the force was necessary to impress upon all races that good order would be preserved, and that our alien enemies who quietly pursued their ordinary vocations and observed strictly their obligations as residents of this country would receive adequate protection [sic].[54]

Indeed, the war impacted the RNWMP drastically as after the outbreak of war the maintenance of internal security and order became an important part of their duties. The police placed German and Austrian nationals under close surveillance. In effect, all German and Austrian nationalities in the provinces were treated as prisoners of war on parole. They could not travel without authorization issued by the Registrars of Alien Enemies or by the police.[55] They had to report regularly to and register at the nearest police detachments or the Registrars of Alien Enemies in the cities. If they failed to provide satisfactory reasons for not doing so, they would be interned and sent to a detention camp. The "alien nationalities" were forbidden to possess or to carry firearms. Every offender was prosecuted and found guilty.[56]

During the period of 1914–16, the police spent a tremendous amount of time investigating the cases concerning the activities of the "alien enemies." Most accusations were found to be baseless. However, they did find minor cases in which the accused persons either used seditious words or traded with the enemy.[57] A person who ridiculed His Majesty or expressed sympathy with His Majesty's enemies could be found guilty and fined $150 or three months imprisonment. Occasionally, a fine went as high as $250 or one year hard labour.[58] Of course, the offenders did not have to be of German or Austrian nationality. One Scotsman was convicted of using seditious language. The officer who reported the case remarked that he "has no patriotic sentiments towards Germany, and his pro-German attitude can only be attributed to a dislike of the British Empire rather than a love for the Teutonic."[59]

Figure 1.1 The RNWMP Strength in Saskatchewan, 1906-1918

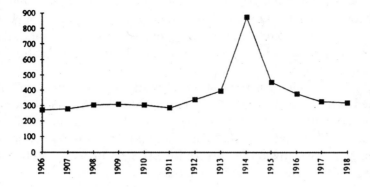

Figure 1.2 The RNWMP Strength in Alberta, 1906-1918

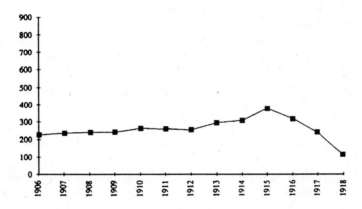

The first year of the war was a peaceful one in the prairie provinces. Commissioner Perry in his 1915 annual report remarked that "no disturbance of the public peace has taken place and the provinces of Saskatchewan and Alberta during the past twelve months have been singularly quiet and orderly."[60] By the end of the first year, many of the force's temporary recruits had taken their discharges and enlisted for overseas service. At the time, there were large bodies of troops in the provinces under training. The troops could be used to suppress any major outbreak or disturbance. Thus, the Commissioner made a recommendation to the prime minster that it might not be necessary to maintain the strength of the force at more than nine hundred men. Consequently, the recommendation was approved.[61] Under this peaceful condition the agreements respecting the services of the RNWMP in the provinces were again renewed on April 19, 1915. The arrangements were made for an indefinite period for the benefit of the force in the long run. However, either party might terminate the contracts by giving one year's notice of intention, providing that the termination would become effective one year after the following 30th of June.[62]

By the beginning of 1916 the strength of the forces had continually declined as indicated in Figures 1.1 and 1.2; it stood at 103 below the authorized strength of 1,000. This condition arose because many noncommissioned officers and constables took discharges to enlist for service in the army. In order to stop this trend, the prime minister, Sir Robert L. Borden, wrote to the officers and men that

... all members of the force must remember that the service which they are now rendering to the Dominion and to the Empire is not less important than that which they would perform if actually serving at the front. Further, it is a service which can only be efficiently performed by a force which has been trained in the discharge of the duties which it is called upon to undertake. For these reasons the Prime Minister has found himself unable to consent to the retirement from the force of many officers and men who have asked that permission for the purpose of enlistment.[63]

In spite of this, the Commissioner found that "the call to arms is so strong that it has been found irresistible."[64] For the same reason, the force had experienced difficulties in recruiting new police constables. The most desirable candidates had already volunteered for overseas service. The Commissioner hesitated to make a special effort to recruit as he was reluctant to enter competition with recruitment for the Canadian Expeditionary Force in western Canada.[65]

As numbers continued to fall even further below authorized strength, the prime minister issued a warning that a raid by enemy aliens might seriously disturb the order and peace in the western provinces. The prime minister indicated that

It was felt that even a raid on a small scale, whether successful or not, would be detrimental to our best interests, in that it would shake the slumbering sense of security of our people, cause unrest among our enemy nationalities, and create a clamorous demand for severe measures to be taken against all enemy aliens.[66]

The prime minister's apprehensions were justified by a telegram intercepted from the German Foreign Office to the German Ambassador at Washington, D.C., dated January 3, 1916. According to the 1917 Annual Report of the RNWMP, the telegram suggested that the German government had been planning the destruction of the Canadian Pacific Railway at several points to sever traffic completely and permanently.[67]

In July 1916, after consultation with General John Hughes on the subject of internal security in the prairie provinces, Commissioner Perry reported to the prime minister that "there was no danger of trouble internally, that there was no unrest among the enemy aliens, and that there had been no agitation nor any attempt to organize for the purpose of disturbing public security."[68] Probably due to the influence of Hughes, however, Commissioner Perry believed that there was still the potential for danger given the German government's intentions. He explained that "given the right incentive our enemy aliens might throw all precautions aside and venture the most daring attempts. Such incentive was only likely to come from conspiracies against us hatched by German intrigue in the United States."[69]

The United States had not yet entered the war. The Commissioner suggested that the current strength and distribution of the force made it powerless to prevent any disturbances that might be organized in the United States. On October 11, 1916, the Commissioner wrote the prime minister to explain his point of view further in this respect and to urge the federal government to take immediate action to prevent any such disturbance. He explained that

> Owing to the wide distribution and paucity, the Mounted Police cannot be looked upon as defensive; their energies are absorbed in their various civil duties. To render it of more service in meeting war conditions its numbers would have to be largely increased, its ordinary police duties taken over by the different provinces and its distribution revised.[70]

He noted the potential difficulties in terminating the federal-provincial contract without providing the required one-year notice. He further suggested that "if not a complete abrogation [of the agreements], then [the Ottawa government needed] a modification which would relieve the force of many of its minor and comparatively unimportant duties."[71] Based on the Commissioner's recommendation, an Order in Council was passed on November 29, 1916 to terminate the agreements regarding the services of the RNWMP during the war.[72]

THE CREATION OF THE PROVINCIAL POLICE

Neither Alberta nor Saskatchewan anticipated the sudden and immediate termination of the agreements concerning the RNWMP services. The premiers of both provinces attempted to persuade the prime minister to alter the decision, but without success. As indicated in a minute of the Executive Council of Saskatchewan, the Saskatchewan provincial government agreed to assume the responsibility of policing the province on January 1, 1917, leaving almost no time for preparation.[73] This was possible primarily because the government used the Secret Service as an organizational basis for the newly established police force.

In comparison, the Alberta government was not well equipped to take over the duties immediately. For the takeover of police duties the Alberta government had to organize an entirely new police force from scratch. This task could not be achieved instantly. The government requested a two-month deferral to transfer duties. The date of the transfer was moved to March 1 from January 1, 1917, the official date of the withdrawal. The Alberta government was required to pay $50,000 to the federal government for the additional two months of services.[74] On February 2, 1917, the Executive Council of the government of the province of Alberta, upon the recommendation of the attorney general, ordered the creation of the Alberta Provincial Police (APP).

After withdrawing from various civil police duties in the provinces, the RNWMP were not strengthened but were redistributed to concentrate on patrolling the international boundary and to control foreign nationals. They also reserved some strength at Divisional Headquarters for the occurrence of disturbances in their districts.[75] The transfer of the duties went smoothly except for some temporary confusion over jurisdiction. The newly established provincial police forces focussed on the enforcement of criminal laws and provincial ordinances. As mentioned earlier, although it had been widely accepted that cities and towns were responsible for the appointment of their own constables to enforce municipal bylaws, few rural municipalities had their own constables. In practice, the jurisdiction of policing among various police forces was not clearly defined during the period of transition. A letter from John L. Fawcett to the Attorney General of Alberta, dated April 4, 1917, provides a good example. The letter notes that

Since the change between the North West Mounted Police and the Provincial Police one is somewhat at a loss to know before whom to make charges and who is interested in the prosecution. A rather flagrant case of perjury occurred here not long since, a representative of the Macleod Town Police, Provincial Police and the RNWMP were all in the court room and know the circumstances. We hardly know who to take the matter up with. As yet there is apparently no provincial justice of the peace.[76]

After the withdrawal from various civil police duties in the provinces, the RNWMP continued to enforce the federal park regulations in national parks. The provincial police enforced other laws in the same districts. This situation could easily cause confusion over jurisdiction. The Commissioner of the RNWMP decided to request full jurisdiction in the parks to avoid further confusion. For that purpose, the Commissioner asked the government of Alberta to appoint the members of the RNWMP who were stationed in the park areas as special constables so that they could administrate all laws in the district.[77]

CONCLUSION

The creation of the provincial police was a relatively simple process in Alberta and Saskatchewan. It was associated not only with the some of the factors identified by Lane, Silver, Carson, and others (such as heightened immigration, increasing crime, and the expansion of the dangerous classes), but also with the existing legal contexts (especially presence of the federal police force) as well as the outbreak of World War I. The delay in the creation of the provincial police was mainly due to the existence of the RNWMP in both provinces. For convenience and financial benefits, the two provinces employed the RNWMP immediately after the province statuses were granted. Although the RNWMP enforced law and order in the provinces as before 1905, the provincial governments soon recognized that the RNWMP services were problematic in terms of the enforcement of provincial statutes. The RNWMP actually avoided enforcing unpopular provincial regulations because the enforcement tended to create antagonistic attitudes toward the force among the population. However, contrary to the prohibition thesis advanced by Robertson and the Palmers, the war was the most decisive factor in the withdrawal of the RNWMP. This decision was only taken following three specific crises. First, the intercepted German telegram showed the intention of the German government to undermine Canadian internal security by attacking the railways. This added security to the police role. Second, the police had difficulties in maintaining the necessary strength for their existing duties due to the shortage of qualified candidates. Finally, the RNWMP might have faced the increased duties under the provincial liquor prohibition – but they had managed to downplay this previously and, particularly in Saskatchewan, the duties had already been assumed by the province. The key factor appears to have been a thinning of ranks, and prohibition would have contributed to this only obliquely.

The existence of the RNWMP in the two provinces postponed the creation of the provincial police. However, the fact that the RNWMP had policed the prairie provinces before the provinces created their own police actually helped the subsequent provincial forces to develop into a professional force. As the RNWMP had policed in western Canada since 1873, there were a large number of former RNWMP members that the provincial police were able to recruit. These ex-RNWMP officers had a notable impact on the professionalization of the provincial police forces. At the same time, the RNWMP had set up a professional standard for policing and had cultivated an excellent public reputation over several decades. After 1917 the provincial police forces had to work constantly to meet the high expectations of the population.

2   THE ORGANIZATIONAL STRUCTURES AND OPERATION OF THE PROVINCIAL POLICE IN ALBERTA AND SASKATCHEWAN, 1917–32

On February 2, 1917, the Executive Council of the government of Alberta, upon the recommendation of the attorney general, ordered the creation of the APP. The size of the force would not exceed 150 police officers and constables. The APP were controlled and managed directly by the Board of Commissioners. The RNWMP influenced the provincial police considerably in terms of their organizational structure and operation.[1] The RNWMP were organized, according to their creator, Sir John A. Macdonald, following the model of the Irish Constabulary. Through the influence of the RNWMP, the military distinctions of the Irish Constabulary could be observed in the provincial police forces with respect to their organization, operation, and discipline. In this chapter, we attempt to answer a number of questions in the areas of organizational development of the provincial forces, such as, to what extent were the provincial police forces influenced by the RNWMP, to what extent were the forces professionalized in terms of their administration and operation, and what factors were associated with such development?

THE BOARD OF COMMISSIONERS OF THE ALBERTA PROVINCIAL POLICE

The first step in promoting professionalism within the Alberta Provincial Police (APP) taken by the Alberta government was to create the Board of Commissioners as a commanding body of the APP. The idea to use the Board of the Commissioners to manage the police force was intimately associated with the developments of the city police. The first board of police commissioners was created in 1853 to oversee the New York City Police Force.[2] This board was established to "eliminate the political favouritism and ward control which prior to that time had dominated the [police] department."[3] However, the boards of police commissioners in New York did not necessarily work as planned. Stenning points out that "the creation of police boards as institutions of government of municipal police forces may be seen not so much as a measure to *remove the police from politics*, as an attempt to move the control over municipal police forces from one sphere of political interests toward another."[4]

Alberta created the first Board of Commissioners of a provincial police force in Canada. This board was similar to a municipal police board. The Alberta Police Act did not offer an explicit statement that the mandate of the board was to remove the police from political control. Nevertheless, the board was composed of two members of lower judiciary (police magistrates) and one civil servant (the deputy attorney general of the province). The APP were controlled and managed by the Board of Commissioners. The composition of members of the board and its power over the police force were similar to that of current municipal police boards in Canada.

The members of the Board of Commissioners were appointed by the Lieutenant-Governor-in-Council. They were Arthur George Browning, deputy attorney general for the province of Alberta and secretary of the board; Gilbert E. Sanders, police magistrate for the City of Calgary; and Philip Carteret Hill Primrose, police magistrate for the City of Edmonton, who was appointed as chairman of the board. These appointments were stipulated in the 1917 Alberta Provincial Police Act.

The board possessed a considerable degree of autonomy in its decision-making process.[5] It appointed, promoted, dismissed, and discharged all police personnel and fixed the sums to be paid to the members of the force. It also issued the order to establish detachments and formulated rules and regulations regarding transportation. The board purchased various equipment, and established and administered pension funds.[6]

On February 9, 1917, the board appointed Edward Grobst McDonnell as superintendent, and John Daniel Nicholson as assistant superintendent to administer the force.[7] Section 11 and 12 of the Act stipulated that "the superintendent shall perform such duties as are assigned to him by the Board of the Commissioners, and shall be subject to the control, order and authority of the Board of Commissioners."[8] The Act also provided that "the duty of the members of the force [is] subject to the orders of the Superintendent."[9] This vertical command system was designed to insulate the police from outside influence.

However, the board was extremely short-lived. After only a two-year operation, it was abolished by the Police Act of 1919. The authority of the control and management of the force was transferred to the attorney general of the province. The major reason for the abolition was that the board enjoyed little popularity due to a series of controversies surrounding the force. In its first year, about sixty-six police personnel resigned. Superintendent McDonnell explained that "a considerable number left shortly after engagement presumably after finding themselves unsuited to the work; others claimed unable to live on their pay; lately a few have been drafted."[10] But other evidence suggested that there was considerable dissatisfaction among the constables because of inadequate management by the superintendent and disappointment with city-police-style uniforms, which were of extremely inferior quality.

The resignations of two senior officers, Assistant Superintendent Nicholson and Inspector A.H. Schurer commanding "A" Division, partially illustrate the discontent of the rank and file with the superintendent. Nicholson complained that he was asked for a resignation without being given any reasons. The superintendent failed to assign proper duties for him. He felt that the superintendent had in every possible way "acted in such a manner as to make my position as useless a one as possible."[11] Schurer's complaint about the superintendent buttressed that of A.S. Nicholson. Schurer said that "whilst I have been appointed Commanding Officer of the "A" Division day after day orders were given by [the superintendent] to noncommissioned officers and men under my command, without any reference to me whatsoever."[12] This situation had made it impossible for him to maintain discipline within the division. Schurer grumbled that the APP were unable to match the excellent reputation held by the RNWMP because of "the unjust, overbearing and discourteous treatment meted out by the Superintendent."[13] The complaints also impugned the board because it operated solely on the information provided by the superintendent.

The large number of resignations on the force and the controversies surrounding the superintendent induced some criticism of the management of the APP. In the provincial legislature, the government was compelled to defend the force and the board against the attacks from the Opposition. On February 28, 1918, A.E. Ewing and J.W.S. Kemmis demanded a public investigation into the administration and operation of the provincial force because of "the unsatisfactory conditions" prevailing among the police.[14] In rebuttal, the government emphasized the achievement of the Board of Commissioners. Premier Stewart stated that

The fact of the sudden withdrawal of the Royal North West Mounted Police by the Dominion Government early in 1917 rendered it necessary to establish at once a Provincial Force in war time, when the man-power most suitable for such Force had been enlisted for Military Service overseas, this House is of the opinion that the Provincial Police Commission is to be commended for having organized so efficient a Police Force in such a short space of time.[15]

One week later after the APP became a controversial topic in the provincial legislature, Superintendent McDonnell tendered his resignation on the grounds of ill health, while, at the same time, he accepted a position of inspector at Peace River. However, the resignation of the superintendent was unable to change the unfavourable perception of the force.[16] The government finally abolished the board altogether and reorganized the force to improve its popularity.

Unlike the APP, the Saskatchewan Provincial Police adopted the commissioner system that was similar to that of the RNWMP. The Saskatchewan government used the Saskatchewan Secret Service as an organizational basis for the Provincial Police. The former head of the Secret Service, Charles Augustus Mahoney, was appointed as the commissioner of the SPP; and William Robert Tracey, a senior member of the Winnipeg Police, as assistant commissioner. Under this system, all officers and police constables were appointed by orders of the Lieutenant-Governors-in-Council. The provincial police were controlled and managed directly by the commissioner and assistant commissioner. However, they were subject to the control, order, and authority of the attorney general of the province.[17] Theoretically, this system placed the police under the control of elected politicians. There were no regulations specifying the power of the attorney general. The system opened a door for the politicians to manipulate the police for political purposes. After the abolition of the Board of Commissioners of the APP by the 1919 Alberta Police Act, the Alberta Government also employed this command system.[18]

THE QUASI-MILITARY ORGANIZATIONS OF
THE PROVINCIAL POLICE FORCES

The provincial police forces, as successors to the RNWMP, adopted its military organizational structure and discipline. Such organizations are, at least in theory, capable of minimizing unsuitable attitudes within and influence from outside. Macleod suggests that the military demeanour can promote police legitimacy. He writes that "social standing and prestige were intimately connected with the ability of the police to command public support and cooperation in law enforcement."[19]

Following the RNWMP's practice, the provinces were divided into a number of districts and subdistricts. The forces were divided into divisions to police those districts; five divisions in Alberta and four, later changed into five, in Saskatchewan. The basic units of the force were individual detachments. Typically, an inspector who was in charge of a division administered about twenty detachments. This system is virtually identical to the structure of the RNWMP and the Irish Constabulary. A detachment was composed ideally of two or three noncommissioned officers or police constables. However, due to the deficiency in strength of the provincial police forces, most detachments had only one constable, although it was obvious to the police officers that single constable detachments were not effective from either a disciplinary or policing point of view. The provincial forces did not create a depot division where new recruits could be trained as the RNWMP and Irish Constabulary had done. But "A" Division provided a similar function to depot training.

The provincial police forces followed the report systems of the RNWMP. Constables in a detachment recorded their daily activities and forwarded the journal to their divisional inspectors weekly. The journal also recorded local weather, road conditions, agriculture reports, ranching conditions, and the movement of the population. Inspectors composed divisional annual reports based on the information provided by the detachments. They reported not only district conditions, but also analyses and recommendations for solving the problems in their districts. The commissioners of the forces forwarded the divisional reports and their annual reports together to the attorneys general of the provinces. Those reports provided the attorneys general with valuable information about agricultural and industrial development, and population conditions. Based on the information, the attorneys general made important decisions about the provincial forces, such as the deployment of the police detachments. Those reports showed that the police not only reacted to crime, but also watched every activity of the population in the communities, especially in those settled by foreign immigrants, who were regarded with suspicion.

Every police officer and constable, with the exception of special constables, had to be a British subject with a sound constitution, active habits, and able-bodied. He was to be not less than twenty-one nor more than thirty-five years of age and able to read English and to write it legibly. Unlike the police forces in other former colonies, the members of the provincial forces were relatively well trained. This was not because the forces had the resources to train the recruits, but because most of the members had experience with other police forces before becoming members of the provincial police. About 70 per cent of the members in each provincial force were ex-members of the RNWMP and about another 20 per cent of their members had experience with other police forces or the military. Except for the commissioner and assistant commissioner of the SPP, almost all the commissioned officers in both police forces were ex-officers of the RNWMP. This appears to be the primary reason why the provincial police forces were so extensively influenced by the RNWMP. After the formation of the police forces, according to the regulations of the forces (the two provincial police forces had similar rule and regulation books), the constables would be given periodic training. Due to the deficiency in the strength of the forces, it was impossible for the inspectors to devote time to drill.

Many military distinctions that were explicitly displayed by the RNWMP can be observed in the provincial police forces. However, those characteristics were largely modified to adapt to fiscal restrictions and to other practical needs of the provinces. The forces were armed, but not heavily. Smith & Wesson .38-calibre revolvers were issued to constables in both forces. The plainclothes officers and constables of the APP used .35-calibre Colt automatic revolvers. The officers in the SPP were armed with .52-calibre Savage automatic pistols. Each Divisional Headquarters of the APP had six Winchester 30.30 rifles. The Headquarters of the SPP kept two Thompson submachine guns. These heavy weapons were kept in the event of serious trouble, such as hunting down dangerous criminals.

Both provincial forces issued quasi-military field uniforms. The SPP had a similar outfit: a Stetson hat with the brim turned up on the left side closely resembling the South African bushman's hat. It turned out that the hat was designed by an inspector who had fought in the Boer War in South Africa. The uniform also consisted of a long khaki tunic with a military-type close neck collar, khaki breeches with a red stripe, and boots. The uniforms of the SPP were chosen largely by the members who had served with the RNWMP.

In the early days, both the SPP experienced some difficulties in outfitting their members; it took the SPP almost half a year to outfit their policemen. This was also the case with the APP. At first, the APP created city-style police uniforms that were similar to those of the London Metropolitan Police. They were blue in colour and were composed of helmet, tunic, riding breeches, serge, and greatcoat, which were manufactured by prison labour at the Fort Saskatchewan Gaol to reduce expenses. The quality of the material for the uniforms was extremely inferior as after six months, the uniforms became very shabby. The quality and the pattern of the uniforms had generated so much discontent, particularly among the ex-members of the RNWMP, that some members of the force had purchased their own uniforms.[20] Others resigned during the first few months in disgust. Only after strong demands from the officers, the APP finally adopted the uniforms consisted of a khaki jacket with military-type close neck collar, cord breeches, boots, and a pea jacket; the headgear was a pony Stetson hat.

The officers in both the APP and SPP were concerned with not only their appearance, but also the quality of services provided by and the reputation of the force because of the deficiency in strength of their forces. Before the withdrawal of the RNWMP from the prairie provinces, the strength of the RNWMP stood at 312 in Alberta and 362 in Saskatchewan. However, in 1918, the APP had 155 officers and staff, and it only reached 205 in 1931 before it was disbanded. The strength of the SPP was even weaker than the APP. In 1918, the SPP had only 106 officers and police constables and in 1927 only 133. In fact, the problems associated with the deficiency in strength in both forces worsened over the years. Because of the continual influx of immigrants and railway expansion, the forces were constantly overburdened by their ever-expanded duties.

Indeed, a general description of the duties of the police was provided in the provincial police acts respectively. The acts declared that they were crime prevention forces. For instance, the Provincial Police Act of Alberta states:

It shall be the duty of the members of the force ... to perform all duties which now are or thereafter shall be assigned to constables in relation to the preservation of the peace, the prevention of crime, and of offenses against the laws and Ordinances in force ... , the criminal law of Canada and the apprehension of criminals and offenders and others who may be lawfully taken into custody.[21]

In addition, the provincial police had the duty to "execute all warrants, perform any duty and services required under laws and ordinances."[22] The provincial police also carried out many other multifarious duties: each member of the forces was ex officio a game warden under the provisions of the Game Act; a fire guardian under the provisions of the Prairie and Forest Fires Act; an attendance officer under the provisions of the School Attendance Act; and an inspector under the provisions of the Vehicles Act and the Theatres and Cinematograph Act. They enforced more than thirty provincial ordinances.[23]

Like the RNWMP, all commissioned officers, including commissioners, assistant commissioners, and inspectors, also exercised considerable judicial power. They were ex officio justices of the peace and coroners in the provinces. Nevertheless, the provincial police officers rarely used the judicial power, except in dealing with the members of the forces who violated the police acts. This practice was different from that of the RNWMP before 1917. The RNWMP officers frequently acted as justices of the peace to try various offenders possibly because of the shortage of civilian justices of the peace at that time.

In addition to the duties set out in the police acts, the police forces also performed tasks that were not stipulated in the police acts. The governments used the forces as convenient administrative tools, although many government departments had already been established. The forces regularly assisted other departments, such as the Department of Justice and the Department of Immigration. The assistance rendered by the forces in some cases was massive, and it often taxed the strength of the forces to the utmost limits. At times such tasks were regarded as serious interference with other more important work. Some officers regarded this assistance to other government departments as "extra" work for the police. One such task for the APP was to escort a large number of prisoners and "lunatics" from cities and town police to the penitentiary. The inspector of "A" Division complained that "I cannot see any reasons for this extra duty being enforced on this force. As far as I know, there is no order that we should take over these prisoners. It is only an old custom, as carried out in the old NWMP days and continued till the present time."[24] Other divisional inspectors suggested that the prisoners from the cities be escorted by city police to the penitentiary.

Obviously for the police, some tasks were more desirable than others. Police officers and constables regard the prevention of crime and the prosecution of criminals as their primary tasks. The rural communities had distinctive policing requirements. The police were concerned constantly with the incidence of stock and horse stealing. Those duties were the real work of the forces compared to other service tasks. For this reason, the officers of the APP suggested that the government spend more money to employ well-trained and experienced lawyers as crown attorneys.[25] They could best prepare the cases and secure a higher conviction rate.

Although the provincial police were influenced by the RNWMP in their organization and operation, the changing community had led the provincial police to have policing priorities different from those of the RNWMP. In comparison, the major tasks of the RNWMP were to assimilate the natives and the new settlers into Canadian society. However, the primary duties of the provincial police were to control serious crime and to maintain social order threatened by the growth of radical movements. Crime increased following the growth of population; more serious violent crime emerged, such as train robberies and safecracking, which had not been seen before then. These types of serious crime posed new dangers to society and consumed considerable time and energy of the police forces. Following the outbreak of World War I, many radical groups, including communists, became higher priority problems. They were regarded as the main source of labour unrest in the Alberta mining communities. It became a new task of the forces to assume a role in internal security to prevent those radical organizations from overthrowing the government of Canada.[26] These shifts in priority in policing will be explored further in the latter part of this book.

THE ADOPTION OF TECHNICAL INNOVATIONS BY THE APP AND THE SPP

The emerging tasks of policing serious crime had a profound impact on how the provincial police organized their routine activities. Both provincial police forces indeed employed traditional methods used by the RNWMP and the Irish Constabulary in their work; but at the same time, they also adopted new technologies that could be used to promote police efficiency, including innovations in communications, transportation, and criminal investigations. These technical innovations were not available previously to the RNWMP or the Irish Constabulary.

Like the RNWMP before 1917, both the APP and the SPP in 1918 still employed a large number of horses for transportation to patrol the vast territories of the provinces, although both railways and automobiles were used. The APP had sixty horses and nine cars. Automobiles were used primarily to suppress the liquor traffic. The police constables of the APP frequently found themselves in the embarrassing situations where bootleggers got away easily because they used more powerful cars than the police.[27] This became an important incentive for the forces to promote the employment of automobiles. In order to promote use of automobiles, a policy was adopted by the forces that the governments would pay ten cents per mile to the APP members and thirty cents per mile to the SPP officers who owned cars and who were willing to use them on police work.[28] This policy enabled nearly 70 per cent of members of the APP and 50 per cent of the SPP members to own their own vehicles and use them in police work. As a result, both provincial forces saved the substantial expense previously incurred in hiring vehicles, and the efficiency of the forces was improved considerably. It moderated the problems of policing the vast territories of Saskatchewan and Alberta with a considerably smaller number of men compared to the RNWMP.

The APP also seriously considered employing other technical innovations, such as an aircraft for patrolling the international border and for other emergency uses. The commissioner proposed that a few air patrols through the Crow's Nest Pass to run down whisky runners would pay for the aircraft.[29] The APP also installed a radio broadcast system to speed up communication between superior officers and subordinates in 1929.[30]

There were some differences between the APP and the SPP in the development of police efficiency. Apparently, the APP were eager to improve efficiency particularly in the areas of organizational structure and training in police work. They created three specialized branches to improve their services: the Identification Bureau, the Criminal Investigation Branch, and the Liquor Branch. These branches dealt intensively with specific cases by concentrating the efforts of experienced police officers and constables who developed expertise in these fields. The specialization of police organizations brought the police up to a higher standard of efficiency. The commissioner of the APP also emphasized the importance of providing police officers with training in police work and law at the University of Alberta. A strong argument for such professional training was that, in the process of prosecuting criminal cases, the police officers' opponents were highly trained and highly paid defence attorneys.[31] For lack of training in law, police officers often found themselves at a disadvantage.[32]

The establishment of the programs was an important step in professionalizing the forces. It reduced the high turnover rate due to relatively low salary and made it possible to retain experienced members for longer periods of service. The APP also established a pension program shortly after the force was created. But the SPP established its pension program too late to carry out as the force was disbanded in 1928. In 1918, likely because of the low pay of the police constables, the board of the commissioners decided that the APP constables could draw and retain the cost of the cases prosecuted by constables. This measure possibly alleviated the problem of resignations by the constables who found difficulties in supporting their families with their meagre salaries ($110 per month on average), although this measure contradicted the stipulation of the Criminal Code of Canada. According to the Code, those fees could be used as remuneration only for constables who did not draw a salary.[33]

The adoption of those institutional and technical innovations in the APP was obviously influenced by other police forces. The University of California, at Berkeley, had created courses in law and criminology for California policemen. The British Columbia Provincial Police not only advised the APP on radio communication technology, but also helped install the equipment.

POLICE INDEPENDENCE FROM COMMUNITIES AND POLITICS

In the early days of police development, policing seemed to be unavoidably involved in local politics. To correct this problem, the RNWMP and the Irish Constabulary adopted a policy separating the police from the community to which they were assigned to shield them from political intervention. The police separation from communities and politics would enable the police to enforce law impartially and efficiently and cultivate the sense that the police acted for the protection of all classes in the community. Consequently, this system would help the police forces to legitimate their power with the public.

The provincial police also adopted this system. However, the adoption was modified largely by practical needs of the communities and the political circumstances. The Regulations of the Provincial Police emphasized the impartial enforcement of law and regulation. They stipulated that

Towards the attainment of complete police efficiency, it is essential that the members of the Force should cultivate and maintain the good opinion of the country at large, by prompt obedience to all lawful commands, by pursuing a steady and impartial line of conduct in the discharge of their duties, by their cleanly, sober and orderly habits, and by a civil and respectful bearing to all classes.[34]

According to the provincial police acts, members of the force had to swear to "impartially execute and perform the duties" before becoming constables.[35] But how did this emphasis on impartiality work in practice?

Stationing police in barracks that were situated outside of the community was not feasible. This is because the police did not have the resources to build their own barracks; the barracks of the police forces were typically rented houses or buildings on the main streets of the urban or rural municipalities. According to the police regulations, to maintain impartiality of policing, detachment constables were subject to periodic changes in their districts or detachments. But, in practice, these regulations were rarely implemented as the transfer from one detachment or district to another was very expensive. Nevertheless, the change of a detachment was a common measure for a constable against whom a complaint had been filed. At the same time, the police regulations prohibited a police constable from serving in a district in which he had family connections or from taking part in the liquor trade or other kinds of business. The case of constable Harper of the APP demonstrates that the APP did follow this rule closely. Harper was transferred out of the detachment at Vulcan because he was the son of a local justice of the peace and was well-acquainted with that community.[36] However, this rule could not be observed without difficulties. Unlike the RNWMP, most of the members of the provincial police were married men. In Saskatchewan the policy was not followed at all, or only rarely. The family of Inspector Simpson commanding Weyburn Division ran a small business in the district where he was assigned. The inspector's family supplied the milk to the Weyburn Mental Hospital in his wife's name. As a favour to the hospital, he frequently violated the regulations to act as a coroner for the hospital when a civilian coroner was actually available.[37]

Police constables were also prohibited from declaring their political affiliation. Provincial police acts treated "wearing a society or party emblem whilst on duty" and "manifesting any political partisanship" as serious offences.[38] Political interference seemed not to be a serious issue with the APP. But the independence of the SPP in law enforcement had been seriously questioned after Mr. Cross became the attorney general of the province in 1921 (a point we shall return to later).

At the beginning of the creation of the SPP in 1917, the attorney general of Saskatchewan, W.F.A. Turgeon, particularly emphasized the importance of insulating the police force from political influence when the SPP were formally commissioned. This emphasis was directly associated with the attorney general's experience with the former Secret Service, the old provincial police force. The Secret Service had been frequently attacked as a political organization serving the interests of the incumbent political party. The organization had no credibility. For this reason, Premier W.M. Martin instructed that the newly established SPP was to be one branch of the civil service. The administration of the police should be left to the chief of police.[39] This policy marked a significant departure from Premier Walter Scott's (1905–16) Liberal government's old partisan practice regarding the police as a part of political establishment in the previous decade. During the period 1917–21 when Turgeon was the attorney general, the commissioner of the SPP enjoyed considerable autonomy in managing the police.

However, after 1922 when Charles A. Dunning (1922–26) became the premier of the province, he resumed Walter Scott's practice of establishing party organization by using patronage appointments and contracts. James Cross, the attorney general, altered the policy set up by the former attorney general, Turgeon, and Premier Martin. Cross was especially interested in the police and assumed a very active role in the administration of the force. Consequently, Commissioner Mahoney's authority was subverted, and he became "a cog in the wheel" in Mahoney's own words.[40] The assistant commissioner, Tracey, believed that the practice led to political manipulation of the force. He noted that

The policy was a mistaken one and did not operate to the best interests of either the police force or of the government, because it brought the administration of the police in such proximity to the political side of the Government as to be too likely to encourage designing persons to try and affect it on political grounds, while it laid the government too easily open to the imputation that the police were subject to political control.[41]

Indeed, the evidence showed gross and open political interference with the force so that in 1930 the Saskatchewan government established a royal commission to inquire into the political interference with the SPP. The commission consisted of two judges from the Saskatchewan Court of Appeal and one from the Court of King's Bench.[42] Inspector Duckworth stated that, for some Liberal politicians, "it was of prime importance that a member of the Force should be politically fit, that he should exercise his influence and office for the advancement of party interests...."[43] The case of Inspector Duckworth was indicative of this point. In a provincial election, Duckworth did not go to vote because his doctor warned him to stay inside as he might get a serious infection on such a cold election day. Some party activists accused him of being a Conservative. Under much pressure, he was forced to write a report to the attorney general to clarify his Liberal Party affiliation.[44] The Liberal politicians frequently required police constables to act in the interests of the party. Under this circumstance, some constables were actively engaged in political work in some federal or provincial elections; others virtually became Liberal Party workers.[45]

Improper political influence was exercised personally by Attorney General Cross and the deputy attorney general of the province. They not only interfered with appointments, dismissal, and placement of constables, but interfered with their performance of their duties. During both federal and provincial elections, constables were frequently ordered to refrain from normal law enforcement with a view to benefiting the Liberal Party.[46] The 1930 Royal Commission Inquiry showed that political interference with the SPP was surprisingly extensive. The commission investigated seventeen incidents of improper conduct of police officers and politicians in the interests of the Liberal Party. The effect of political manipulation was detrimental to the force. Inspector Duckworth testified that, during the period when he was an inspector in the SPP, it was his experience that

Owing to the continual political interference during the latter years of the Liberal administration, it was an impossibility to enforce the law impartially. Political expediency took priority over principles. Such interference also ruined the morale within the Force. Members of the Saskatchewan Provincial Police force dabbled in politics and were encouraged and in some cases required to do so by "heelers" and the greater their efficiency in this respect rather than in their abilities as police officers was what frequently counted when it came to promotions. For the same reason men who had showed themselves unfit for the service could not be dismissed or transferred to some other point.[47]

Evidence in the report also shows that the police officers, including the commissioners and inspectors, expressed their concern with the fact that extensive political interference with the police was actually detrimental to both police efficiency and popularity. Some Liberal politicians not only treated the complaints of the police officers about the political interference as disloyal to the party, but also retaliated against officers, such as Duckworth, who attempted to resist the intervention. One result of the political interference was a growing public discontent: Cross was defeated in his Regina riding in the 1925 election, although the government soon found him a seat later in another constituency. However, the premier was warned that the attorney general was unpopular and the police force had lost the confidence of the public.

An immediate question, then, is why the SPP, not the APP, were manipulated by the politicians for political purposes. For the twenty-four years (1905–29) after the creation of the province, Saskatchewan was under the government of Liberal Party. The first premier of the province, Walter Scott (1905–16), emphasized the establishment of the Liberal Party organization using methods such as the allocation of various government jobs and contracts. The Saskatchewan Secret Service was established under the Scott government. The chief constable position went to C.A. Mahoney, "a Roman Catholic and a Strong Liberal."[48] As a result, the Secret Service not only enforced the liquor law, but also provided valuable assistance in establishing Liberal Party organization in the province. However, the second premier of the province, William Martin (1916–22) radically modified the former premier's practice by emphasizing the establishment of an efficient government. He insisted on separation of the SPP from party organization after 1917. Primer Charles A. Dunning (1922–26) and later Premier James G. Gardiner (1926–29), however, altered Martin's policy and resumed using the police to establish Liberal organization until the disbandment of the police in 1928.

By contrast, the Liberal Party of Alberta (1905–21) also used patronage appointments and some government departments to establish the party organization, but not to the extent to which the Saskatchewan Liberal Party did during the periods 1905–17 and 1922–28.[49] During the period 1921–35, the United Farmers government of Alberta had an official policy that "the elected members should not have anything to do with operating the political (i.e. electoral) machinery."[50] This might be a major reason why politicians in Alberta did not manipulate the APP for their own political interests. The different approaches to organizing governments and political parties in Alberta and Saskatchewan appear to have been responsible for the differences in the relationship between the police and politics in the provinces. This suggests that police autonomy was determined by individual politicians as much as by the principles of government.

The political interference with police work had profound effects on the daily activities of the police forces. As political interference with the SPP became more widely known, judicial confidence in them also declined. Justices of the peace frequently refused to be swayed by individual policemen or other party heelers in discharging justice. An uncooperative relationship developed between the members of the provincial police and the local judiciary, including police magistrates, justices of the peace, and juries in some districts.[51]

There was already significant animosity between the judiciary and the police. The police complained that justices of the peace and magistrates neglected their duties by being too lenient with "the prisoners," and that juries gave them too much of the benefit of the doubt.[52] The police also suspected that some witnesses for the defence perjured themselves to save their fellow citizens from the law.[53]

On the other hand, some justices of the peace and magistrates were not satisfied with the policemen either. Some of them had taken opportunities to censure constables in the presence of the accused.[54] They charged the police with trying to convict the accused at all costs. Such complaints about the police may have been well-founded. One of the most important criteria for the police in evaluating the performance of the justices was whether they always convicted the accused.[55] The Inspector of "C" Division of the APP explained that

In connection with Police Magistrates and JPs we have been fairly well upheld, very well by some, others appear to be somewhat weak-kneed. There is nothing that gives a police officer greater satisfaction than to know that when he has given his very best, worked night and day to bring his case to a successful conclusion, and proved the same to the satisfaction of the court, to see a good stiff sentence handed out. When it is not, he has not the same spirit to face all dangers and difficulties when he knows that he is not going to be upheld.[56]

Police frustration was not always unfounded either. There were many justices of the peace and magistrates who had little education, not to mention legal training.[57] At the same time, many justices of the peace were businessmen whose cases supplemented their business income. Therefore, they were subject to a great deal of external influence in the process of making their judicial decisions.[58] The police recommended that the government should appoint salaried travelling magistrates who could deal with the cases more independently.

CONCLUSION

Our investigations of the organizational structures and operation of the APP and SPP suggest that both police forces made considerable efforts to professionalize their operations by adopting various organizational structures, rules, and regulations. Clearly, there was a continuity between the provincial forces and the RNWMP. The SPP and APP adopted many of the same organizational structures, rules, and regulations to isolate the forces from external influence and to improve efficiency – which were created initially by the RNWMP. This significant influence of the RNWMP on the provincial police was conveyed through a large number of the former members of the RNWMP who joined the APP and SPP.

However, the professionalization of the police organization was an uneven process. The organizers of the APP showed more eagerness than those of the SPP to experiment with an organizational structure to promote police autonomy and independence. The APP were also more willing to adopt new technical innovations to improve police efficiency. The SPP enforced rules and regulations that could promote professionalism of the forces less strictly than the APP. The most important difference between the SPP and APP was that the former experienced more political interference by members of government, especially after 1921.

The Saskatchewan case might also imply that the attainment of police autonomy depends largely on the political culture. Concerns with professionalism within the forces may mitigate the extent to which they can be manipulated politically. But it is not a factor that can alter the ultimate fate of a police force in the face of a political machine with little concern for autonomy. Concern with professionalism among officers themselves may be a significant factor in the struggle over the autonomy and independence of police organization, as in nineteenth-century Toronto, but it is not determinative by itself.[59] Although the SPP were manipulated by politicians, this does not mean that the police had lost their legitimacy entirely. In fact, the police enjoyed a relatively favourable reputation as the political interference with the force was known widely to the public only after the 1930 Royal Commission Inquiry. This suggests that police legitimacy might be associated more with the police image and the services they provided for prairie settlers than with political reality.

It is interesting to observe that, although the social conditions justifying a quasi-military police force no longer existed as the provinces modernized, the provincial police still valued military traditions. They also possessed considerable judicial power and provided extensive assistance to the government departments. These features of the forces suggest that they still possessed some of the virtues of colonial police. They acted to preserve the peace and to uphold justice, even in Saskatchewan where their record was blemished. However, the switch from the federal force to the provincial forces was accompanied by a greater attention to the provincial agenda, aside from questions of direct interference. Then, the questions are: what is the object of control of the provincial police and what are the differences in the object of control between the provincial police and the RNWMP?

3   THE SHIFT IN THE OBJECTS OF POLICE CONTROL IN THE PRAIRIE PROVINCES

As we discussed earlier, to understand the objects of police control is important for our investigation of the police professionalization process. Existing studies in the objects of police control are based primarily on the analysis of the relationship between police and crime in urban communities. There is as yet no study on the question of how the objects of police control were transformed in rural communities while a police force undertook the professionalization process. The empirical study of the shift in police control has been based primarily on the analyses of arrest rates and police strength available in the annual reports of various urban police forces. This approach is based on the understanding that police behaviour could adequately account for the variations in arrest statistics.[1] Monkkonen, as an exponent of the theory, claims that "the variations in the arrest rate came from changing police behaviour ... rather than changing criminal behaviour."[2]

Employing Monkkonen's perspective, we examine the objects of provincial police control through analyzing crime trends as well as their correlation with police strength during 1906–50. This forty-five-year time frame allows us to understand changes in the function of the provincial police and the differences between the RNWMP and the provincial police in terms of their policing priorities. For these purposes, six variables concerning arrests for various crimes and police strength were created from the police annual reports.[3] The variables are (1) total arrest rate for crimes under the Criminal Code of Canada, (2) arrest rate for serious crime, (3) arrest rate for public order offences, (4) arrest rate for offences against the person, (5) arrest rates for offences against property, and (6) police strength rate.[4] These crime rates measure only crime trends in rural areas in Alberta and Saskatchewan because the RNWMP and the provincial police had jurisdiction over rural areas, including villages and rural municipalities. Major cities, such as Calgary, Edmonton, and Regina had their own city police.

The variable "total arrest rates" includes all arrests for crimes committed under the Criminal Code of Canada. Serious crime is equivalent to the variable "arrests for crime with victims" in Watts' study, which includes offences against the person and offences against property.[5] It differs from Monkkonen's variable "crime with victims," which is inflated with non-victimous elements, such as prostitution, gambling, liquor-related offences, and narcotic law violations.[6] This is because Monkkonen creates this variable by subtracting public order offences, including disorderly conduct, drunkenness, and vagrancy from total offences.

Consistent with definitions in Watts and Boritch and Hagan, the variable "public order offences" consists of offences concerning not only public disorder but public morals as well.[7] Specifically, it consists of offences against public order (carrying offensive weapons, prize fights, sedition); offences against public morals and public convenience (such as drunkenness, disorderly conduct, creating a disturbance, swearing and threats, vagrancy, prostitution, gambling, and game house keeping and frequenting); offences under Dominion statutes (such as violations of Indian Act, Railway Act, Lord's Day Act, and Juvenile Tobacco Act); and offences under provincial statutes (such as violations of the Liquor Act, Insanity Act, School Attendance Act, and Pool Room Act). The provisions of these federal and provincial statutes show that the intention of the legislative authorities was to regulate the lower orders of society, the groups dubbed as the "dangerous classes" in the nineteenth century. During the period from the beginning of the twentieth century to the 1930s, in the prairie provinces this class of people was primarily composed of the non-British immigrants who were subject to intense and sometimes constant surveillance by the police. Our examination of changes in the objects of police control will focus on a comparison between the trends in arrests for serious crime versus for public order offences.

In order to understand the trends in serious crime, we separate the variable "serious crime" into two variables: offences against the person and offences against property. The former is made up primarily of murder, attempted murder, manslaughter, rape, various assaults, and unlawful carnal knowledge. The offences against property include common theft, theft of cattle and horse, theft of grain, robbery, forgery, breaking and entering, false pretenses, and fraud.

THE OBJECTS OF PROVINCIAL POLICE CONTROL

During the period 1880–1970, Canada witnessed an ever-increasing trend in crime rates with a series of small fluctuations.[8] The rise in crime was so significant that Blanchard and Cassidy called the increase "exponential" in nature. Evidence suggests that rural crime trends in Alberta and Saskatchewan are not identical with the national pattern, although some similarities exist.

Figure 3.1 shows that in Saskatchewan, by and large, there was an overall increase trend in the aggregated arrest rates under the Canadian Criminal Code during 1906–50, which was similar to Canada's national pattern. Note that in Saskatchewan there were several large fluctuations during this period. In the first ten years after Saskatchewan became a province, beginning in 1905, the total arrest rates showed a slight increasing trend due to a crime wave during 1914 just before World War I. Over the period of 1917–28, the crime rates remained relatively stable. This suggests that during the twenty-two-year period from 1906 to 1928, Saskatchewan experienced a stable period in crime and violence compared to the period 1929–50. During 1929–41 the province witnessed an escalation of crime. In 1941 the arrest rates reached a record high 3,800 arrests per 100,000 population. This peak was followed by a long-lasting gradual decline during the period 1942–50. However, in this second decreasing period, the per capita rate of arrests on average was much higher than in the period before 1928.

In comparison, there are some similarities between Alberta and Saskatchewan in their patterns of arrest. In Alberta there was also a crime wave around 1914, and it was followed by a downward trend until 1917. During 1917–32, the crime rates showed a moderate but gradually increasing trend. The next crime wave came around 1933 and 1934. Then, the arrest rates fell again during 1935–46, but with large fluctuations. Therefore, from 1917 to 1940 a very gradual and long-lasting increasing trend can be observed.[9]

Whatever the overall changes in the trends in both Figures 3.1 and 3.2 may be, there are several shallow depressions during 1917–32 in Alberta and 1917–27 in Saskatchewan. Obviously, these depressions in arrest rates coincide with the periods when the provincial governments created and employed provincial forces. The coincidence between the depression and the duration of policing by provincial forces seems to support the argument that police organizations and policies were associated with arrest statistics.

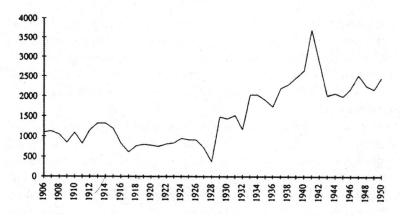

Figure 3.1 Arrests under the Criminal Code per 100,000 Population in Saskatchewan (Non-Urban)

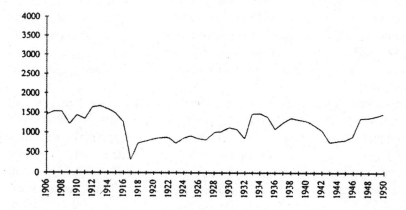

Figure 3.2 Arrests under the Criminal Code per 100,000 Population in Alberta (Non-Urban)

These depressions in crime levels result from significant changes in police strength during the period (as noted in the last chapter) and from the changing policies of the provincial forces, which set priorities on the enforcement of provincial legislation. These policy emphases may have reflected greater provincial government control of the police agendas. The crime "waves" during 1932–33 in Alberta and 1928–31 in Saskatchewan were closely associated with the transition from the provincial police back

Figure 3.3 Police Strength per 100,000 Population in Alberta and Saskatchewan (Non-Urban)

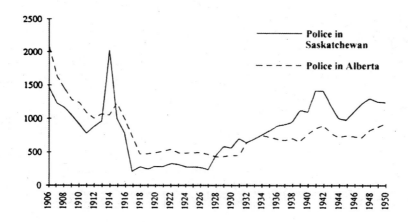

to the Mounties. The higher arrest rates beginning in 1928 in Saskatchewan and 1932 in Alberta (compared to previous periods) appear to be related to the RCMP's larger number of policemen, as indicated in Figure 3.3, and the RCMP's greater preoccupation with criminal matters.

Let us further analyze the crime trends in the two provinces by examining two disaggregated arrest rates: for crime with victims (serious crime) and for crime without victims (public order offences). Because these separate arrest rates have their own dynamics (complaint- versus police-initiated) in their relationships, we do not expect the trends of these separate arrest rates to follow each other closely.

This is because the provincial police were expected by the provincial governments to devote significant resources to the enforcement of provincial statutes, consisting primarily of public order offences, while the RNWMP were more interested in enforcing the Criminal Code (concerned more with serious crime) and federal statutes. Therefore, we would expect that during the period of 1917–28 in Saskatchewan and 1917–32 in Alberta, the arrest rates in public order offences would not surpass the arrest rates for serious crime. As we shall see, only after 1928 in Saskatchewan and 1932 in Alberta did the arrest rates for serious crime exceed the arrest rate for public order offences. This argument is based on our understanding that public order offences are a most unstable category of crime. They frequently reflect the values and norms of social elites and religious groups in society. Very often, scholars do not regard these offences as "real" crimes at all.

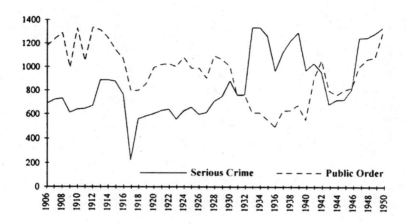

Figure 3.4 Serious Crime and Public Order Arrests per 100,000 Population in Alberta (Non-Urban)

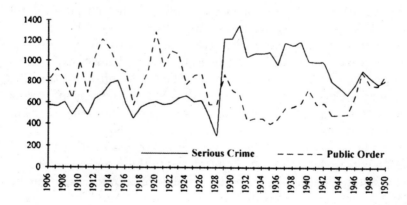

Figure 3.5 Serious Crime and Public Order Arrests per 100,000 Population in Saskatchewan (Non-Urban)

In Alberta (Figure 3.4) arrest rates for public order offences show a steady decreasing trend during the forty-five-year period, 1906–50. This trend is similar to the trend in public order offences in Canada as a whole. In Canadian history, liquor-consumption-related offences played an important role in determining the trend in public order offences. Drunkenness and disorderly conduct constituted about 56 per cent of total public order offences between 1869 and 1889.[10] According to Thorner, liquor-related offences constituted about 40–50 per cent of all crimes committed in southern Alberta around 1900.[11] Drunkenness and disorderly conduct rose dramatically before 1900. There was a similar situation in rural Alberta in the first two decades of the twentieth century. From 1906 to 1917, drunkenness and disorderly conduct made up about 23 per cent of the annual public order offences on average. After 1917, these offences were incorporated into violations of the Alberta Liquor Act, which continually accounted for a significant proportion of public order offences. In addition, vagrancy also constituted a significant percentage of the public order offences (about 14 per cent) at this time, although from 1917 to 1923, the number of vagrants arrested decreased. However, after 1924, the arrest rate for this offence rebounded to its pre-1917 level.

In comparison, in Saskatchewan (Figure 3.5) arrest rates for public order offences also show a downward trend during the forty-five-year period. This pattern is consistent with that in Alberta. In rural Saskatchewan, like in Alberta, vagrancy and offences related to liquor (such as drunkenness and disorderly conduct) accounted for a large proportion of the public order offences. Drunkenness and disorderly conduct accounted for about 23 per cent of the public order offences and vagrancy for about 13 per cent before 1917. After 1917, arrest rates for vagrancy increased, accounting for about 22 per cent of the public order offences. The offences of drunkenness and disorderly conduct virtually vanished from the returns in the police annual reports when they were treated as violations of the Saskatchewan Temperance Act.

Figures 3.4 and 3.5 also suggest that, compared with public order offences, there were upward trends in serious crimes, including offences against the person and offences against property, in both provinces. In Alberta, a dramatic increase in serious crime occurred around 1932, coinciding with a sharp decrease in public order offences. Similarly, in Saskatchewan, the largest increase started in 1928, while public order offences fell off sharply. Arrest rates for serious crime for the first time exceeded public order offence arrests in 1928 in Saskatchewan and in 1932 in Alberta. Figures 3.6 and 3.7 show a percentage comparison of arrests for serious crime versus public order offences in the two provinces. An important question for our investigation is: What exactly caused these changes?

There are two possible explanations for the shifts in the focus of police control: the policing policy thesis and the serious crime thesis. We argue that these two theses are not mutually exclusive, but complementary in accounting for the shift.

Figure 3.6 Percent Comparison of Serious Crime and Public Order Arrests in Alberta (Non-Urban)

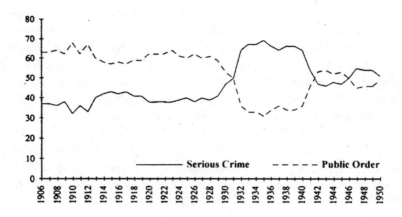

Figure 3.7 Percent Comparison of Serious Crime and Public Order Arrests in Saskatchewan (Non-Urban)

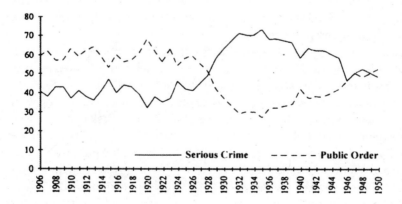

THE POLICING POLICY THESIS

This thesis suggests that the change from the provincial police to the RCMP in Alberta and Saskatchewan was associated with a shift in focus of control away from the dangerous classes. Figures 3.1 to 3.7 indicate that the transformation in police function in western Canada was intimately associated with the changes in police organization and, consequently, by implication, policing policy. This is suggested by the coincidence between the drastic decreases in public order offences and the transitions from the provincial police to the RCMP in 1932 in Alberta and 1928 in Saskatchewan.[12]

As noted in the last chapter, the Mounties traditionally had not been very interested in controlling public order offences. The data concerning the relationship between the arrest rates for criminal code offences and those for provincial statutes shows that the provincial police gave greater priority to enforcing provincial statutes over the Criminal Code of Canada. This does not mean that the provincial police let serious criminals "get away with murder." Rather, there were many public order offences in the Criminal Code, such as vagrancy, drunkenness and disorderly conduct, offences concerning houses of ill-fame, and other similar offences. Figures 3.8 and 3.9 indicate that, after 1917, there was an immediate increase in arrests for offences under provincial statutes while public order offences under the Criminal Code decreased in both provinces. This suggests that in exercising their discretion the provincial police gave more attention to public order offences stipulated under the provincial statutes than to the public order offences in the Criminal Code. Under the provincial mandate, the provincial police not only appeared to have received instructions to enforce certain provincial statutes vigorously, but also felt more pressure from both the public and the politicians to enforce policy-related provincial statutes.

The enforcement of liquor legislation by the provincial police is a good illustration of how the provincial police were increasingly pressured to enforce provincial statutes. The annual reports of the provincial police forces during these periods show that the police were constantly pressured by the provincial politicians to enforce the prohibition legislation. Figures 3.10 and 3.11 suggest that there was a drastic decline in arrests for public order offences under the Criminal Code after 1917, while liquor-related offences increased to a great extent. Before 1917 Criminal Code arrests for "offences against public order" and "offences against religion and

Figure 3.8 Arrests under Provincial Statutes vs. Public Order Offences under the Criminal Code per 100,000 in Alberta (Non-Urban)

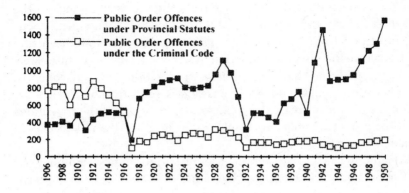

Figure 3.9 Arrests under Provincial Statutes vs. Public Order Offences under the Criminal Code per 100,000 in Saskatchewan (Non-Urban)

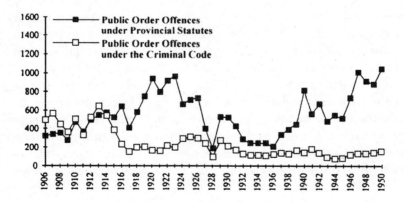

public convenience" accounted for about 53 per cent of the total public order crime in Alberta while liquor offences accounted for less than 10 per cent. When the APP policed Alberta (1917–32), these offences accounted for just about 20 per cent of the total public order offences, although the decrease in public order offences was not drastic. "Offences against public order" and "offences against religion and public convenience" in Saskatchewan also accounted for a large proportion (about 48 per cent) of

Figure 3.10 Liquor Offences vs. Public Order Offences under the Criminal Code per 100,000 in Alberta (Non-Urban)

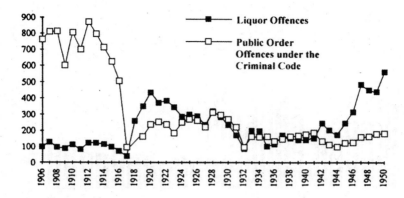

Figure 3.11 Liquor Offences vs. Public Order Offences under the Criminal Code per 100,000 in Saskatchewan (Non-Urban)

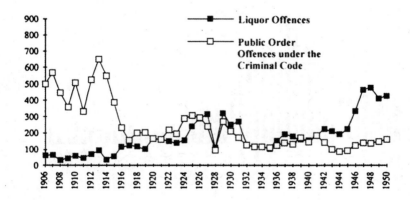

the total public order offence arrests before 1917. However, in the period 1917–28, they accounted for only 24 per cent of the public order offences. Offences under the liquor laws made up a predominant proportion of the public order offences after 1917 in both provinces. The enforcement of the pubic order provisions of the Criminal Code was overshadowed by the enforcement of liquor legislation.

Figure 3.12 Arrests for Public Order Offences per Police Officer in Alberta (Non-Urban)

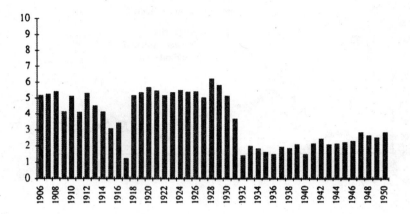

Figure 3.13 Arrests for Public Order Offences per Police Officer in Saskatchewan (Non-Urban)

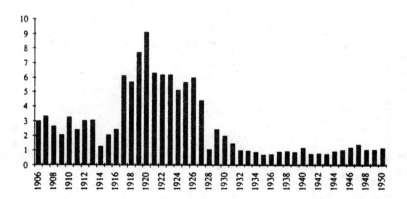

The RCMP, like the earlier RNWMP, were not interested in enforcing the provincial statutes, particularly the notorious liquor laws. As a federal force, the Mounties were more concerned with the enforcement of the Criminal Code. This is borne out by the findings from a statistical analysis using the Alberta and the Saskatchewan data. Our analysis suggests that the change in police organization from the APP to the RCMP in 1932 had a significant impact on the arrests for public order offences in the following years; in fact, arrests for public order offences decreased by 317 in 1932 and the number of the arrests stayed in this new lower level afterwards. Similarly, in Saskatchewan, the change in police organization from the SPP to the RCMP also had a significant impact on the level of public order arrest. The change in police organization in 1928 reduced the arrests for public order offences by 455. After that time, the arrests for the offences remained at the new level.[13]

This policy change was reflected in an instant decline in arrests for public order offences in both provinces, even after we take into account the changes in police strength. Figures 3.12 and 3.13 suggest that the average number of arrests for public order offences by each provincial police officer was approximately five as opposed to two arrested by each RCMP officer.

CHANGES IN CRIMINAL BEHAVIOUR

The second explanation of the shift of the objects of police control is concerned with changes in criminal behaviour. This thesis argues that an increasing trend in the incidence of serious crime helped the RCMP focus their attention on serious crime. Police arrests for public order offences are *proactive*. These arrests "depend on a [police] department's willingness to sanction, although public pressure can spur the police to action from time to time."[14] In practice, the police have great flexibility in apprehending offenders against public order and morals, and the arrest rates for these offences were indeed an index of the police reaction to criminal behaviour. This means that the changes in police policy can have a significant impact on arrests for public order offences.

However, this could not be the case for serious crime. Arrests related to serious crime (i.e., crime with victims) are *reactive*. These arrests are made because the police follow victim complaints rather than initiate arrests proactively. The seriousness of violent crimes and the demands for assistance from victims leave police little flexibility in dealing with these cases. In fact, because the prestige of the police is associated with combating serious crime, the police readily claim that preventing serious crime and apprehending dangerous criminals are their top priorities. These views were repeated by the superintendents and the commissioners of the RCMP and of the provincial police. This implies that an increase in the arrests for serious crimes may have reflected an increase in the actual incidence of serious victimization.

This argument can be examined empirically. The police can only make a finite number of arrests given that the police strength is fixed. As a result, if the incidence of serious crime increases, the police will devote more time and resources to apprehending serious criminals and, residually, spend less time and resources on the control of public order and moral offences. Therefore, the variations in the arrests for public order offences could be an inverse function of the arrests for serious crime. Statistically, if this assumption is correct, the arrest rates for serious crime over the long run would account for the variation in the arrest rates for public order offences and would do so independently of short-term policies that promote proactive control of public disorder. In order to examine this argument with statistical methods, we form the following two working hypotheses: (1) that the variable "police strength" varies systematically with the levels of serious crime and public order offences over time, and

(2) that serious crime was associated with the level of public order offences in the long run. The purpose of the first hypothesis is to examine the effect of the changing level of police strength on crime statistics.

The statistical methods employed in our analysis are the co-integration test and the error-correction model. These methods were developed by econometricians in the late 1980s to analyze time series data with auto-correlated error processes in linear regression and, at the same time, to avoid the problems in inferential statistics associated with conventional correction methods (such as the Cochrane-Orcutt approach to serial correlation). These methods allow us not only to estimate long-run relationships, but also to model short-run dynamics between time-series variables. (Appendix B provides a detailed explanation of these methods for readers who are interested in time-series analysis.)

The findings from the statistical analyses in Appendix C indicate that there was no long-run relationship between the variable "police strength" and arrest rates for serious crime or public order offences in either Alberta or Saskatchewan. The absence of a long-term causal relationship between police strength and serious crime in both provinces reveals that the trends in serious crime and public order offences could be explained only by factors other than police strength. These results contradict Monkkonen's observation that there was a long-run causal relationship between crimes and police strength. Arrest rates are more influenced by what police do than by their numbers.

The fact that police strength does not explain the levels of serious crime in the Alberta and Saskatchewan data may be due to inflexibility in police numbers, especially during the period where the provincial police controlled the provinces. Because of financial constraint, over more than a ten-year period, police strength hardly changed, despite fluctuations in crime. This stability in police strength may have contributed to the absence of any causal relationship between police strength and changing levels of serious crime.

Concerning the hypothesis of the relationship between the incidence in serious crime and public order offences, the findings from the time-series analysis confirm our initial theoretical argument that changes in police function were due to an increase in the actual level in serious crime, in addition to changes in police policies and police regimes. This is supported by the fact that the changing level of arrest rates for public order offences can be related systematically to arrest rates for serious crime over time.

Theoretically, the existence of the long-run relationship between the increasing trends in the incidence of serious crime and public order offences in Alberta and between property and public order offences in Saskatchewan suggests the presence of a mediating factor, which in this case is policing. The increase in the incidence of serious crime led the police to devote more time and resources to the apprehension of serious criminals and, residually, fewer arrests for public order offences resulted. This would result in high arrest rates for serious crime and low arrest rates for the public order offences. Similarly, when the incidence of serious crime came down occasionally, the police might have given more attention to the arrest of public order offenders, and consequently, the arrest rates for public order offences would be relatively high. This provides an explanation for the common fluctuations of arrest trends in serious crime and public order offences over time. Police behaviour appears to be the force (also called "common attractor" in econometrics) drawing arrest variables for various crimes to move together and to behave in a systematic and causally related way.

CONCLUSION

A shift in the focus of police control from the dangerous classes to serious crime is an important process in the professionalization of policing. Evidence suggests that there was indeed a transformation in police function from class control to crime control in the prairie provinces during the first half of this century. The transformation was a gradual but steady process beginning in the early stages of the tenure of the provincial police. However, only after 1932 in Alberta and 1928 in Saskatchewan did the police complete the shift, as indicated by the fact that arrests rates for serious crime exceeded those for public order offences.

There are two existing explanations given for the factors that promoted the shift in the objects of police control. Following Monkkonen we have examined police policies and police strength. Our findings suggest that the changes in police policy were a direct consequence of the transition from the provincial police to the RCMP. This policy change shifted the police focus away from the public order offences and the dangerous classes. However, the statistical analysis suggests that there is little evidence that police strength *per se* accounted for the change.

At the same time, we have argued that an increase in the incidence of serious crime was another factor reinforcing the shift. Our statistical analysis confirms that the gradual long-term decrease in arrests for public order offences can be explained by the increase in the incidence of serious crime, particularly by increasing trends in offences against property. Consequently, this finding suggests that the change in criminal behaviour as displayed by the increase in serious crime helped the police focus their attention on controlling serious crime. Thus, we can draw the conclusion that the two theses – the police policy thesis and the thesis of changes in criminal behaviour – jointly account for the shift in the focus of control from the dangerous classes to serious crime during the period 1906–50 in the prairie provinces. The two theories are complementary. The police policy thesis better explains why the provincial police were preoccupied with public order regulations; the theory of changes in criminal behaviour accounts for the RCMP's subsequent attention to serious crime.

However, the transformation in the objects of police control toward serious crime did not completely eliminate the police role in controlling the marginal elements of society. In fact, the repressive police role in this area was gradually replaced by police as providers of social services. In other words, the nineteenth century's dangerous classes were increasingly redefined as the twentieth century's "vulnerable classes." Social services assisted the police to maintain their legitimacy and to co-opt the dangerous classes, i.e., immigrants, into Anglo-Canadian Society.

4 PROVINCIAL POLICE ACTIVITIES IN CONTROLLING THE "DANGEROUS CLASSES" AND SERIOUS CRIME, 1917–32

Over the period 1917–32, police work was concerned decreasingly with what historians call the "dangerous classes" and increasingly with serious crime. In this chapter, we examine in greater detail what was entailed in police control over these two areas. More specifically, we shall examine the complexities of multifarious police activities in the control process through our attempt to answer the following questions: why did police focus on immigrants as the embodiment of dangerous classes on the prairies; what was the police role in "Canadianizing" immigrants; what were police activities in controlling serious crime; and what was the relationship between the increase in crime and other social factors in the provinces?

THE INFLUX OF FOREIGN IMMIGRANTS

The changes in the objects of provincial police control were intimately associated with the influx of foreign immigrants in the first quarter of the twentieth century. Although Sir John A. Macdonald initiated the policies of national development via western expansion and completion of the transcontinental railway in the late nineteenth century, the North-West Territories did not attract large numbers of settlers until the end of the nineteenth century. In the 1890s, guided by economic and nationalistic motives, Clifford Sifton, a cabinet minister responsible for immigration and Wilfrid Laurier, the prime minster, made tremendous efforts to appeal to immigrants.[1] As a result of their efforts, in 1911 there were 1,128,941 immigrants in the western provinces (including Manitoba, Saskatchewan, and Alberta) who were from the United States, the British Isles, and continental Europe. However, these efforts to attract immigrants were charged with racist prejudices. Palmer and Palmer observe that

> Widely held notions of a world-wide racial hierarchy based on social Darwinism, which circulated as scientific fact in the English-speaking world in the late nineteenth century, were firmly embedded in Canada's immigration policy. During this period of British imperial ascendancy, British immigrants were considered "best." Anglo Canadians gloried in the exploits of the British Empire, believing in loyalty to God, king, and country. They had been taught that the Anglo-Saxons and the British government were the apex of biological evolution and human achievement.[2]

The 1931 Census of Canada suggests that during the first three decades of the twentieth century, the majority of the population in Alberta and Saskatchewan could trace their roots to Britain. Foreign immigrants of non-British origin represented about 35 per cent of the total population in Alberta and Saskatchewan, as shown in every national census conducted between 1901 and 1931.[3]

Table 4.1: Total Population by Origin in Alberta[4]

Birth Place	1901	1911	1921	1931
Canada	41,782	161,86	315,090	425,867
British Isles	7,643	68,252	97,505	106,781
Foreign Born				
Austria	5,712	10,583	9,981	4,083
Germany	1,186	6,102	4,606	8,148
Russia	2,439	10,011	11,572	15,561
Poland	-------	5,816	3,073	8,202
Sweden	1,609	6,345	6,535	7,431
Norway	-------	5,761	6,681	8,820
Denmark	302	1,380	2,353	5,500
Other	12,186	96,713	129,171	139,228
Total	73,022	374,295	588,454	731,605

Table 4.2: Total Population by Origin in Saskatchewan[5]

Birth Place	1901	1911	1921	1931
Canada	55,084	248,751	457,833	603,240
British Isles	10,506	80,177	99,166	99,730
Foreign Born				
Austria	7,695	15,878	17,039	11,382
Germany	992	8,300	6,409	9,832
Russia	12,146	23,084	28,315	31,382
Poland	-------	8,797	12,989	29,594
Sweden	484	6,209	7,381	7,580
Norway	-------	7,625	9,240	10,721
Denmark	67	982	1,515	2,947
Other	4,173	91,735	116,434	114,106
Total	91,279	492,432	757,510	921,785

Many of these immigrants were from southern and east-central Europe. The largest groups of immigrants were Slovaks, Hungarians, Ukrainians, Poles, and Romanians from central and eastern Europe and from the Austro-Hungarian Empire.[6] Historical evidence from this period suggests that many Anglo-Canadians regarded east and south European immigrants as culturally inferior.[7] Nevertheless, they believed that these immigrants could be eventually assimilated into Canadian society. Therefore, the term "foreign immigrants" was often used to refer to those peoples whose origins were the least anglicized, i.e., from southern and east-central Europe. Most Anglo-Canadians judged foreign immigrants on the basis of how quickly they could be assimilated into Canadian society; immigrants from east-central Europe were not quickly assimilated and were thought to be in need of a "Canadianization" campaign.[8]

The provincial police were particularly troubled by the fact that foreign immigrants were lacking in knowledge about Canadian law and order. Commissioner Bryan of the APP in 1921 stated that

The province of Alberta owing to its cosmopolitan population is hard to police, alien settlements being scattered all over it. These people banded together as they are, and in a good many instances retaining the customs and mode of life they lived in their own countries before coming to Canada, are not as yet educating themselves with regard to the laws of this country, it is impossible to obtain evidence from them, and they are too prone to look upon any policeman as an enemy instead of a friend.[9]

The police believed that an important method of educating the immigrants to observe laws was to enforce laws among them. This often led the immigrants to complain about justices of the peace and police constables who punished them severely over trivial disputes. The demand to remove the justice of the peace, Mr. Woolly, and Constable Varzari by local residents in Andrew, Alberta in 1917 was a case in point. A report by the inspector of Edmonton Division from the investigation into the complaint concluded that the justice of peace and the constable only carried out their routine duties involving prosecutions and trials of cases concerning local Russian nationals. He noted that

I am informed that the petition circulated and signed was done at the instance of certain parties who are in opposition to the proper enforcement of the Canadian law among the Russian People.... In this district there is a large community of extremely ignorant people. Administer the law as it is administered among our Canadian people, and these people may some day be spoken of as intelligent. Cease to administer it ... these people will never be good citizens or have any respect for the laws of the country.[10]

Opposition to enforcement of laws only strengthened the police belief that foreign immigrants had to be educated (i.e., arrested) to establish the rule of law.

The immigration booms during the period 1896–1914 in the Northwest Territories and the prairie provinces were correlated with the rise of three interrelated social and moral reform movements: the social gospel movement, the prohibition movement, and the women's rights movement. Concerning the immigrants, the urban middle-class Anglo-Canadians who led these movements argued that the new immigrants possessed a series of social and moral defects. They argued that immigrants were more inclined toward crime, violence, prostitution, family breakdown, and political corruption than the rest of the population.[11] Alberta historian Howard Palmer identified this anti-immigrants sentiment as "nativism" – a mixture of prejudice, racism, and nationalism.[12]

The police echoed this nativistic sentiment in order to garner support. They frequently suggested that immigrants were inclined to crime as they had little sense of law and order. They argued that the level of immigration was a predominant factor that determined the levels of various crimes in different districts. Higher crime rates in districts were correlated with higher levels of foreign immigrants.[13] The increase in the number of both serious crimes (such as murder, assault, and theft) and public order offences was attributed primarily to the foreign population. APP Inspector J.S. Piper of Division A in the Edmonton area reported to the commissioner in 1928 that "the increase in the number of both murder and stealing can be attributed to the foreign population mostly, who often think they have the right to take the law into their own hands, and settle any dispute that may happen to arise."[14] Commissioner Mahoney of the SPP, in his 1919 Annual Report to the attorney general, expressed a similar view. He claimed that "a large percentage of the crimes committed can be traced to persons of foreign extraction."[15]

No doubt the police's assertion of the existence of the inherent association between crime and immigration population is completely baseless.[16] However, these views had important policy implications. For example, police detachments were located to ensure surveillance of immigrants. In the mining communities where foreign immigrants were concentrated, the police deployed more detachments and had more policemen in each detachment than in any other place. However, police control of foreigners was actually quite complex. The police found that each policing situation was different and required different policies and approaches. To say police control of foreign immigrants was suppressive is an oversimplification of the complexity of the relationship between immigrant populations and the police.

POLICING STRIKERS, VAGRANTS, AND RADICALS

During the period from 1917 to the 1930s, strikes in mining communities in both provinces, especially in Alberta, were fairly common. Immigrant workers played a prominent role in those strikes. Because so few English-speaking Canadians were interested in such socially undesirable work, immigrants made up a large proportion of the miners.[17] As a result, they played a prominent role in strikes. Concurrently, radical organizations realized that working-class communities with their large numbers of foreign components provided good grounds for organizing radical political activities. APP Superintendent McDonnell observed in 1919 that many strikes in coal mining districts were organized by "agitators of the [One Big Union] who visited all the mines in the district holding meetings and they soon had the foreign element in line with them, the latter being in the majority in the unions."[18] Consequently, in Alberta and Saskatchewan, mining communities became a central concern of the police.[19] In his 1918 Annual Report, APP Inspector Brankley in the Calgary region called mining towns, such as Drumheller, "hot bed[s] of the disease"[20] because the foreign immigrants repeatedly precipitated the industrial strikes in those areas. For the police, labour unrest posed significant difficulties for law enforcement and the maintenance of order in mining communities. However, their role was not one of simple suppression. To win the confidence of the workers, the police also played the role of industrial mediators. This is shown in the "rules of engagement" during strikes.

The police were legally required and instructed by the commissioners or superintendents to execute their enforcement duties in an impartial manner in industrial disputes between strikers and owners or managers. According to the SPP Annual Report of 1920, the Criminal Code of 1920 stipulated that "it is lawful for workmen to combine in a strike in order to get higher wages, and persons who aided or encouraged such strike would not be committing an unlawful act because they were endeavouring to bring about something that is legal."[21] The policemen who were involved in maintaining order in strike areas were frequently instructed to abstain from all acts of interference in the labour disputes. Their duties in connection with a strike were strictly to protect life and prevent the destruction of property. The SPP constables were specifically instructed not to display their sidearms unless in a situation where a riot occurred.[22]

However, historical evidence suggests that the police identified with the property owners. Many policemen regarded strikes as harassment of property owners, which they would have strictly forbidden. APP Inspector Brankley in charge of the Calgary Division suggested in 1918 that there had been few strikes and that the mining industry had been operating in full swing. This condition was not because the miners became more reasonable, but because the operators had acceded to practically all the demands levied by employees who had been anything but reasonable. The inspector reported that "in fact the operators are practically at the mercy of the Miners Union, which, when consideration is given to the fact that same is composed almost wholly of alien enemies, is a most regrettable state of affairs to be tolerated."[23] It should be pointed out that the union radicals were not entirely composed of "alien enemies" as police alleged. In fact, many of union organizers were British subjects.[24] The major reason for the police to single out "foreign immigrants" as the union radicals is that the police attempted to invoke, once again, nativism and get support from the general public in their control of the radical union activities.

Although the police were sympathetic to the property owners in the industrial disputes, this did not mean that the police acted only in the interests of property owners or managers during industrial disputes. The owners and operators of the mines under a strike often requested police protection. However, for the police, the occurrence of a strike was not a sufficient reason to send constables to the areas. One of the important criteria for providing police protection was the existence of threats to life and destruction of property. Typically, mine operators complained that they did not receive enough protection from the police. The police believed that the mine operators frequently exaggerated their situations and were trying to use the police to break picket lines. These differences in perception certainly caused friction between the police and the mine management. Sometimes, mine operators directly petitioned police protection or complained to the press or the premiers of the provinces about the inaction of provincial police. When this occurred, the provincial police believed that mine operators were trying to embarrass them politically.[25]

Frequently, the police did gather a few constables from the vicinity detachments and send them to the strike areas. The police presence often had the effect of pacifying the strikers. Subsequently, the police had to explain to the mine operators that they could not station the constables any further as there were no threats to life or property.

Given these tensions, the police were clearly compelled to present themselves as a neutral mediator. The police often informed the workers that they were allowed to form a picket line as long as there was no violence involved. In 1925, APP Commissioner Bryan advised a group of miners from the Red Deer Valley Miners Union, including the well-known union activists, Messrs Jenkins, Hall, and Metcalfe, that "as long as no force or violence was attempted, they would be allowed to walk along the road in the vicinity of the mines but that law and order would be maintained if it took a thousand men to do it."[26] Occasionally, the police even gave some practical advice to the union leaders concerning how a labour impasse could be resolved. In the Drumheller mining strikes of 1925, the commissioner of the APP advised radical union leaders to step down in order to achieve settlements with the operators.[27]

There *were* occasions where the police acted more as suppressors than mediators. On the morning of January 4, 1923, a picket line was formed by eighty men and forty women at the public road to the Bush Mines in the Edmonton area. The picket line was eventually driven back. During this melée, Constable Engel was struck over the head and lost consciousness. Constable Keen was struck in the face. When the order was given to the mounted section to clear the strikers away, several mounted men were struck by rocks. Constable Farthing sustained a deep cut over the eye and one on the nose. Constable Marks had a serious cut on the head. Batons were used freely by the mounted and dismounted policemen. The strikers were eventually dispersed. Obviously, many strikers were also injured. But this fact was not entered in the police records.[28]

Police crackdowns on labour movements and strikes were limited by the Criminal Code. However, in interpreting and enforcing provisions in the Criminal Code, police discretion and prejudice played a significant role. There were many instances in which the police used sections of the law to harass the organizers and leaders of the labour movements. According to sections 132 and 134 of the Criminal Code, police constables were instructed that

> ... where the ultimate purpose of the strike, as declared in public speeches and propaganda was revolution to overthrow the existing form of government in Canada and the introduction of a form of socialist or Soviet rule in its place, which was to be accomplished by general strikes, force, and terror, and if necessary bloodshed, the conspirators of such a strike are guilty of seditious conspiracy.[29]

Unlawful assemblies and riots were dealt with by sections 87 and 90; and nuisances by sections 221 and 222.

One important tactic that the police used to break strikes and to arrest their organizers was to connect industrial action to the Communist Party of Canada. This approach resonated with the fears of class warfare among the middle- and upper-class Anglo-Canadians aroused by the Bolshevik Revolution. Strikers and political radicals were often viewed as part of the criminal classes. Such characterization justified the use of greater force than the public might have accepted otherwise and led to the frequent detention of strikers and their leaders. The 1930 Annual Report from the headquarters of the APP states that the strikers at Mercoal were composed mostly of a very radical element and communist leaders from Toronto.[30] The report from "A" Division referred to the same group of workers as the "mob." To break the picket line and reduce potential violence, the police arrested five workers on charges of being members of an unlawful assembly. They were found guilty of the charge and sentenced to one month in Fort Saskatchewan Jail and a fine of $50. In addition, some of them were also found guilty of common assault, riotous conduct, and obstructing a peace officer. These punishments had the effect of quelling all the radical elements in the mining areas in the province.[31]

In fact, the police also implicated the communists in violent criminal behaviour. Two cases in point were the dynamiting of a fan house and box car loader in the Elgon Mine of Alberta in 1927 and the dynamiting of William Hopkin's house near Newcastle Mine in 1925. In spite of the most strenuous investigations involving several police officers, no evidence was discovered that incriminated labour activists. However, in a general remark, the inspector in the Calgary District stated that

... [the Communist Party of Canada] is small but very energetic, and has been at the back of most of the labour trouble during the past summer. They were undoubtedly responsible for the theft of dynamite from the Newcastle mine, also for the explosion which occurred outside, and partially wrecked the house occupied by William Hopkins, with fortunately no loss of life. This case, I regret to report, has not been brought to a successful conclusion, but we hope to arrive at a successful solution. The dynamite was found about forty feet to the rear of the Communist Headquarters, by some children who were playing, and the discovery prevented any further outrage which might have been perpetrated.[32]

The police also noted the significant influence of individual organizers on "foreign elements" and the labour movement. After Lewis McDonald (a.k.a. "Kid Burns"), a local Communist Party leader, was sentenced to the penitentiary at Prince Albert, the police found that both communist propaganda and the intermittent outbursts of violent strikes vanished in Drumheller. Lewis McDonald was not only a party leader but also possessed influence with foreign immigrants.[33]

The police role vis-à-vis the mining community was complicated. They were required to permit lawful strikes and to act impartially during the strikes. However, they were opposed to industrial mass action and were frequently exposed to danger in suppressing it. In addition, there was deep animosity towards the union because of their foreign elements and their communist sympathies. This combination in facts exacerbated conflicts and fomented violence in labour struggles. On the other hand, the police resented manipulation of their function by the mine owners who attempted to co-opt police control to break strikes, and, when that failed, to embarrass the police politically. The outcome was a situation in which the police were drawn into suppression of unionists during periods of conflict while trying to maintain a semblance of neutrality and by occasionally mediating tensions to forestall violence.

In contrast, police activities in controlling the unemployed and vagrants were concerned primarily with maintaining public order and with preventing serious crime. For the police, there was a close correlation between vagrancy, unemployment, and crime; vagrancy involved the unemployed foreign elements. As a result, the provincial police made vagrancy a priority.

In rural areas, charges for vagrancy were very much seasonal offences associated with harvesting and threshing periods. Usually, a large number of harvesters poured into rural areas during the fall from the cities and from other provinces. Towards the end of the season, the provincial police expected the harvesters to leave for home. After the end of harvesting season, police arrests for vagrancy usually increased as some harvesters drifted without a fixed address.

The police attributed the vagrancy problem to two factors. First was the policy of neighbouring provinces towards the floating or unemployed elements of their population. In 1924, APP Inspector E.W. Bavin in the Lethbridge area explained that

Owing to the fact the large cities in B.C. and Manitoba have been endeavouring to keep their unemployed moving, they have been drifting through the west, and a number of them are a very useless type. Consequently, we show an increase in the number of vagrants handled.[34]

The second factor was the availability of government relief. When seasonal work was finished, some labourers remained in the provinces because they intended to collect relief from the provincial governments or look for new employment.[25] In either case, they were unwelcome. Police enforcement of the vagrancy law suggests that they must have been aware that enforcement was not only to maintain public order, but also to discipline labourers. When other jobs were available at the end of the harvest, the police always charged the persons for vagrancy who refused to accept other jobs, usually in mining or lumbering. However, in those years where the inclement weather reduced harvesters' income to the extent that there were few jobs available to them, the police were actually sympathetic towards them and reported that many of them deserved government relief.[36] Despite limited amounts of relief, the police were reluctant to turn away the deserving applicants. On the contrary, they always rejected applications from persons who refused to accept a job or who were found drunk.[37] In controlling the unemployed foreign immigrants, the police were quick to link the activities of the unemployed directly to the Communist Party of Canada. In 1928, about eight hundred men arrived at Edmonton, demanding government relief. The police estimated that over 85 per cent of the protestors were foreign immigrants from central European countries.[38] The police believed that the protest could cause social disorder because the organizations had "red elements." Commissioner Bryan of the APP reported in 1928 that

There is no doubt that Edmonton has been made a central point for these [the unemployed] to congregate, where they are engineered by the Communistic Party. I am endeavouring to secure some data on this, and it will be reported to you later. I do not anticipate any trouble but it is rather hard to anticipate what might happen when a bunch of ignorant foreigners are harangued by one or two fiery and radical orators in their own language.[39]

In 1925, one hundred and twenty-five unemployed in Calgary marched and boarded a freight train to Edmonton demanding work or subsistence from the government. Upon their arrival in Edmonton, they were arrested by a squad of police on a charge of stealing a ride on the railway. After a brief interview by government officials, they were placed in cars attached to the midnight express and returned to Calgary under police escort.[40] The leader of the organized march was A.J. Bolter, who was identified as an extreme radical.[41] The report from the commissioner of the APP emphasized that radicals were dangerous to the maintenance of the public peace. They intended to exploit the situation of the poor and unemployed by fomenting trouble among the working class. It was said that the radicals even intended to educate children in communist ideology. The police complained that "while our men were marching, mounted or dismounted, out to where they were training at Drumheller, children would line up on the sidewalk and sing the *red flag*."[42]

The police often dispersed the meetings attended by the unemployed by accusing the speakers of being communists. In 1931, at a meeting of the unemployed, when the police attempted to arrest one of the speakers, they were attacked with stones and other projectiles. Constable Carter was severely injured after being struck on the head with a brick. The offenders were arrested. On that evening, the police raided Communist Party headquarters in Calgary and arrested several of its members.[43] This connection between the unemployed and the communist movement was used to justify police action. However, what it amounted to politically was an attempt to deprive the unemployed of their right to express grievances through collective protests.

Because the ranks of the unemployed were comprised mainly of foreign immigrants, the police carefully watched this group. Relief registration among the unemployed was usually conducted by the Criminal Investigation Branch in Alberta.[44] In fact, APP Detective Furser at the Calgary District, along with other detectives, was appointed as relief officer in charge of caring for those left destitute by unemployment.[45] The police believed that these people had an explosive capacity that could result in social unrest. However, such incidents never occurred.

For the police, one way to reduce the influence and potential danger of social unrest by foreign immigrants was to increase the proportion of English-speaking employees who would offset the effect of foreign immigrants in industrial and mining communities. Inspector W. Brankley in the Calgary area said that

One desirable thing accompanying the return of the soldier from overseas, is the average increase in the number of English speaking people who are finding employment there. The big proportion of employees has been foreign born, Italian and Austrian for most part, with a sprinkling of other nationalities, and the English speaking element as it grows in percentage will offset, and subdue the Bolshevik tendencies of the others.[46]

"CANADIANIZING" FOREIGN IMMIGRANTS

To this point we have seen how the police were used to combat foreign influences in the areas of labour disputes, vagrancy, and radical politics. The police also had a more general and unwritten mandate to impose Anglo-Canadian values and norms on immigrants to assimilate them into Canadian society. Similar to the police in nineteenth-century England, the provincial police committed great time and resources to controlling immigrants' leisure time. Leisure activities, such as drinking, gambling, and dancing, were monitored to meet Anglo-Canadian moral standards. The police routinely attended public activities, such as fairs, picnics, roundups and stampedes, dances, and boxing bouts. Pool and billiard rooms were inspected regularly.

Enforcement of the School Attendance Act and enforcement of the Liquor Law are the most interesting areas in which we can see not only the police attitudes and activities in enforcing moralistic law, but also the reactions of the population to the imposition of morality by the state. Many Anglo-Canadians held that the major defect of central and eastern Europeans was their lack of education. The assimilation of the immigrants would have to be achieved through the enforced attendance in the Canadian school system. This was required by the School Attendance Act in Saskatchewan and the Truancy Act in Alberta. These laws made parents accountable for the failure of children to attend school. Many parents were prosecuted for violation of the law. The majority of them were convicted and fined for child non-attendance. More than 75 per cent of those parents summoned for violating the provision of the laws were foreign-speaking immigrants, primarily Russians and Mennonites.[47]

These laws were not popular pieces of legislation for many citizens of the provinces. Many immigrant parents from central and eastern Europe disliked sending their children to either tax-supported denominational or public schools where only English was taught. They viewed school attendance as a threat to the survival of their culture.[48]

In fact, the police did not enjoy enforcing the school law either, particularly in Saskatchewan. During the early period of the force, the SPP investigated and prosecuted as many as 1,500 cases annually.[49] This consumed a considerable amount of police time and resources. Several division inspectors complained that the enforcement of the law should not be part of police duties. For instance, the inspector of Weyburn Division argued that

> During the past few months, a great number of reports requiring investigation and prosecution have been received from the Department of Education, under the School Attendance Act, and a considerable amount of valuable time has had to be given to these cases by the constables in charge of detachments and I have often thought if there was any way in which the Department of Education could appoint their own investigators as I believe you will agree with me that prosecutions of this nature do not enhance the good name of the police force ... people begin to think that the police are running around looking for this kind of petty case instead of looking after cases of a serious nature.[50]

The inspector of Saskatoon Division in 1919 had a similar complaint. He suggested that "the enforcement of the School Attendance Act does not harmonize with general police work and as no increase of the Division has been made to meet this extra work, in a good many instances the investigation of crime has suffered."[51] In answering the request of the Banff School Board for the enforcement of the Truancy Act of Alberta, the Board of Commissioners of the APP also indicated that the APP could enforce the act only "so long as such work did not interfere with the regular duties of the constables."[52] However, the number of cases concerning the violations of the School Attendance Act declined gradually after 1920 in the annual reports of the SPP.

Another aspect of the Canadianization of immigrants was the provision of a variety of services that could assist immigrants to live in a "Canadian" lifestyle. Generally, the police function was associated with crime. However, the provincial police had a very complex set of mandates. They acted as game wardens, fire and theatre inspectors, organizers for prairie fire fighters, child protectors, advisors to newcomers, and vehicle and road inspectors. Due to the introduction of automobiles, patrolling highways and regulating traffic for public safety quickly became additional important but time-consuming duties.[53] Occasionally, the police also enforced sanitary regulations to restrain the spread of diseases. In 1919, for instance, the APP rigorously enforced the quarantine regulations associated with the Spanish influenza epidemic. This was an urgent task and the police put every available officer into enforcement of the regulation. Many special constables were used. Routine work was neglected and scheduled trials were postponed. At the same time, it was also a dangerous task. Several policemen caught the disease and died.[54]

During the recession following World War I, many people became destitute. The police were in charge of caring for these persons in the rural areas. Some police officers were appointed as relief officers who distributed rations to the destitute. Searching for missing persons was another time-consuming service rendered by the police. For this purpose, the police travelled countless miles. Frequently, such searches proved fruitless. They were also charged with the duty of investigating and reporting all sudden or accidental deaths, including suicides. Subsequently, they also compiled an inventory of the deceased's estate for public administration. The police also routinely engaged in traditional duties that had been performed by the RNWMP before 1917 in western Canada, such as providing escorts for persons who were mentally ill and for visiting dignitaries, and being in attendance at coroners' requests. In addition, the police conducted a large number of inquiries and investigations on behalf of various government departments, such as investigations into whether employees were justly entitled to compensation.[55]

According to the statistics from APP annual reports for 1930, the police put about 43,026 hours into social service activities. Although the service work probably amounted to less than 10 per cent of total police working hours, the police recognized that these activities were important to the public. The police claimed that "this is a part of our work which is of great public value and importance," though it did not result in prosecutions.[56] In fact, such social services served multiple purposes, including providing valuable assistance for the newcomers, helping to integrate immigrants into Canadian society, and generating police legitimacy.[57]

POLICING SERIOUS CRIME

In the last chapter we examined how the proactive elements of policing were associated primarily with trends in public order offences. In the above discussion we have attempted to elaborate how proactive policing was directed at the immigrant population. However, we also discovered in the last chapter that the most serious cases of crime appear to come to police "reactively," i.e., as victim complaints. Now we shall answer questions such as what was the nature of police control in the area of serious crime, what did it entail, and what did the police do and think about it?

Serious crimes consisted of offences against the person and property stipulated in the Criminal Code of Canada. Offences against the person included crimes such as murder, rape, and various assaults. The offences against property were composed of thefts, robbery, and breaking and entering, etc. The police believed that crime prevention and apprehension of serious criminals were an essential part of their duties. These activities often generated or reinforced the police's image as an impartial law enforcement agency. Formal rules and procedures directed the police activities. We begin our exposition by outlining how the police controlled three of the most serious categories of crimes: domestic violence, homicide, and crimes against property.

Violent crimes were common social problems of the day. The police paid special attention to violent crimes against women and presented them under the subtitle "crime against women" in their annual reports. In some districts, such as remote areas of Grande Prairie, Alberta, the police sensed the constant existence of violence against women. The crimes included rape, incest, carnal knowledge, seduction, etc. Probably the largest category of crime against women was wife assault. Nevertheless, the police hardly detected such crime except in circumstances where other deadly violent crimes, such as murder, were involved. The police frequently came to the realization that serious wife abuse had already existed in the family for a long period of time. The attempted murder committed by John Dobek in the Lethbridge area in 1926 is a case in point. While Dobek was drinking, he started to assault his wife. When his hired man intervened on the woman's behalf, Dobek indicated his intention to kill him. When Dobek's wife objected, he shot her. After the shooting, the woman ran outside, but Dobek brought her back and struck her over the head with the barrel of the rifle. When the police found the woman, she was in a state of collapse with her shoulder shattered by a .44-calibre bullet. The police were informed that this was not the first murderous assault Dobek had made on his wife.[58] Both Gray and Carrigan correctly pointed out that many cases of wife-beating were alcohol-related. This may have been one reason why women were strong supporters of the prohibition movement during the 1910s and 1920s.[59]

At the same time, women rarely reported the violent abuse they experienced. In many cases, after the police arrested their abusive husbands, the women refused to testify against them. Charles Kereschtien in Regina District in 1918 beat his wife, inflicting, in all, ten wounds. The crime was the outcome of a drunken brawl precipitated by Mrs. Kereschtien's accusation that her husband was keeping company with other women. After the accused was committed to stand trial, his wife, the victim, spared no effort trying to get Charles Kereschtien released. She refused to testify against her husband at his trial.[60]

Robert Jamerson's case in the Edmonton area further suggested that wife abuse had reached an intolerable state. In 1921, Jamerson inflicted an eighteen-inch-long cut on his wife's back because she would not help him find one of his socks.[61] There were also cases of men killing their wives because they were not happy with their lives. In 1931, Richard Wooght in the Edmonton region killed his wife and two children, aged six and eight, because he was unemployed and in financial difficulties.[62] There were also many cases in which husbands killed their wives out of jealousy.

On the other hand, many women also killed their husbands, apparently in protest against long-lasting and violent physical abuse at their hands. Zoska Kaminski, who lived in the Edmonton area in 1924, killed her husband with a monkey wrench and attempted to commit suicide. The note that she left for her daughter showed that the murder was a result of lifelong abuse. Kaminski wrote in the note: "goodbye my neighbour, and do not bury us in one grave as my husband might illtreat me there as well...."[63] This woman was found guilty of manslaughter by a jury. However, there were three cases in which previously abused women were acquitted by juries of murdering their husbands.[64] Apparently, juries have long understood and accepted the battered wife syndrome.

Police investigations also revealed excessive violence against children in families residing in rural communities. The case of William Hisabeck is another case in point. The police regarded this case as "one of the most cruel and heartless cases that has ever been brought to the attention of the public." William Hisabeck beat his little son aged seven to death and severely wounded his nine-year-old little daughter. According to the girl, her father whipped them first with a quirt, then with a piece of board.

Her father also burnt her brother's private parts with matches and beat his head on the floor. Hisabeck was sentenced to be hanged, but later the sentence was commuted to life imprisonment.[65]

In addition to the murder cases occurring within families, most murder cases happened within an intimate circle of relatives, friends, and acquaintances. Usually, the police had little difficulty in bringing the criminals to justice. Often, the murderers actually waited for the police to come. For instance, Marshall Douglas in Prince Albert in 1923, after he killed his wife and two children, called the police himself and waited for police in his home.[66] Of course there were cases that cost the police much time and energy, sometimes even policemen's lives, to apprehend the murderers.

Many murders were often committed on the spur of the moment over trivial matters. Clarence Johnson, who resided in the Edmonton area in 1921, killed a man who lived near the accused, over a dispute that arose over a fork belonging to the accused. The accused pleaded not guilty. The judge on this case angrily pointed out that "it would be absurd for everyman to be the judge of whether his neighbour should live or die" regardless of how much of a nuisance he or she was.[67] Another case was that of Alfred Brunetle, who shot and killed his employer, an operator of a lumber camp at Styal, over $1.00. The accused later committed suicide.[68]

Probably, the most sensational murder cases were ones in which the police were involved directly. In 1922, an APP constable, Stephen O. Lawson, was murdered during the investigation of a rum-running case in Lethbridge District. In the process of chasing Steve Picariello, son of Emilio Picariello, a well-known rum-runner in the Crow's Nest Pass area, Lawson shot and wounded him in the hand. Later, learning that his son had been arrested, Emilio Picariello decided to go to Coleman, where the detachment was located. Florence Lassandro, wife of his close friend Charles Lassandro, insisted on accompanying him. According to witnesses, Emilio Picariello met Lawson and insisted that Lawson accompany him to find his son. When the officer refused his demand, Emilio threatened the constable with a gun. Lawson grappled with him and Mrs. Lassandro fired at Lawson in fear and panic. After a long series of trials and appeals, Emilio Picariello and Mrs. Lassandro were hanged at the Fort Saskatchewan Jail on May 3, 1923.[69]

Indeed, liquor seemingly played a role in many violent crimes. In the annals of the provincial police, there were several murder cases where crimes were committed while the perpetrators were under the influence of alcohol or the killing was a result of drunken brawls.[70] APP Commissioner

Bryan again blamed such cases on the foreign immigrants.[71] The police believed that foreign criminals lacked a sense of law or a sense of right and wrong. Worse still, they felt that immigrants *per se* did not have these senses either. Herbert Jeffrey Martin shot and killed one Mr. Neilson because Martin thought that Neilson was going to assault his wife, Mrs. Neilson. The shooting was witnessed by three other people. The jury actually acquitted Martin. Chief Justice Simmonds in the Supreme Court in Edmonton said that

Herbert Jeffery Martin, you have been tried by six of your countrymen, and they have brought in a verdict that sets you free. I think you should consider yourself somewhat fortunate under the circumstances, because I feel it is my duty to say it is not a verdict which, in my opinion, fulfils the requirement of the law of the land. In doing so, I am not reflecting on the honesty or integrity of the jury; it is simply a question of different opinion, and I regret to say it. In giving the case the consideration that my experience gives it, I do not think there was any excuse for you taking the life of your fellow countryman.[72]

The inspector in charge of Saskatoon believed that the jury in the John Bronch murder case acquitted the accused because the jury made the decision based on the "unwritten law" of their native land – a country of central and eastern Europe – rather than Canadian laws.[73] The police often drew their opinions about immigrants from eastern and central European countries based on particular cases. From the murder case of Gregory Hminiuk of his father-in-law, the police concluded that

This case presents many features common to the character of the Austrian race and the motive, though obscure to the casual eye, is quite apparent when the mode of living, such as jealousy and lack of moral principle and the disregard for the value of human life, are enquired into.[74]

For the police, the people from eastern and central Europe were obviously suffering from a diminished moral sense.

A large proportion of police work was also directed at crimes against property without violence, such as cattle stealing, grain stealing, arson, breaking and entering, and petty theft. In rural communities, stealing cattle or grain was very easy since both were located far from homesteads.[75] The beneficiaries of police services in the control of property crimes were the general population, including immigrants. This does not imply that foreign immigrants owned much property. In rural communities, many things, from small items such as grain or a fork to large items like cattle, were subjects of theft. Of course, police protection of property meant more to established well-to-do settlers than newly arrived immigrants as, very often, the older settlers were ranchers, and cattle and horses were the main chattels that the police protected.

The police devoted a considerable amount of time and resources to investigating the theft of cattle or horses. Prior to the mid-1920s, cattle and horse stealing were very serious offences. Such cases were tried in the supreme courts of the provinces. The sentences for such crimes usually ranged from one- to five-year imprisonment. In one case, an offender was sentenced to fifteen years in prison. For the police, severe punishment was the primary deterrent of criminal activities. In 1920, the inspector of Weyburn Division complained that many judges and justices took far too lenient a view of crime. They attributed the decline in cattle stealing in Saskatchewan to the late A.L. Safton and his brother, Chief Justice Harry Safton, who dispensed long-term sentences to bands of cattle and horse thieves.[76]

Police work in controlling cattle stealing was concerned primarily with professional cattle rustlers, who killed the cattle to sell the beef. Occasionally, they cut out the brand and stitched the flesh up again before bringing the cattle to market. In order to capture the rustlers, several police officers were appointed as stock inspectors. At the same time, the police also frequently hired people with knowledge about cattle, often ranchers, as stock detectives to search for suspects. The police routinely executed their search warrants at the suspect's residence at midnight. Frequently, the police discovered the carcass of beef, hide, or heads of young cows. The hides with brands were important evidence leading to convictions.

In many cases of cattle theft, the police experienced difficulties in tracing missing animals. Occasionally, even the discovery of stolen animals was not sufficient to lead police to their owners. According to police sources, this situation was created by laxity on the part of owners in branding their stock. In one case, the police were in the position to apprehend a suspected person, but they were unable to locate the owners of the alleged stolen property. After an eight-month investigation, the police finally found the owner and convicted the criminal. The police complained that "had these animals been branded a great deal of unnecessary work and useless expenditure would have been avoided."[77]

To the police, the large number of unbranded cattle created great opportunities for cattle rustlers. In one case, Clive Curtis stole fifteen unbranded horses.[78] The existence of many unbranded cattle was also a major source of confusion between stealing cattle and mistaking other people's cattle for one's own. Most cases reported to the police concerning cattle or horse stealing were proven later to be just a matter of strays. Usually, ranchers turned their cattle out to pasture in the spring. By winter, many cattle had strayed a considerable distance. The ranchers then complained to the police of theft.

This situation led the police to pressure these ranchers to change their customs of raising cattle. Locating stray cattle consumed precious police time and resources, especially when some cattle were found in the possession of other ranchers. In these cases, the prosecution usually followed even where the cows were branded. The purpose of the prosecution, the police explained, was not to stop cattle rustling *per se*, rather to establish negligence on the part of the defendant in branding other people's cattle without making a thorough examination first. Such cases usually ended with dismissal or withdrawal.

However, from the mid-1920s onward, theft of cattle and horses declined as the high prices for beef declined and automobiles gradually replaced horses as a means of transportation, and theft of automobiles gradually replaced theft of horses. For the police, auto theft was the easiest of any crime to commit since there was little legislative regulation of the use of automobiles in the 1920s. As car theft became more prevalent each year, the police strongly suggested legislation to curb the illicit trade.

Among the property crimes that the police were kept busy with, the most serious ones were robberies. These were cases that the police tried to avoid, not only because the crime usually involved violence and property damage, but also because the police usually had difficulties in bringing the criminals to justice. Such cases were rare, but they had a detrimental effect on the reputation of the police. A 1920 CPR passenger train robbery in the area of the Crow's Nest Pass presents a case in point. On August 2, 1920, Tom Bassoff, George Arkoff, and Ausby Holloff (all Russian immigrants), armed with heavy automatic revolvers, managed to hold up the conductor and passengers of a CPR passenger train at Sentinel, Alberta, and robbed them of their money and jewellery. After leaving the train, all three men hid themselves in the heavy bush in that vicinity. Five days later the Bellevue detachment of the APP received information that Bassoff and Arkoff were lunching in the Bellevue Cafe. Constables Frewin and Bailey of the APP, and Constable Usher of the RCMP, immediately went to arrest the two men. The police, with the assistance of Mr. Robertson, JP, exchanged shots with the two robbers. Constables Bailey and Usher, and

Arkoff were killed in action. The sight of two policemen being murdered stunned Constable Frewin. He did not recover until Bassoff ran off. Five days after the shooting, Bassoff was arrested by CPR constables at Pincher Creek station without offering any resistance. He was subsequently sentenced to death and was executed on December 22, 1920, at the common gaol in Lethbridge. Ausby Holloff was not arrested until 1924 in Montana, at which time he was sentenced to seven years in prison.[79]

In August 1920, the APP district office was under close media scrutiny in Lethbridge. The press reported that the three men who pulled off the train robbery were supposed to have belonged to a "bad Russian Bolshevist gang" that resided in the Crow's Nest Pass. The APP Commissioner questioned the RCMP's ability to monitor the activities of Bolsheviks and other extreme radical elements in the Crow's Nest Pass. For the APP, the most damaging part of press reports was that the bandits were assisted by other foreigners. This implied that the immigrant population under the APP's mandate were also part of the criminal problem. Press coverage was extremely detrimental to the immigrant community, but it also had a damaging effect on the APP's reputation. The commissioner of the APP denied the allegation that the police had not properly socialized immigrants in the area. In the 1920 Annual Report, the commissioner of the APP stated that the wounded Bassoff went to a Canadian woman for help rather than to an immigrant. The robbery was planned in Great Falls, Montana. Although there was a large immigrant population in the Lethbridge area, according to the report, these were not criminals. Also, according to the report, the condition during the period was a hundred per cent better than in 1905–12, when it was under the RNWMP.[80]

However, paradoxically, a similar train robbery case actually rendered a rather favourable result to the SPP. On the evening of February 1, 1923, Canadian National Train Number 6 operating between North Battleford and Regina was robbed by a lone bandit with a revolver. After about a month-long intensive investigation following a clue left by a handkerchief used to gag Venzke, the CNR Express Messenger, a detective of the SPP, van Gorder, arrested the bandit, a former CNR employee. He was subsequently sentenced to eight years imprisonment and all the money and securities that he robbed from the CN train were recovered. The SPP's successful handling of the train robbery case garnered favourable public opinion for the police.[81]

Typically, serious property-related crimes consumed a considerable amount of police time and resources. The 1921 case of robbery and murder illustrates this point. According to the APP, this was one of the worst crimes in the annals of the province. It involved John Kozdrowski, a man seventy-four years of age, and his wife, Mary, a woman of sixty-five, who resided on their homestead in the Chipman area of Alberta. After they had retired, they heard someone knocking at the window and a voice said "come outside." John Kozdrowski got up and went to the door. As soon as he opened the door, the man outside started shooting. Kozdrowski at once shut the door. The man outside attempted to push it open. Kozdrowski called for his wife to assist him. As Mary was getting off the bed, she was shot in the shoulder by a bullet fired through the window. The man then burst the door in and set fire to the house. Mary managed to escape by crawling on the floor to get outside, where she then hid in a straw stack and watched the house burning. After being in the stack all night, she was later discovered and moved to a hospital, where she remained for some time in a precarious condition.

The house had been burnt to the ground. On searching the ruins, some of the remains of John Kozdrowski were found. Dr. Archer, the coroner, suggested that the remains (bones) had been dismembered before being burnt. The police believed that the motive was robbery. In this case, two constables spent almost six months on the investigation and trial. Finally, Peter Kaezure was convicted of robbery and murder on purely circumstantial evidence. The accused was hanged later in 1921.[82]

Another type of serious property offence was safe cracking and bank robbery. In 1922 a crime wave occurred around southern Saskatchewan, particularly in the Weyburn policing district. There were eight bank robberies and safe-blowing cases in total, seven in Weyburn and one in Prince Albert. There was also a series of minor robbery cases. In most of them, the criminals were unsuccessful in opening the safe. In one case, robbers blew the safe seven times and left without obtaining the money. However, both robberies of the Union Bank in Regina and the Bank of Montreal in Weyburn yielded about seven thousand dollars in cash and a large amount of grain tickets and securities. These bank robberies caused a considerable amount of panic among the public. A good deal of publicity was given to the cases in the press from time to time under the headline "Another Wave of Crime."[83]

The SPP officers believed that the safe-cracking wave was associated with the rum-running (e.g., liquor-smuggling) business and that the robbers were Americans. Through fingerprinting, the police were able to trace several robbers who had committed crimes in other parts of the country. These criminal elements, in many areas, belonged to the bootlegging fraternity, who entered the province pretending to be threshers or land speculators. In all cases, the robbers were heavily armed. In a case of safe-blowing in Weyburn, when a loud explosion occurred, the town policeman rushed out to investigate whether youngsters had set off fireworks again. The robbers ordered the officer to go back inside and shot in his direction. One bullet lodged in the officer's thigh.[84]

From various investigations, it was determined that the robberies and the attempted robberies were carried out by armed criminals with modern high-powered automobiles. For this reason, the police failed to catch any of the robbers involved. It is noteworthy that just as soon as the police became mobile enough to chase them in their newly acquired modern cars, the robberies ceased. From these experiences the police emphasized the necessity of being as well-equipped as the criminals with whom they had to deal.[85]

A similar safe-blowing wave hit Alberta in 1924. A gang of safe-blowers drifted into Alberta and made Edmonton their headquarters. Several safes were blown, and money and other securities were taken. Like the SPP, the APP did all they could to capture the criminals but to no avail. The only thing they could do was to advise postmasters not to put money in safes.[86] This was because the criminals were very skilled safe-blowers who covered their tracks so well that, in most cases, not even the slightest clue could be obtained in terms of their identities.[87] Unlike in Saskatchewan, there was little evidence suggesting that the robbers had connections with rum-runners. Instead, the police believed that these bandits were a well-organized band of "yeggs" (twenty-four of them in total) from the west coast. After they made their headquarters in Edmonton, they sent out "spotters" along the railway lines to pick out the places that were to be robbed. The men sent out were chair menders or cripples selling laces or begging. Although the police did not have direct evidence showing that these people were associated with the safe-blowers, they arrested them and removed them from the province under the catch-all offence – vagrancy.[88]

Police annual returns on crime suggested that serious crimes against property were on the rise while homicide and other serious crimes against persons remained relatively stable during the period 1917–32. The police were very interested in the issue of why the various criminal activities varied. The police observed that World War I had a direct and immediate effect on crime. The impact of the war on crime was reflected in the increase in juvenile delinquency. Due to the absence of many fathers at the front, many children were neglected and young women adopted "loose" lives. The police reported that young girls from the country drifted into the cities in great numbers and fell for the seduction of easy money. Consequently, there was an increase in both car theft by the youths and in the number of illegitimate births. The long-run effect of the war observed by the police was that there was the creation of well-organized and efficient bands of thugs who had been juvenile delinquents during wartime.[89]

According to the police, another source of criminals was the floating population. They were mainly the harvesters brought into the provinces from around Canada and the European countries during the fall. According to the police, "some of these gentry no doubt meant well – others came here for what they can accomplish in the way of getting (not earning) an easy living."[90] Occasionally, the people who could not find other employment after the harvest seasons and were refused relief by the governments drifted towards crime. However, there were few cases in which serious crimes were committed by the harvesters. Usually, they were regarded as a nuisance or as undesirable by the local population in villages or towns. As noted earlier, they were controlled by the vagrancy law.

The police also observed that, contrary to the common wisdom that poverty leads to an increase in crime, in rural communities an improvement in the economy often was thought to result in crime. The inspector of "D" Division of the APP in the Lethbridge area suggested that the better crop would cause an increase in crime as "the more money some people have, the more apt they are to get into trouble, this is especially true in relation to cases of intoxication and gambling."[91]

Probably the most interesting observation by the police was that the number of arrests by the police and convictions by the courts, particularly in the area of public order offences, did not necessarily reflect an increase in criminality. More often, occasional increases in crime were due to police efficiency, the number of policemen on the force, and the availability of other resources.[92] Concerning the higher level of charges and convictions in Alberta compared to other provinces of Canada (almost equal those of Ontario, a province with five times the population of Alberta), Commissioner Bryan argued that "this does not mean that the citizens of Alberta are less law abiding than those of the other provinces. Its real significance is that the Provincial Police of Alberta have by far the most efficient organization of the kind in Canada."[93]

Commissioner Willoughby Charles Bryan, the Alberta Provincial Police, 1920; ex-staff sergeant with the Royal North-West Mounted Police, appointed Commissioner of the APP in 1922, retired on March 31, 1932 (Glenbow Archives, NA-1177-5).

Group of Alberta Provincial Police; front row, W.C. Bryan, 3rd from left, E.W. Bavin, 3rd from right, ca. 1920s (Glenbow Archives, NA-2899-19).

Funeral of Constable E. Usher of the Royal Canadian Mounted Police and Constable E. Bailey of the Alberta Provincial Police, Fort Macleod, August 11, 1920; Constable Usher and Constable Bailey were shot while attempting to arrest train robbers Tom Bassoff and George Arkoff (Glenbow Archives, NA-2320-6).

Illicit still seized by Constable Everett, E. Markerison and special Detective Vernon Shaw of the Alberta Provincial Police, near Cardston, Alberta, early 1920s (Glenbow Archives, NA-2899-13).

Saskatchewan Provincial Police boat at Nipawin, Saskatchewan, 1921 (Saskatchewan Archives Board, R-A4165-1).

Corporals Kistrack, Rod S. Pyne, and Art Bond, SPP Moose Jaw, 1927/28 (Saskatchewan Archives Board, R-A7535-2).

Corporals Rod Pyne and Andy Anderson, Robsart, Saskatchewan, 1926 (Saskatchewan Archives Board, R-A7537).

EMPIRICAL EXAMINATION OF THE CORRELATION BETWEEN IMMIGRATION AND CRIME

We have pointed out that police officers and social and moral reformers attributed the steady increase in crime and violence in the prairie provinces to the immigrant population. Why was there an apparent correlation between immigration and crime? Hurd argues that "the propensity to crime is in some measure at least a product of racial background"; the correlation between immigration and crime could not be eliminated by improving their living conditions.[94] Some police officers attributed the correlation to some alleged characteristics of immigrants, such as immigrants' use of intoxicating liquor and noxious drugs, their insensitivity to the law, jealousy, and desire for revenge.[95]

However, a study in policing and immigration in Canada as a whole showed that the influx of immigrants was associated only with the level of public order offences, specifically drunkenness, but not associated with serious crime. This was because "men arrived in advance of their wives and children. Hotels and salons, bars and billiard rooms were dominated by a bachelor culture of young men many of whom were European. In the combined context of the prohibitionist sentiments and the fear of foreigners, the latter became a prime subject for police control."[96] However, there is no evidence suggesting that immigration was a primary cause of increases in serious crime. In this section, I hypothesize that immigration was associated with the level of pubic order offences, but not with serious crimes in Alberta and Saskatchewan over the period 1906–50.[97] This contradicts the accepted wisdom of the time, but it is consistent with the conclusion in the last chapter, which suggests that public order offences may fluctuate due to proactive policing, while serious crime is less a result of police behaviour than criminal acts.

The statistical findings (from the analysis in Appendix D) confirm our hypothesis that the shifting levels of immigration during the period 1906–50 are partially responsible for the trends in public order offences. An increase in public order offences could be attributable to the growth of the immigrant population in both provinces over the long run. Consequently, this suggests that the police indeed used public order offences as a method to regulate the conduct of immigrants and to control this segment of the population. The police as law enforcers were the prime agency that arrested public order offenders. It was the police who used their discretion to decide who needed to be arrested. As discussed previously, the content of the law, the public concern, and the alien culture and customs of the immigrants led the police to identify them as a dangerous class. The historical and statistical records suggest that the police used public order offences to regulate, educate, discipline, and assimilate the alien newcomers. Therefore, it was the police who created the stable long-term relationship between the two variables and adjusting the relation constantly to meet public concerns in the name of preventing serious crime.

However, the findings from this analysis demonstrates that in fact there was *no* long-run relationship between serious crime and immigration levels. The absence of a statistical relationship between immigration and serious crime reveals that changes in immigrants were *not* a cause of the changing levels of serious crime as suggested by the police. The historical condemnation of immigrants as dangerous criminals was unfounded. Our findings support the alternative view – that immigrants were the prime subject of police control under highly discretionary public order offences and that arrests for such offences varied systematically with immigration.

CONCLUSION

In this chapter, we have examined provincial police activities in controlling the dangerous classes and serious crime. The provincial police played an active and important role in regulating and shaping the prairie society during the 1910s, 1920s and 1930s. The police activities were primarily directed by the provincial governments and by the pressure from Anglo-Canadian society. At the same time, the police activities were also concerned with their legitimacy among the policed population. These police concerns determined the diversity of routine police activities.

From our discussions in this chapter, we can see that the police activities in controlling the dangerous classes – i.e., "foreign immigrants" – were governed by the provisions of the Criminal Code of Canada and the instructions from the police commissioners. But police discretion, based in part on prejudicial attitudes toward immigrants, played an essential role in their decision-making in connection with the regulations of the conduct of immigrants. Consistent with Anglo-Canadian attitudes, the police acted more as agents of control than as mediators of friction in the regulation of the "foreign"-dominated labour movements. The police vigorously suppressed the collective activities of unemployed immigrants and workers by using the catch-all offences – vagrancy and public disorderly conduct. The alleged links between immigrants and the Communist Party of Canada enabled the police to justify their exercise of suppressive power over these segments of the population.

At the same time, the police also acted as a "domestic missionary" in the prairie provinces during the period under study. They actively imposed an Anglo-Canadian moral order and values over immigrants from central and eastern Europe by surveillance of all phases of the life of the immigrants. In this process, immigrants obtained direly needed assistance through relief efforts operated under the auspices of the police. This humane dimension of their work enabled the police to receive the cooperation of the immigrants and to assist their transition into Canadian schools and Canadian society.

It is worth noting that the police observation on the relationship between crime and police behaviour is rather instructive. In addition to the influx of immigrants, the police officers recognized that there were many social factors that could contribute to increases in crime, such as the war and economic activities. The police noted that police behaviour, including police efficiency, had significant impact on crime statistics. The statistical analysis with data on crime and immigration suggests the existence of an association between immigration and public order offences. We have argued that this correlation indicates that the Criminal Code was used to regulate the conduct of immigration, but only in the areas of great police discretion. In the area of serious crime, immigrants were wrongly attributed a role they did not play.

5 THE POLICE ENFORCEMENT OF PROHIBITION LAWS, 1917–24: LEGITIMATION CRISIS

The influx of immigrants from central and eastern Europe in the first quarter of the twentieth century had profound effects on police activities in the provinces. At the same time, the prohibition movement and the police enforcement of law associated with it also played a significant role in the development of both the provincial police forces. The prohibition movement, as part of the nation-building process,[1] attempted to regulate and reshape moral values and the conduct of not just foreign immigrants, but also subordinate groups of Canadians. The movement attempted to inculcate in the population the sober and hardworking ideals that middle-class Anglo-Canadians valued. For such a purpose, the prohibitionists actively made use of the legal process, including the police, to impose "official" Canadian virtues on the lower segments of the population. Through this movement, the Canadian state presented itself as a neutral participant. Nevertheless, the police, as state employees, were deeply involved because they were mandated to enforce what was essentially moralistic legislation.[2] The enforcement resulted in what Habermas calls a "legitimation crisis." In this chapter, we attempt to answer the questions as to how the police enforcement of prohibition laws and the resulting public attitude towards the laws and their enforcement affected police legitimacy and how the police legitimation crisis affected other areas of police activities.

Liquor problems had haunted politicians in both the Dominion and local governments even before the formation of the provinces of Alberta and Saskatchewan. One of the Dominion government's purposes in creating the North-West Mounted Police in 1873 was to eliminate the whisky trade in the North-West Territories. It was believed that the drinking habits of the native population produced many undesirable results, including crime and violence.³ The 1878 Scott Act of Canada allowed voters to decide what liquor policy each city or municipality would adopt. As early as 1880, the first Total Abstinence League of Saskatchewan was organized at Prince Albert to urge the Territories government to crack down on the liquor traffic.⁴ In Alberta, the Temperance and Moral Reform Society was first established in 1907 to push for government control of liquor sales among the natives and general population.

After Alberta and Saskatchewan became provinces in 1905, in response to the pressure of the temperance groups, both provincial governments frequently amended the liquor law with respect to penalties, inspection procedures, and policies regarding the confiscation of illegal liquor. The Alberta government adopted and then revised the North-West Territories ordinances respecting the sale of liquor in almost every other year between 1907 and 1915 to tighten up government control over the issuing of liquor licences. Nevertheless, these amendments had little effect on the actual *liquor condition* in Alberta as the RNWMP were extremely reluctant to enforce provincial liquor legislation. In 1907, the Saskatchewan legislature enacted its own Liquor Licence Act regulating the sale of liquor, and it created a Liquor Licence Board to assist in the enforcement of the Act. In 1910, considering the RNWMP's reluctance to enforce the Act, the Saskatchewan government created a small detachment especially to enforce the Liquor Licence Act. The force was referred to as a "Secret Service" because it consisted exclusively of undercover special constables.⁵

Although temperance groups had been urging the governments on the prairies to crack down on the liquor traffic, the temperance movement only began to have some effect on the government and general population just prior to World War I. One major reason for this occurrence was the influx of immigrants from central and southern Europe. Many western historians, including James Gray and Frank W. Anderson, point out that liquor abuse was serious in many immigrant communities on the prairies.⁶ Many immigrant men came to western Canada ahead of their families. The loneliness and hardship of frontier life often led men to seek solace in drinking. For temperance organizations, the drinking habits of the immigrants were undesirable. They connected drinking to a variety of social problems – spousal abuse, family breakdown, absenteeism, crime, and violence. In Alberta, some prohibitionists complained that the immigrants' taste for alcohol made them more vulnerable to election bribery.⁷ James Gray suggests that "[the temperance groups] concentrated their attention on a single target – Temperance, unaware perhaps of the intolerance, racism, and bigotry that were often the nether side of their movement."[8] *The Moose Jaw Times* summed up the drinking habits of foreign immigrants in this way: "among the Canadians there are many who do not drink at all. Among the French there are very few who do not drink. Among the Germans and Half-breeds there are absolutely none at all."[9]

With the massive influx of immigrants that peaked in 1912 and 1913, public support for the prohibition movement increased and increasingly more people came to accept the notion that heavy drinking was a serious problem. James Gray observes that even some drunks worked very hard with the prohibitionists; they were convinced that if distillery and brewery operations could be eliminated, their bad habits would go with them.[10] The temperance groups launched a series of effective campaigns in both provinces. In Alberta, the movement obtained support from the United Farmers of Alberta. In response to the pressure generated by these campaigns, in October 1914, the government of Alberta decided to hold a plebiscite regarding the sale of liquor on July 21, 1915. After six months of intensive campaigns by both the prohibitionists and the moderationists, about 61 per cent of Alberta voters approved total prohibition of liquor sales on voting day, with the exception of the population in the Lethbridge area where the majority voted against it. The government subsequently passed "An Act Respecting the Sale of Intoxicating Liquor," prohibiting sales and consumption of liquor in public places on April 19, 1916. The prohibition law came into effect on July 1 of that year.

In Saskatchewan, the prohibitionist and moderationist forces seemed to be evenly split. This situation led the government conveniently to adopt a law abolishing all bar and club licences for liquor sales and establishing the government liquor dispensaries to control liquor sales on July 1, 1915. This policy satisfied both sides temporarily.[11] The abolition of liquor sales in bars and clubs was justified as a wartime measure, subject to ratification in a referendum that would be held after the war. However, encouraged by the fact that Alberta became a "dry" province in July 1916, the prohibitionists in Saskatchewan renewed pressure on the government. Subsequently, the government held a plebiscite on the issue of prohibition in December 1916. As a result of the vote, Saskatchewan also became a "dry" province on January 1, 1917.[12]

In Saskatchewan, the newly formed provincial police undertook enforcement of the Temperance Act when they replaced the RNWMP on January 1, 1917. In fact, the RNWMP had never paid much attention to the enforcement of provincial liquor laws, despite pressure from prohibitionists and some politicians to do so. This was the reason Saskatchewan created the Secret Service to begin with. It was only in 1917 with the newly minted provincial forces that the provincial laws were seriously enforced.

THE PROHIBITION LEGISLATION

The general prohibition of retail liquor sales was contained in the Alberta Liquor Act of 1916 and the Saskatchewan Temperance Act of 1917. The enforcement of these laws eventually brought down the police popularity. The Alberta Liquor Act of 1916 and the Saskatchewan Temperance Act of 1917 shared many characteristics.[13] Both were complex and complicated pieces of legislation. The former consisted of seventy-four sections, while the latter was composed of eighty-four sections. The essence of the laws was to prohibit the sale and consumption of intoxicating liquor (with more than 2 per cent alcohol) in public places, including bars, liquor houses, hotels, and restaurants. However, the Acts contained so many loopholes that their original purposes could not be easily achieved. The Acts prohibited sale and purchase of liquor within the provinces of Alberta or Saskatchewan. But, the Acts allowed the possession and sales of liquor for medicinal, scientific, or sacramental purposes.[14] They also permitted the purchase or sale of liquor interprovincially or internationally by government-licensed businesses. Brewers and distillers were allowed to manufacture liquor and sell it anywhere outside the province. Private dwelling houses were permitted to have liquor on the premises purchased from other provinces through mail-orders. The legislation permitted a person to consume intoxicating liquor at home.[15]

The punishments for violations under both the Acts were relatively severe. In Alberta, the penalty for a first offence was not less than $50, nor more than $100; in default of immediate payment of the fine, the penalty would be imprisonment for not less than thirty days, nor more than two months. The fine for a second offence would be not less than $200 and no more than $500. However, the profit from bootlegging was so large that the APP officers soon found out that the punishment stipulated in the law could not deter the violation of the Act at all. The bootleggers usually charged ten times what they had paid for illicit liquor.[16] A police officer in the Red Deer area observed that

The liquor Act is a drastic piece of legislation, but the penalties attached do not concern, very much, the people engaged in the liquor traffic, owing to the exorbitant price charged and obtained for their goods. A few days ago I was shown by one of our operators a bottle of *Hennessy's Three Star Brandy* made locally, which cost $1.50 to make and sold for 15.00 per bottle.[17]

Consequently, the offenders were prepared to pay their fines and to resume their old bootlegging businesses immediately following sentencing. This situation seriously undermined police efforts to enforce the Act.

Under pressure from both the APP and the prohibitionists, the government of Alberta amended the Liquor Act of 1916 in April 1917. According to section 12 of the amended act, the fine for first time offenders was doubled; for a second offence the fine was not less than $250, nor more than $500, or three to six months imprisonment. However, Inspector Hancock in charge of the Peace River Division continued to complain that the heavy fine still did not deter offenders.[18]

The Saskatchewan Temperance Act had a rather complicated penalty system that provided different punishments for different types of offenders.[19] The Act stipulated only maximum penalties, while magistrates could impose any penalty within the maximum according to their discretion. The penalty in the Act ranged from a $100 fine or one month imprisonment for individual offenders, to $1,000 for an offender that was an incorporated company. The Act also stipulated that the officers empowered to enforce the Act who received any money for performing or failing to perform their duties in connection with the administration of the Act were liable to a penalty of $100 or imprisonment for three months.

The major differences between the Saskatchewan Temperance Act of 1917 and the Alberta Liquor Act of 1916 was that the former contained a section stipulating how the act should be enforced.[20] Police officers, constables, or any other persons who may be appointed by the Attorney General had the power to enforce the Saskatchewan Temperance Act. The Act gave the enforcers a wide range of powers to enforce the Act, such as the power to search without a warrant hotels or restaurants where police believed liquor was being sold illegally.

Law enforcement personnel in both provinces realized that the offenders created by the prohibition legislation consisted not only of members of the criminal classes or "crooked" men as most people believed, but also many respected businessmen and medical professionals, including doctors, druggists, and veterinarians. In their annual reports, the police constantly reminded politicians that many medical professionals were profiteering handsomely from prohibition and that the punishment imposed by the acts did not deter violations at all.

POLICE ENFORCEMENT OF THE PROHIBITION LAWS

In the first APP Annual Report presented to the Attorney General, the police inspectors suggested that there were serious problems in the enforcement of the law. The penalties imposed by the law did not deter its violation since the profit from bootlegging was exorbitant. The Alberta Liquor Act of 1916 was violated by so many people and so frequently that Inspector Piper in the Edmonton area in 1918 expressed his doubt that prohibition was a proper way to alter people's drinking habits. He stated that "I am of the opinion that prohibition tends to increase crime in some lines and that restriction is the right solution to the control of the liquor traffic."[21] Because they were unable to stop liquor traffic, the police hoped that Montana would go "dry" so that one of the major sources of illegal liquor into Alberta might be eliminated.

SPP Commissioner Charles Mahoney seemed to hold a more positive attitude towards the enforcement of the prohibition law in Saskatchewan. He apparently believed that enforcement was necessary to reduce crime since crime was correlated with the consumption of liquor. He said that "the use of intoxicating liquor and noxious drugs is indirectly responsible for about 50 percent of all crime committed in the province."[22]

Although official attitudes towards the law between the provinces may have been somewhat different at the onset of prohibition, their actual enforcement of the law was rather similar. Both the SPP and APP adopted a reactive policing strategy. This was because most policemen in the forces were known to the bootleggers. Even new undercover policemen, who acted as special constables, could not get evidence because very few bootleggers were naive enough to sell liquor to strangers.

Police investigations typically arose from complaints about persons who were selling or keeping liquor illegally. Many of these complaints were lodged originally with various authorities, including the attorneys general of the provinces. They would turn these complaints over to the police commissioners and instruct them to investigate. The majority of these complaints provided very little information about the offenders and were often anonymous and may have come from temperance activists. On occasion, the persons who signed the complaints anxiously wanted to withhold their names. The police investigation of such complaints was not only extremely costly in terms of time and money, but also often bore little fruit. Many complaints consisted of hearsay evidence or arose from personal grudges. When the police successfully identified the location of an alleged bootlegging operation, they often obtained little assistance from local citizens.[23] As a result the police had little success in getting evidence against bootleggers, and most of the charges and convictions secured by the police were actually against the people who purchased liquor from the bootleggers.

The police were fully aware of the fact that the prohibition law was unpopular. The issue of how to enforce this law was directly concerned with the relationship between the police and the public. The police noted that most complaints came from the areas where the majority of the population voted for prohibition. Police enforcement would be better accepted in these areas than in places where people voted against prohibition. Using their discretion, the police confined their investigations to the areas where people made complaints rather than the places where they got no complaints – independent of whether bootleggers were active there.[24] This significantly reduced police efficiency in their enforcement of the law.

The difficulties that the police experienced in enforcing the laws were also multiplied by a variety of tactics used by bootleggers to circumvent the liquor law and to avoid police detection. These tactics included spying, bribing, and the use of freight trains to conceal illegal liquor. An important reason why the police were inefficient in controlling liquor traffic was that bootleggers established an effective spy system. This considerably nullified police efforts to enforce the law proactively. The spy system used by the bootleggers was efficient because they appear to have spent substantial money to support it. The movement of the police was noted by spotters and telephoned from one locale to another. Every stranger going into any of the small towns and settlements where there was illicit sale of liquor was looked upon with suspicion. Even with undercover policemen, it was impossible to stop the traffic.[25]

The bootleggers were able to trace police movement by using railway men in various railway stations as informants. Because the primary means of transportation used by the police was the railway, the railway men were always able to identify the police who were travelling on trains to investigate liquor cases throughout the provinces. Therefore, the railway men could wire information ahead about police movement to various points along the line. Because of such an effective espionage system, bootleggers could identify plainclothed policemen and avoid police raids.

Another effective tactic used by bootleggers was bribery. In the 1921 Annual Report, the APP reported that, among twenty-seven constables who were engaged in policing the liquor traffic, three were convicted for corruption. In 1921, one constable who tampered with a barrel of beer ordered confiscated by a justice of the peace was dismissed. Two other members were required to submit their resignations as they were suspected of associating with bootleggers in Calgary.[26] There was also evidence that the Bronfman brothers in Saskatchewan attempted to bribe customs officials.[27] The case of Constable Smith illustrates just how vulnerable the police were to bribes. Police were offered bribes that sometimes were worth more than forty times their monthly salary ($120). Stationed at Coutts in 1918, Constable Smith was offered $5,000 to absent himself from his detachment for two days to leave the border unguarded.[28] Nevertheless, he refused the offer.

Bootleggers were also able to recruit city and town police and other officials to work in their espionage system. In the Crow's Nest Pass, the mayors and the chiefs of police of some towns committed themselves to watching strangers and provincial police coming into their towns.[29]

A more disturbing fact was that the names of some mayors and chiefs of police of some towns were found among the list of the convicted bootleggers. The provincial police charged and convicted the mayor of Coleman, Mr. Johnson, twice for illegally selling liquor. The chief of police of St. Albert was convicted and fined $100 for bootlegging. The town councils did not remove the offenders from their official positions even after their convictions. This showed that the violation of the liquor law was not only extensive, but it was also publicly acceptable.

Bootleggers also shipped illicit liquor by freight trains, concealing the liquor in cars containing many goods, including lumber, fence posts, and coal. The police found it extremely difficult to detect the contraband. The police were sometimes informed that there was one car containing illicit liquor among seven or eight cars containing lumber or coal. In these cases, the police had to unload several cars of lumber or coal before they obtained the liquor. Naturally, they did not particularly enjoy this work. Worse still, although the police were able to confiscate the illicit liquor, since it would never be claimed, no one was ever charged after such a hard day's work![30]

In counterattacking the bootleggers' espionage system, the APP established a Liquor Branch (LB) in 1919 and the government of Saskatchewan formed the Liquor Commission (LC) by an amendment to the Temperance Act in 1920. These new branches of the attorneys general used the plainclothed policemen to replace the uniformed officers to enforce the law.

According to the 1920 amendment to the Saskatchewan Temperance Act of 1917, the Liquor Commission was not an alternative to the police; rather, it was entrusted with the responsibility of coordinating administration of the new Act in conjunction with the various police forces. However, the Commission could appoint inspectors and enforcement officers to carry out the provisions of the Act. The members of the Commission, inspectors, and enforcement officers might call upon any municipal or provincial police officer at any time for the purpose of obtaining assistance in the enforcement of the provisions of the Temperance Act. In fact, the SPP were very often called upon to provide such assistance. The Liquor Branch of the APP was responsible for the enforcement of the Liquor Act in Alberta. The police officers in the LB were deployed mainly in the cities, especially in Calgary and Edmonton.

The establishment of the LB and the LC largely relieved the uniformed policemen from liquor law enforcement. It was designed for two purposes. First, the plainclothes recruits, consisting mostly of special constables, could avoid detection by the bootleggers' espionage system and could more effectively enforce the law. Second, the transfer of responsibility to the LB and LC was supposed to shift public hostility away from the uniformed police and enable them to regain some popularity so as to perform other important duties more effectively. In reality, there was little evidence indicating that the creation of the new organizations achieved either purpose.

Matters were not helped by the fact that the special constables who enforced the law had an unsavoury reputation. Because the liquor law and its enforcement were extremely unpopular, the special constables were viewed with suspicion. As a result, those who took the jobs were often men of "less than exemplary character." Inspector Hodgkins of the LB apologetically explained the situation by saying "particularly the kind of work these men [the members of Liquor Branch] have to do leads them to all kinds of temptation, and the work is of such a nature that it is very difficult to get the better class of men to do the work."[31] The establishment of the new agencies to enforce the laws necessitated considerable government expenditure. In 1921, the Liquor Branch of the APP spent about $19,413.18 (out of a total budget of $478,855.79).[32] In 1923, the SPP spent a total of $10,039 (out of its total budget of about $300,000) to assist with the enforcement of the liquor law. Stewart and Hudson and Pinno have pointed out that it was expensive to enforce the law.[33] However, the enforcement of the liquor law was also a rich source of revenue for the government. In 1921, the police attached to the Liquor Branch of the APP collected $64,722 in fines and confiscated $62,800 worth of liquor. This is in contrast to the $23,000 required to purchase the building for the Weyburn Divisional Headquarters of the SPP. The Inspector of the

Weyburn Division noted that it could easily be paid for by $24,231 worth of confiscated liquor that was seized by the police in that division in 1920.[34] After 1920, this income was removed from the police and placed at the disposal of the government.

To counteract the bootleggers' spy system, the police also began gradually to use automobiles for transportation whenever they wanted to make a raid on bootleggers. Initially, the police hired taxis for such purposes. Many policemen bought private vehicles and used them to do police work. Police tactics used to control bootlegging were very much shaped by their reaction to the bootleggers' innovations to circumvent the law and avoid police detection.

Most illicit liquor was illegally sold in hotels, pool-rooms, dance-halls, game houses, and drugstores, particularly in mining towns (such as the Drumheller and the Crow's Nest Pass), lumbering camps, and construction centres. The police noted that the undercover policemen had to pretend to be drinkers in order to secure evidence for conviction based on direct observation of liquor infractions. In other places, police frequently used search warrants to obtain evidence. The police emphasized that searches had to be conducted in the utmost secrecy. In searches of private residences the police encountered ongoing public objections. The police eventually adopted a policy of not searching private houses unless they were absolutely sure that the evidence of bootlegging could be secured.[35]

Because of the lack of strength in the Liquor Branch of the APP and the difficulties in enforcing the Liquor Act, the APP eagerly sought to pass the duties of enforcing the law in cities to municipal police. In 1918, the Board of the Commissioners of the APP adopted a policy recognizing the jurisdiction of municipal police in Edmonton, Calgary, Lethbridge, and Medicine Hat over liquor infractions in their cities. This had been provided for in the 1918 amendments to the Liquor Act of 1916.[36] According to the APP, it was more appropriate for the city police to check on violations of the Act in liquor stores and hotels as most of these were located in the cities. However, the city police of Calgary questioned the legality of this new obligation, and the Board of Commissioners recorded in 1918 that the city commissioners "refuse[d] to be primarily responsible for the enforcement of the law in connection with liquor."[37] The evidence also suggested that the rank and file of the city police had no interest in enforcing these laws. In 1924, Calgary municipal authorities called upon the APP to crack down on violations of the liquor laws. The Calgary press were sceptical about the inability of the city police to enforce the laws.[38]

On the other hand, the power of city police to enforce the prohibition law in city jurisdictions led to a certain amount of resentment in smaller towns and villages which remained under provincial police jurisdiction. The people who lived in small centres were aware that since the large cities managed their own affairs concerning the Liquor Act (which was referred to as "home rule" by some local people), the people living in the large cities were allowed to drink whatever they wanted. Simultaneously, in the country, where the APP enforced the act, the only liquor available was home-brewed moonshine. They argued that the APP discriminated against people in the country. The police observed that because of this resentment, the complaints about violations of the Liquor Act from small towns fell off in 1921. By 1922, in order to appease the resentment, many small-town police forces requested and received authority from the attorney general to enforce liquor laws locally.[39]

Violence was also a feature of the bootlegging business, particularly in the rum-running activities along the border. In Alberta, the most famous instance in which violence was involved was the Emilio Picariello case in 1922. An APP constable, Stephen O. Lawson was murdered during the investigation of rum-running in the Lethbridge district.[40] In Saskatchewan, Harry Bronfman's brother-in-law was murdered in the process of conducting the bootlegging business.[41] There were also rumours that the rum-runners were responsible for a wave of bank robberies in the 1920s. However, there was no evidence suggesting this was a case. Much liquor flooded into the prairies from Montana, although police watched the trails from south of the border day and night for the law breakers. In connection with rum-running, bootleggers often used the most expensive high-powered cars. The police often found themselves in a situation where the hired taxis simply could not pursue and intercept the bootleggers. Frequently, all they could do was to watch the bootleggers driving away with the illicit liquor. APP Inspector Hodgkins noted in his 1920 report that

Owing to the lack of a car on two occasions I lost the Metropole Liquor Co. On the first occasion two of the men who were watching this place hired cycles, but were unable to keep up with the Dodge Car which had the liquor. I then hired a Ford Car with the same result.[42]

In order to enforce the law effectively, many amendments to the liquor legislation were suggested directly by the police or the Liquor Commission. For example, according to the Alberta Liquor Act and the Saskatchewan

Temperance Act, private dwelling houses were permitted to have any quantity of liquor on the premises. Many bootleggers took advantage of this and converted their cellars into trading warehouses. On the strong recommendation of the police in Alberta, in 1917, the government amended the Liquor Act to provide that private dwellings would not be allowed to possess more than one quart of spirituous liquor, and two gallons of malt liquor. In 1922, the police further suggested that the Act should stipulate exactly the maximum quantity of fermented liquor that a person was entitled to keep in a private dwelling. Legally, the liquor in private dwellings could be imported from other provinces through mail order. The police found that this was not always the case. Much of it came from liquor export warehouses within the provinces that were diverting supplies manufactured for export into the local market.

SOURCES OF ILLEGAL LIQUOR: LIQUOR EXPORT
WAREHOUSES AND ILLICIT STILLS

Police had difficulties in eliminating bootlegging. It was mainly because there were two sources of illicit liquor that the police could not effectively control: liquor warehouses and illicit stills. Allowing importation and export of liquor by liquor warehouses was the biggest loophole in the prohibition law in both Alberta and Saskatchewan. Both the Alberta Liquor Act and Saskatchewan Temperance Act permitted liquor warehouses to conduct interprovincial or international trade in liquor.[43] These stipulations were consistent with those of the Canada Temperance Act of 1914, 1916, and 1917. At the same time, both the governments of Alberta and Saskatchewan enacted laws regulating liquor warehouses such as the Alberta Liquor Export Act of 1918 and Saskatchewan's "An Act to Prevent Sales of Liquor for Export" of 1917.

In 1918, however, the Dominion government invoked the War Measures Act to prohibit the manufacture of liquor for beverage purposes and the transportation of liquor into any part of Canada.[44] In May 1919, the Dominion government introduced legislation to extend prohibition of liquor sale and manufacture for an additional year. The legislation passed the House, but was voted down by the Senate on the basis that it was an infringement of provincial rights. The interprovincial shipment, importation, and export of liquor again became legal, and this development was a major blow to the prohibition movement in Canada and the United States.[45] Liquor export warehouses sprang up rapidly through Canada and interprovincial trade resumed. In fact, just before the restoration of interprovincial trade, the Dominion government amended the Canada Temperance Act in November 1919 in order to address conflicting liquor legislation in the provinces.[46] The amendment allowed provinces (in which there was a law in force that prohibited the sale of intoxicating liquor for personal consumption) to prohibit the importation of liquor into the province by means of a plebiscite.

Consequently, in April 1920, in response to the demands levied by temperance groups, the Alberta government, without holding a plebiscite, amended the 1918 Liquor Export Act, stipulating that the importation of liquor into Alberta was illegal.[47] The amendment forced most liquor warehouses out of business except for the Gold Seal Liquor Co. of Calgary. The company took legal action in the courts and questioned the legality of the amendment in the absence of a plebiscite. On the second of

July 1920, after a three-month legal battle, the Appellate Division of the Supreme Court of Canada ruled that the 1918 Liquor Export Act and its amendment prohibiting the importation of liquor from other provinces of Canada into Alberta were *ultra vires*, that is, they surpassed the legal authority of the Legislative Assembly of the Province of Alberta.[48] A similar law passed by the Saskatchewan government received the same ruling from the Supreme Court of Canada in 1920. Because of this ruling, the police were required to return all the liquor that they had confiscated earlier in the year. However, after the Liquor Export Act of Saskatchewan and of Alberta and their amendments were proclaimed *ultra vires*, there was no law by which the police could regulate the warehouses effectively in the provinces.

The police knew that almost all liquor export warehouses had been involved in bootlegging. But the police had difficulties getting evidence substantiating their views. One way to establish that a warehouse had been bootlegging was to find discrepancies in the quantity of liquor imports and exports. However, this simple information was not readily available. In practice, the export companies imported stocks of liquor in bulk or in barrels. Before the liquor was shipped to other provinces, the companies bottled the liquor under various names. This process made it impossible for the police to check up on the actual amount of liquor that was shipped out of the province. Even when there were some shortages in goods, they were always accounted for by breakages.

With the intention to eliminate liquor importation, the governments of Alberta and Saskatchewan finally decided to hold plebiscites on importation at the end of 1920. As a result, importation became illegal in February 1921 in Alberta and February 1922 in Saskatchewan. But liquor export warehouses continued to exist allegedly for exporting liquor. The new law gave the police greater powers to oversee the illicit activities by liquor export warehouses. However, in 1922, the Dominion government also amended the Canada Temperance Act, which permitted the use of automobiles as common carriers for the direct delivery of liquor.[49] This proved to be a very serious blow to the police effort to enforce the prohibition law in both provinces. This provision created a new loophole enabling liquor export warehouses to bootleg.

Bootleggers could load up liquor in an automobile and deliver it to a purported buyer in another province or state south of the border. If there were no police in the vicinity, the bootleggers would drive carloads of liquor to some place within the province for illicit sales. Even if the police were tipped off, bootlegging under this scheme was very difficult to prevent. After many attempts over four years to use the new legislation controlling the illicit sale of liquor, Inspector Stott of the Liquor Branch of the APP admitted that the police failed to eliminate the sale of liquor in public places because the liquor export warehouses were the "supply depots of a large number of bootleggers."[50] This was also the case in Saskatchewan. The police believed that the best way to stop illegal liquor traffic was to close all liquor warehouses. This was never done and prohibition was doomed to failure.

The second major source of illegal liquor was illicit stills. The number of illicit stills appears to have correlated inversely with the existence of legal liquor export warehouses in the provinces over time. During the period 1917–20, when the import and export of liquor was prohibited under the War Measures Act, there was a relatively large number of convictions for operating illicit stills. In 1920, the increase in the excise duty on alcohol from $2.40 during wartime to $9 a gallon gave the home-brewing industry another incentive to exist and expand. The operation of stills presented difficulties in police control in both legal and practical senses.

In many situations, illicit still spirits (often called "household remedies") were made for home consumption. They were plentiful among foreign immigrants and many rural residents made moonshine for themselves and their neighbours. Inspector Stott of the LB remarked in 1922 that "the immigrants drink anything with a 'kick' in it."[51] However, English-speaking communities were relatively free from such home remedies as they could afford to purchase liquor from other provinces through mail orders legally.[52]

Although the police estimated that there were a considerable number of illicit stills, they were very hard to find because many of them were hidden in the bush, around lakes or ponds or unoccupied farmland. Although police searches were most successful during the holiday seasons, they were frustrated by the fact that, while they might find the stills, they could not identify their owners and prosecute the offenders.[53] The practice of making still spirits was usually confined to the country, but a large number of people in the towns and cities were also in the habit of making wine and beer at home with the advance of prohibition. Ingredients, such as malt and hops, could be easily purchased from drug stores.

The enforcement of law concerning illicit stills by the police was also complicated by many conflicts in jurisdiction. Manufacturers of liquor were regulated by the Inland Revenue Act. The enforcement of the Act was the responsibility of the federal Inland Revenue Department. The provincial and the city police were involved only when the illicit stills moved into the retail markets. However, it was the SPP and the APP that often uncovered illicit stills in the process of enforcing the prohibition legislation. Before 1922, when this happened, the provincial police had to notify the attorneys general of the provinces who would inform the Inland Revenue Department. Then, the department often called upon the assistance of the provincial police or the RCMP to make an arrest. The Superintendent of the APP believed that the Inland Revenue Department should ask for assistance exclusively from the RCMP because the Inland Revenue Act was a federal law.[54]

The practical problem for the provincial police in helping the Inland Revenue Department to suppress illicit stills was that they had no authority to prosecute offenders. Under federal law, only Inland Revenue Officers could initiate charges of illicit manufacture of liquor. After the provincial police seized stills or mashes, they often had to wait for months to get an Inland Revenue officer to arrive and initiate the prosecution of the offenders. In 1922, in order to solve this difficulty, several APP and RCMP officers in Saskatchewan were sworn in as Inland Revenue officers with powers to enforce the Inland Revenue Act.

In most instances, the police assisted the Inland Revenue Department in seizing illicit stills, whisky and brandy mashes, and other articles necessary for manufacturing moonshine liquor. The spirits were manufactured out of every available crop: raisins, sugar, barley, corn, and potatoes. The stills were made from all kinds of utensils, including old copper kettles, boilers, and zinc buckets. In one instance, a still was made from the radiator of a Ford automobile. The home-distilled whisky was reportedly quite potent due to extremely high alcohol content, not to mention the toxic metals. The police noted that one or two drinks of such spirits could send a drinker crazy. Occasionally, the drinkers had to be sent to a hospital or a place of restraint.[55]

PHYSICIANS AND DRUGGISTS AS BOOTLEGGERS

The police complained that the prohibition laws created many criminals. From the beginning of the prohibition era, medical professionals, including physicians, druggists, and veterinary surgeons quickly turned to bootlegging. In fact, it was suggested in the annual reports of the LB that doctors and druggists were among "the worst offenders" of the prohibition laws.[56] Everybody knew that much of the liquor consumed in the provinces was sold legally by prescription.

According to the Alberta Liquor Act and Saskatchewan Temperance Act, physicians were allowed to issue written or printed prescriptions permitting patients to purchase intoxicating liquor from druggists. The physicians might also sell liquor themselves in those areas where druggists were not available.

As a result of this loophole, many thirsty patients paid two dollars a visit to see a doctor, not for medical advice, but for a liquor prescription allowing them to purchase a bottle of liquor. It was widely known that, if a physician refused to issue such a prescription, he was liable to lose a considerable amount of business to other doctors.[57]

The laws that permitted physicians to prescribe liquor did not explicitly stipulate the number of prescriptions that a physician could issue within a limited time period. Many physicians issued prescriptions indiscriminately and some of them made the issuing of prescriptions their sole business, given the amount of money involved. Some doctors even went so far as to simply sell their prescriptions in bulk to druggists. The druggists filled in the name of the person to whom the liquor was sold. Since veterinary surgeons in small towns were allowed to have a certain amount of liquor in their possession, they also bootlegged occasionally.[58]

Since the law created a legal avenue via prescriptions, bootleggers started to access supplies by forging prescriptions. The prescription forgery could be sold for two to three dollars on the market.[59] To curb the forgery of prescriptions, the 1919 amendment to the Alberta Liquor Act empowered the government to change valid prescription forms frequently and at its discretion.[60]

The government also used legislation to restrain illicit practices of physicians in both provinces. Under the 1917 Saskatchewan Temperance Act, physicians could lose their privilege of prescribing liquor after a second conviction for writing an illicit prescription. The 1920 amendment to the Act further provided that purchases by physicians were restricted to one quart at a time and each prescription was limited to eight ounces of brandy or rye whisky.

The 1919 amendment to the Alberta Liquor Act stipulated the same. Alberta's 1921 amendment provided more severe penalties for those doctors who violated the Liquor Act. The fines ranged from $400 to $1,000 for first-time offenders and six months imprisonment for subsequent offences without the option of a fine. In addition, a physician could not use more than a hundred forms for liquor prescriptions per month.[61] The APP noted that these legal changes did not seem to affect the illicit liquor traffic among physicians. This is because in most cases the police could not collect sufficient evidence against them.

Although the police were aware of such widespread illicit practices, they could not do much to control them. Even in cases where the police did have evidence that physicians were engaged in illicit practices, magistrates rarely convicted them. This was because of the important status of medical professionals in the community. The courts sympathized more with doctors than with the police.[62] Nevertheless, the APP did manage to convict four doctors of illegally selling prescriptions in bulk in 1920, four in 1921, three in 1922, and one in 1924.[63] When doctors were convicted, they typically received the minimum fine. This was much lower than the penalties that were received by career bootleggers. The minimum fine could be $5 or $10 in Saskatchewan since the Saskatchewan Temperance Act only stipulated a maximum penalty of $100.

If physicians could make money by selling liquor prescriptions, druggists were in an even better position to do the same. It was the druggists who actually handled liquor directly. According to the Alberta Liquor Act and the Saskatchewan Temperance Act, druggists were entrusted to sell intoxicating liquor by prescription. However, sales without prescription were prevalent during the prohibition period. The APP commented that "the majority of the drug stores are nothing more than legalized blind pigs."[64] Of course, many druggists were also frequently harassed by numbers of "thirsty men" who tried to obtain liquor without a prescription. Druggists who operated strictly in accordance with the law lost old customers to other druggists who had fewer scruples.

According to the police, many druggists appeared to have made a lot of money by bootlegging. Inspector Brankley of the Calgary district observed that

It is well known to us where drug clerks with very limited salaries, and practically no financial backing, have opened up a drug store, and have become independently well-off in a year or so, and it is not the amount of drugs they dispose of but the great amount of liquor that passes through their hands at very large profits.[65]

As in the cases with physicians, the police were typically powerless to obtain sufficient information to prosecute druggists. The 1919 amendment to the Alberta Liquor Act stipulated that drug stores were allowed only to purchase liquor from government vendor stores. The stores had to account for the quantity of liquor by doctors' prescriptions. However, the amendment still did not prevent druggists from bootlegging. Many druggists purchased liquor from the government vendors in bulk. By diluting or adulterating liquor before it was bottled, the druggists were able to make up the shortage due to illicit selling that was not accounted for by prescriptions. By so doing, the druggists could easily avoid police detection of illicit traffic by checking prescriptions.[66] At the same time, drug stores were frequently supplied with illicit liquor from the export warehouses.

Although the number of druggists who were convicted of bootlegging was small, the police knew that illicit liquor traffic was widespread in both the rural and urban areas. There were differences in respect of the extent to which bootlegging was conducted by druggists between cities and rural areas. The police observed that, as in the big cities, very few druggists in the country would sell a bottle of whisky to a stranger without a prescription. The druggists in the country suspected every stranger of being with the liquor police. Although bootlegging was more prevalent in urban areas than in the countryside, the police had a similar difficulty catching druggists who bootlegged. This is because druggists in both country and urban areas had their regular customers and there was no point in taking a chance by selling liquor to strangers who might be undercover liquor policemen.

In order to curb the excessive profits going to the druggists, the 1919 amendment to the Alberta Liquor Act allowed government vending stores to sell liquor by prescription as well. Druggists who were convicted twice of selling liquor without prescription could lose their privilege of selling any liquor by prescription.[67] The 1922 amendment further restrained the druggists' capability of bootlegging by allowing them to sell only government-sealed bottles of liquor by prescription and the penalties to offenders became more severe.[68]

In Saskatchewan, the 1920 amendment to the Temperance Act adopted a drastic and complex measure aimed mainly at preventing bootlegging by druggists. The amendment stipulated that the Saskatchewan Liquor Commission would henceforth have complete control of liquor imports for medical purposes; all orders for liquor from druggists to wholesalers were to be sent directly to the Commission for approval. When approved, such liquors were to be forwarded by the Commission to the designated wholesalers. No liquor could be sold unless its package contained the seal of the Commission. Druggists were required to keep complete records of all prescriptions filled, and these records were to be available to the liquor inspectors.[69]

When druggists did not comply with the regulations, their liquor permits were subject to cancellation in both provinces. As a result of some intensive investigations, in the last week of August 1920, twenty-seven Alberta druggists lost their liquor permits. The APP officers observed that the 1922 amendments to the Alberta Liquor Act effectively reduced druggists' bootlegging. But some druggists continued to conduct illicit traffic, albeit in a smaller way.[70] Eventually, the provinces abandoned prohibition in 1924 and replaced druggists altogether with government-controlled retail and wholesale operations.

PUBLIC DISCONTENT AND POLICE UNPOPULARITY

The police experience of controlling illicit liquor suggests that their difficulties in enforcing the liquor prohibition came primarily from two sources: the loopholes and complexity of the prohibition legislation and a large number of people who participated in illicit liquor trades. Indeed, the largest obstacle to the enforcement arose from the fact that a substantial proportion of the population did not support the law. The police noted that women tended to give more support to prohibition than men, but general public resistance made the public uncooperative with the police in the enforcement of the law. APP Inspector Brankley in the Calgary area reported in 1921 that

... the enforcing of [the Liquor Act] is a bone of contention with us. The act is on the Statute Books, and has to be enforced, but where you have pretty nearly 50 per cent of the population against you, and throwing every barrier in the road to frustrate justice and to shield guilty parties, make it very arduous for us.[71]

Even the "better" class of citizens who never violated any laws showed no hesitation to violate liquor legislation. APP Inspector Fisher of the Red Deer district noted that the Liquor Act was so unpopular that it appeared to be "more honoured in the breach than in observance in the public."[72] Most of the public actually did not think that the violation of the liquor regulation was a crime. Inspector Brankley (Calgary area) reported in 1921 that "I have had on more occasions than one some of the very best citizens tell me that they did not think it a crime or offence to break this act – in fact, they loved to do so."[73] It was "smart" to circumvent the prohibition law and get a drink or bottle of whisky. The law had little or no moral authority.

In spite of public resistance, the police were required to enforce the laws in both provinces. However unpopular, the laws were on the provincial statute books and some politicians from strong prohibitionist constituencies often urged the police to enforce the acts vigorously. At the same time, there were many people who complained about liquor violations in their towns and villages.

The police often found themselves in the centre of conflicts between the prohibitionists and anti-prohibitionists. Typically, the police were instructed by the attorneys general of the provinces to investigate violations of the prohibition laws when a complaint was lodged. When the police got to the localities, they could not get any assistance, not even from the complainants. Sometimes, the police faced violent opposition from townspeople. In the 1921 report, APP Inspector Stott complained that

> We have had complaints from people about the *terrible conditions* that exist in their town, and when we have investigated the complaint and caught the offenders, the whole town was up in arms, wanting to hang, draw, and quarter the detective who was responsible.[74]

A direct consequence of the hostile public attitude towards the laws and their enforcement was that the police failed to enforce the law efficiently because they could not get evidence that could be adequately presented in the courts to secure convictions. Inspector Hodgkins of the Liquor Branch of the APP noted that in his two-year experience working in the Branch, there was not a single person who was willing to provide information about the violation of the Liquor Act and give evidence supporting a prosecution.[75] The results of most police investigations were disappointing.

If the public was reluctant to cooperate in investigating liquor offences, magistrates and justices of the peace were barely lukewarm in trying such cases. Justices of the peace often dismissed cases because the police could not provide sufficient evidence or because the evidence was secured using improper methods. Furthermore, justices of the peace often refused to convict the accused on the verbal evidence collected by special constables or on the evidence provided by informants who were hired by the Saskatchewan Liquor Commission. Very often, these hired informers or special constables were crooked men themselves with dubious credibility. When this happened, some justices of the peace did not restrain themselves from criticizing the police. In 1921, the Superintendent of the APP complained to the attorney general that in several instances the justices of the peace took opportunities to censure police constables in the presence of the persons who were charged with violations of the Liquor Act. He believed that their attitudes towards the police were detrimental to the enforcement of the law in general and the prohibition legislation in particular. They tended to encourage law offenders and discourage police enforcement. In Saskatchewan, the Liquor Commission decided that the liquor inspectors were to work in pairs so that the evidence obtained by them would more likely be accepted by the courts.

However, where guilt was established, the police often accused justices of the peace and magistrates of being too lenient on the offenders since they imposed minimum fines on the offenders. This is because they either shared the public's anti-prohibition sentiment or did not want to be unpopular in the town or village where they lived. The police explained that the magistrates' reluctance to dispense justice was associated closely with their pecuniary interest. Most justices of the peace received only $25 per month from adjudicating legal cases. It was necessary for them to have their own business in the town where they lived. Thus, they were afraid for business reasons to dispense justice.[76] In order to solve these problems, the police suggested appointing more travelling magistrates with a relatively higher salary.

A final obstacle to effective enforcement of the law was the lack of cooperation between the different police forces. Both the SPP and APP always received assistance from other police forces concerning matters of "real" crime. But, with the enforcement of the prohibition legislation, this was not true. Inspector Stott of the Liquor Branch of the APP reported to the commissioner that if they depended upon assistance from city police, they should have received few cases.[77] The lack of cooperation between the Saskatchewan Liquor Commission and the SPP and other city police was also evident. According to the Saskatchewan Temperance Act of 1920, the Liquor Commission could call upon the assistance of the SPP. Occasionally, there were conflicts between the special constables appointed by the Liquor Commission and the SPP regarding how the law should be enforced. The efforts of the APP and SPP to enforce prohibition legislation resulted in public contempt for the police. The police were referred to as "spotters" and "whisky sleuths." The relationship between the police and the public was seriously undermined. The public not only refused to provide the police with any assistance in enforcement of this law, but they also were developing an uncooperative attitude towards other police duties.

The enforcement of the prohibition law was detrimental to the police in both provinces. The governments gradually recognized that total prohibition was impossible to enforce, and that the attempts were exposing the police to danger as well as ridicule. The governments in Alberta and Saskatchewan adopted a new approach in 1924. Control by licence replaced retail prohibition. The Liquor Branch of the APP in Alberta and the Saskatchewan Liquor Commission were disbanded. Liquor Control Boards were established in both provinces to administer the Licence Act. Many public places, such as beer halls, hotels, and restaurants, were allowed to sell intoxicating alcoholic beverages again under government-regulated licences. The police had a very positive attitude towards the new changes, and the 1924 Annual Report of the APP suggested that the changes had the wholehearted support of most citizens.[78] The police began to regain their popularity.

CONCLUSION

The prohibition laws of Alberta and Saskatchewan were unpopular pieces of legislation. They were the product of conflicts between the well-to-do middle class and the working class, mixed with an ethnic division between Anglo-Canadians and the immigrants from central and southern Europe. These laws were intended to impose middle-class Anglo-Canadian values on the working class and foreign immigrants and to alter their lifestyle so as to co-opt them into Anglo-Canadian society. The police, who enforced such moralistic laws, were no longer able to maintain their seemingly neutral position in society. Their image of relative autonomy from politics disappeared and their attachment to politicians was overwhelming, as the law reflected the values or aspiration of special interests in society. Under prohibition, liquor prescriptions, the export and import liquor trade, rum-running, bootlegging, and home-brewing flourished. These booming illicit enterprises reflected both the loopholes in the laws and anti-prohibition sentiment among the public. As a result, the laws not only created a large number of criminals who would be law-abiding citizens under normal circumstances, but they also generated a large amount of wealth from illicit liquor businesses. As the enforcers of the law, the police experienced a legitimation crisis – they lost the cooperation of ordinary citizens; they were rebuked by the judiciary; and they frequently failed to obtain the cooperation of other law enforcement professionals.

Public sentiment and opinion towards the laws and their enforcement played an essential role in police enforcement. After all, the extent to which the public accepted the police depended on the nature and content of the law and how it was enforced. Community support was an essential precondition for the police to enforce the laws efficiently. Without this support, the enforcement of laws was impaired and the offences continued. By implication, the ability of the police in the larger historical context to civilize the marginal classes and offensive behaviours is not a one-way street. The police were not only agents of change, but, as in this case, victims of unrealistic policy, and objects of change from social resistance.

CONCLUSION: THE RETURN OF THE RCMP

"Instead of being the end, it is the start of a new beginning." – APP Acting Commissioner Hancock, 1932[1]

The enforcement of the unpopular prohibition legislation was detrimental to the professional image of both provincial police forces. However, the legitimation crises did not ruin the police entirely. In fact, the forces gradually regained some popularity after the prohibition legislation was repealed in 1924. It was budgetary considerations that finally led the provincial governments to dissolve the provincial police and to re-employ the RCMP. The SPP and APP were disbanded in 1928 and 1932, respectively, after policing Alberta and Saskatchewan for more than a decade. The process of disbanding the police forces provided further evidence that the manifold police tasks were shaped directly by government policies and sometimes by individual politicians who happened to be in charge of the police.

Maintaining provincial police forces in Alberta and Saskatchewan was a large burden for the often meagre provincial coffers. Since the establishment of the provincial police forces in 1917, the expenses to sustain the forces had increased exponentially in both provinces.[2] Soon after the establishment of the forces, both provincial governments recognized that the expenditure on policing could be curtailed as there was a federal police force – the RCMP – with more than a hundred policemen in each province, with relatively little work to perform. In fact, following the end of World War I, the RCMP were confined to the enforcement of a few federal statutes, such as the Inland Revenue Act, the Indian Act, and other acts exclusive of the Criminal Code.

As early as 1923, J.E. Brownlee, then attorney general of Alberta, observed that there were overlapping efforts and needless expenses between the provincial police and the RCMP in the enforcement of law and maintenance of order in the prairie provinces.[3] This observation could have been a response to the farmers' call for a return of the RCMP to police rural Alberta due to an increase in cattle theft in the province during the early 1920s. Nevertheless, overlapping duties and duplication in expenses became two important arguments for governments to reform policing in the western provinces.

At the 1927 inter-government conference in Ottawa, the ministers from western Canada formally presented the problem of needless duplication of policing. The provinces could have a single general police force instead of two specialized organizations. Premier J.C. Gardiner and Attorney General J. Cross, both of Saskatchewan, proposed specifically that the provincial police could take over the RCMP work of enforcing Dominion statutes with an allowance from the federal government. Otherwise, the provincial governments could disband their own provincial police forces and pay the federal government to administer justice in the provinces by the RCMP.[4] Considering the general sentiment favouring the RCMP, "an organization of proven efficiency and one with a tradition which is cherished," it was reasonable to assume that if one police force was to be eliminated, the RCMP would certainly be retained.[5] However, on account of the disagreeable relationship between the federal government and the western provinces on many issues, the Saskatchewan delegates were credited with not being particular about which of the two police forces would be retained.[6] This proposal became a starting point for federal-provincial renegotiation on policing. The federal government announced that it had no intention of disbanding the RCMP – "a historical establishment."[7] After the 1927 conference, the dialogue continued between the provincial and federal governments. After some six months of negotiations, on March 22, 1928, an agreement was reached between the government of Saskatchewan and the government of Canada.[8]

Economic considerations were cited as the primary reasons for the disbandment of the provincial force. In its official publication *The Public Service Monthly*, the government of Saskatchewan stated that

> Motives of economy dictated, and the duplication of forces operating in the province necessitated the dissolution of the provincial body. The efficiency of the force was never called in question. That was taken for granted, and abundantly demonstrated. Regina being the training centre of the RCMP, it

necessarily followed that the Dominion Government had to maintain an organization and a fairly powerful force within the province, and the obvious fact that the policing of the province could be more economically undertaken by one body, led inevitably to the negotiations between the provincial Government and the federal government that resulted in the latter agreeing to resume responsibility, through the RCMP of the policing of Saskatchewan.[9]

The federal government corroborated this argument. When questioned about conflict between the SPP and RCMP in 1928, Lepointe, Minister of Justice of Canada, and C.C. Staines, Commissioner of the RCMP, stated that there had been no friction between the RCMP and the SPP in the western provinces. C.C. Staines said that "it is purely a case of the province finding the expenses of the provincial police force too heavy."[10]

However, for D.E. Smith and J.H. Archer, the economic argument might have served as an excuse to break up the force for political reasons.[11] Archer suggests that the reasons for the disbandment were the accusation of political interference with police work and enforcement of prohibition law.[12] Smith argues that Gardiner, the premier of Saskatchewan, recognized the occurrence of political interference in police work, particularly by the attorney general, J. A. Cross, as revealed in the subsequent 1930 *Report of the Royal Commission of Inquiry into Statements Made in Statutory Declarations and Other Matters*. Smith maintains that the premier's real objective in dissolving the force was to remove J.A. Cross's *personal* influence on the force.

Smith's argument is certainly plausible. Premier Gardiner had keen interests in thoroughly controlling the Liberal party organization during his tenure as premier. Even so, the economic factor was a growing source of concern. The police expenses had increased annually. In 1916, the police annual budget was $18,750. By 1921, the police expenditure had increased to $299,686, more than fifteen times that of 1916. Between 1921 and 1927, this trend continued. The 1927 police budget was $402,714, having increased 34 per cent since 1921. Also in the 1920s, Saskatchewan's economy was in difficulties. The province relied predominately on agriculture. In 1925, 92 per cent of the net value of production in the province was still accounted for by agricultural production. Prices for farm products fluctuated greatly. As a result, the revenue of the government was extremely unstable. During 1925–37, the cash income of farmers declined by $92.5 million per year on average. The average annual cash income during this period was only 39.5 per cent of that of the previous nine-year period.[13] This difficult financial situation predated the Great Depression. During the 1920s, the province's deficit and debt increased. The government had to use more than 27 per cent of its total revenue in 1926 to pay the interests on the debt. In 1927, in order to reduce government expenditure, Attorney General J.A. Cross ordered a reduction of twenty-five men, cutting the 1927 police budget by $63,439, 15 per cent of the total $402,714 budget.[14] The government actually saved $200,000 annually by switching to the RCMP contract. This saving was a considerable amount of money for the government of Saskatchewan, whose total annual income revenue was only about $15 million. In light of this economic condition in Saskatchewan, the disbandment of the SPP could be a consequence of both political consideration and economic hardship of the province.

Table 6.1 Police Expenditure in the Province of Saskatchewan

Year	Expenditure
1911	$75,000.00
1916	$18,750.00
1921	$299,686.90
1926	$306,539.38
1927	$402,714.00
1931	$175,000.00
1932	$182,849.72
1931	$177,310.35
1934	$177,885.90
1935	$178,234.97
1936	$178,566.65
1937	$178,840.21

Source: Province of Saskatchewan, *A Submission by the Government of Saskatchewan to the Royal Commission On Dominion-Provincial Relations*, 1937, p. 391.

In Alberta, the potential savings in policing were also very appealing to the government. Alberta was not richer than the province of Saskatchewan in the 1920s and 1930s. However, in 1928, the Government of Alberta actually rejected a similar offer from the federal government. This was partially because the province of Alberta and the federal government could not agree on the amount of money that Alberta would pay for RCMP services. The federal government held that approximately $220,000 annually would be the cost to Alberta as compared to $175,000 annually to Saskatchewan. In Alberta, the RCMP needed to recruit another 90 police officers in order to bring the force up to the minimum of 220 men as promised by the RCMP, as by then there were only 111 RCMP members stationed in the province. However, in Saskatchewan, 70 more police officers would be sufficient to bring the force up to that fixed number.[15] In this case, if the government accepted the offer from Ottawa, Alberta could save $177,606 per year, according to the 1928 APP budget.[16]

However, unlike the government of Saskatchewan, the government of Alberta highly valued the social services rendered by the APP. The possibility that the RCMP might not provide such services was the strongest argument for the government to decline the offer from the federal government. The concern was summarized retrospectively by the press during the 1930 debate on the policing issue: (1) since the federal government maintained that they had to retain the RCMP to administer federal statutes, it was equally important that the Alberta government should maintain the APP for enforcing provincial statutes; (2) there were a number of duties that were imposed on the APP (such as the enforcement of the provincial Game Act), which could not be imposed on the RCMP; and (3) as the province wanted to carry out policies of the government efficiently, direct control of the police had to be retained.[17] In early 1929, J.E. Brownlee, premier of Alberta, stated, "I am not satisfied that the saving would be sufficient to offset the greater advantage of having at all times, control of our own police force."[18]

However, because the government of Alberta was in financial difficulties as serious as those found in Saskatchewan and under the constant pressure from opposition MLAs to cut government spending and reduce the taxpayers' burden, the government cut police expenses through both reorganizing APP divisions and reducing the pay of APP members by twenty dollars across the board in 1928. Red Deer ("B" Division) was closed in April 1928 and its detachments were absorbed into Edmonton ("A" Division) and Calgary ("C" Division). APP Commissioner Bryan indicated that "this change is a very economical one and the work at the present time is being done more efficiently than with a divisional headquarters established at Red Deer."[19] Inspector Duncan, who was in charge of "B" Division, was brought into APP Headquarters in Edmonton and placed in charge of the Criminal Investigation Branch. This reduction in police expenses did not completely ease the financial difficulties the government faced. However, it served to appease criticism from opposition MLAs.

For the opposition, cutting police expenditures through disbanding the APP was a feasible way of reducing the government deficit. This was attested to by the two-year successful cooperation between the government of Saskatchewan and the federal government. In 1930, the Alberta Conservative Party leader, Mr. D.W. Duggan, proposed to replace the APP with the RCMP and reduce costs further. According to his estimate, the government could save $210,000 by using the RCMP to police the province without impairing the efficient enforcement of the law. He pointed out that "the present high state of efficiency now enjoyed would not be impaired by the change. This being the case, the chief concern was one of finance."[20] Mr. Duggan pointed out that provincial police costs were not only higher than RCMP fees but that the APP budget was increasing at the rate of $25,000 annually. Duggan's proposal as a motion from the Opposition party was rejected on a straight party vote in the provincial legislature. Again, the chief argument by the government against turning over police work in the province to the RCMP was that "there were many functions which could not be termed strictly police but which the provincial force was expected to perform."[21] Mr. Perren Baker, a U.F.A. MLA, suggested that "the government believed in extending the functions of the APP to a point far beyond those of a purely police body, which the advent of the natural resources would mean more work of a civilian nature, which would cost much additional money if the RCMP were doing the policing of the province."[22] The APP officers had acted in the capacity of local administrators. In Saskatchewan the RCMP did only straight police work.

However, all government opposition to disbanding the force was put aside in 1931 when the serious financial crisis of the Great Depression hit the province. A report from the government showed that "by the end of fiscal year, March 31, 1931, the province had experience in a very drastic way of the effect of the depression and the disastrous decline in the price of farm products."[23] The revenues of the provincial government dropped by approximately $2 million or by 14 per cent compared to 1930. This was the first time in the history of Alberta that the government had to record a deficit of almost $20 million and use nearly *half* of government revenue to pay debt charges. The politicians had to seriously reconsider the RCMP and the savings that it offered.

Table 6.2 Financial Situation of Alberta (thousands of dollars)

Year	Income Revenue	Expenditure	Deficit	Debt
1926	$11,912	$22,857	$10,945	$93,000
1927	12,263	21,937	9,674	--------
1928	15,265	24,220	8,955	96,000
1929	15,830	26,025	10,195	98,000
1930	15,711	28,907	13,196	74,000
1931	13,492	33,365	19,873	79,000

Source: Mackintosh, *Economic Problems of the Prairie Province*, 70 and 58; and *Case of Alberta*, 346.

Right after the end of fiscal year 1931, the government cut police expenses. An APP Circular Memorandum indicated that the various departments of the government had been notified by Premier Brownlee that expenditures must be cut down to the lowest possible minimum. APP Commissioner Bryan instructed officers that all unnecessary expenditures be curtailed. For instance, a great deal of mileage was incurred in cases where the long distance telephone would probably do. Requests for renovations, office supplies, and other matters, had to be cut down.[24] The government also required the APP to take over work from other social service departments in order to reduce government expenses. A large proportion of work of the Department of Neglected Children was transferred to the APP.[25]

The successful experience of Saskatchewan with the RCMP for more than three years suggested that Alberta would find it equally satisfactory. On March 8, 1932, the government presented to the legislature the arrangement made between the government of Alberta and the federal government for employing the RCMP to police the province. The agreement was subsequently ratified by the legislature with the support of all MLAs except seven opposition members. The APP were formally dissolved on April 1, 1932.

THE FEDERAL-PROVINCIAL AGREEMENTS

According to the RCMP Act of 1927, the federal government was entitled to enter into an arrangement with the provinces of Canada on the administration of justice in the provinces and the attorneys general of the provinces were also empowered to enter such agreements on the behalf of the provinces. The agreements between the federal government and Saskatchewan in 1928 and Alberta in 1932 on policing shared many characteristics. The agreement with Saskatchewan consisted of sixteen provisions, and there were seventeen in the Alberta agreement. The RCMP took over the duties of the SPP on June 1, 1928, and the APP on April 1, 1932. The term of the agreement with Saskatchewan was from June 1, 1928, to the last day of 1935, and the term with the Alberta was from the 1st day of April, 1932, to the 31st day of 1935. The agreement could be terminated under the condition that either of the parties gave the other one year's notice.[26]

The RCMP would remain a federal force and under the control of the federal government. However, in order that the provincial governments could maintain their full jurisdiction over the administration of justice in the provinces, the RCMP Commissioner or an officer appointed by him to be in charge of criminal investigations in Saskatchewan and Alberta would act on their own responsibility under the direction of the attorney general of each province without reference to the superior officers of the force in Ottawa, except where federal statutes or federal police duties were concerned. In this manner, prompt decisions could be given within the provinces without delay. The agreement more specifically stipulated that the administration of justice including the liquor law of the provinces and all other laws in force or thereafter passed, which were formerly enforced by the SPP or APP, would be enforced by the RCMP. They would be enforced in accordance with the wishes and under the direction of the attorneys general of the provinces in the same manner and to the same extent as though the provincial police were still in existence and carrying on their duties theretofore assigned to them.[27]

These provisions emphasized provincial authorities and objectives with regard to the administration of justice in the provinces. These emphases undoubtedly addressed the concerns of the provincial governments with the enforcement of provincial statutes and other duties performed previously by the provincial police. For this purpose, the duty of RCMP assistance commissioner in western Canada was limited to taking charge of all matters pertaining to interior economy, discipline, and personnel.

For policing service provided by the RCMP, both the provinces of Alberta and Saskatchewan would each pay the federal government $175,000 a year, in addition to cost of maintenance and transportation of prisoners.[28] Concomitantly, both provinces would also retain all fines and costs collected by the police under Liquor Acts and the Criminal Code of Canada with all costs collected concerning the enforcement of the laws in the two provinces. The fines and costs were a considerable amount of money for the provinces. They contributed significantly to the revenue of the provinces when the provincial police enforced the laws. This indicates that the enforcement of law and order by the RCMP in western Canada was not for dollars but for symbolic reasons.

Table 6.3 The Fines Collected by and Costs of the Provincial Police

Years	By the APP		By the SPP	
	Fines	Costs	Fines	Costs
1920	$158,957.00	$14,834.79		
1921	$151,452.00	$14,374.28		
1922	$198,791.50	$14,722.74	$107,910.00	$38,019.04
1923	$171,141.45	$14,062.32	$130,449.30	$40,920.78
1924	$98,776.75	$16,187.06	$130,983.38	$32,140.01
1925	$78,286.00	$14,460.28	$173,978.00	$38,553.83
1926	$75,157.00	$14,925.31	$192,901.50	$33,845.11
1927	$65,000.50	$14,353.00	$181,322.59	$55,874.09
1928	$99,149.00	$22,192.10		
1929	$122,775.75	$24,107.26		
1930	$338,909.00	$18,666.74		
1931	$77,741.55	$16,934.72		

Sources: Annual reports of the APP, 1917–1932 and SPP, 1917–1928 for the Attorneys General of the Provinces, located in the Provincial Archives of Alberta and Saskatchewan, respectively. The fines and costs collected by the SPP prior to 1922 are not available.

CONTINUITY IN PERSONNEL AND EQUIPMENT

Since the conclusion of World War I, the RCMP had been charged with the enforcement of federal laws such as the Inland Revenue Act, the Indian Act, and other similar acts, exclusive of the Criminal Code of Canada. In 1928, the RCMP maintained a force of 150 men of all ranks in Saskatchewan. In order to fulfill the additional duties of enforcing the Criminal Code of Canada and provincial statutes, the RCMP agreed to maintain the force at not less than 220 men in Saskatchewan during the life of the contract. The RCMP were forced to recruit an additional 70 men. At that time, the SPP had 120 officers of all ranks. The province negotiated with the RCMP to absorb as many SPP members as possible into the RCMP. The RCMP agreed to recruit from the SPP the 70 men, including three inspectors and one superintendent. Since many SPP members were married, the restriction of the RCMP regulations regarding marriage in the acceptance of members of the SPP to augment the RCMP were not to be enforced. The age limit for original engagement in the RCMP was forty years, and all members of the SPP who were under forty years of age would be eligible to present themselves as candidates for selection, regardless of marriage status. For the members who were over forty years of age, only those who had previously served in the RCMP were deemed eligible for reengagement. In fact, only 67 SPP members forwarded their applications for enlistment in the RCMP.

Regarding the arrangement of APP members, the agreement between Alberta and the federal government provided that "the RCMP shall take over into that force all officers and men presently on the strength of the APP who are in good standing and physically fit to carry on the duties hereby undertaken by the RCMP."[29] In point of fact not all 222 actually qualified. The APP were divided into three classes. Class "A" men would *not* be taken over, including twenty-seven clerks, chauffeurs, and office men. Class "B" men would be taken on probation for one year, including seventeen special constables and liquor enforcement officer. And Class "C" men would be taken for the regular enlistment time of three years, including constables and officers of the APP.[30] Similar to the policies applied to SPP members, the restrictions of the RCMP regulations as to age limit and marriage would not be operative to exclude any member of the APP from admission to the RCMP.

The members of the APP and SPP who were employed by the RCMP would retain their ranks and be given credit for pension and seniority of the service in the two forces and previous service in the RCMP. In fact, the SPP seriously considered establishing a pension fund, particularly in 1927. Attorney General J.A. Cross instructed all members of the force to forward moieties (of fines received from the federal government in connection with cases under the Customs and Excise Act) to Headquarters for the purpose of forming the nucleus of a pension fund for the SPP.[31] This attempt to establish a pension fund was discontinued by the news of disbandment of the SPP in early 1928. Therefore, the provincial government of Saskatchewan had to contribute to the RCMP pension with sufficient funds to enable the recruited SPP members to receive credit for prior service. In comparison, the APP had established their pension fund in 1921. The fund was liquidated under the authority of the Alberta Provincial Police Pension Fund Liquidation Act.[32] The Alberta agreement stipulated that APP members who were engaged by the RCMP had to pay personally into the federal government in the amount fixed by the RCMP commissioner in order to be entitled to get credit for pension for the service performed in the APP.[33]

For SPP members who were not engaged in the RCMP, including constables and officers, the provincial government of Saskatchewan would give a gratuity of one month's salary for each year of service on retirement owing to disbandment of the SPP. This payment cost the government about $50,000.[34] For the remaining APP members, the opposition MLAs suggested that the government make a small land grant to these men. The proposal was rejected immediately by the government. As there were 52,000 other persons employed by the government of Alberta, the government argued that they could not set a precedent such as this one.[35] However, according to the Pension Fund Liquidation Act, the commission for the liquidation was entitled to distribute surpluses of the fund to the persons who were detrimentally affected by disbandment of the APP. Under this provision, APP members who did not join the RCMP could receive a gratuity of money (amount unspecified) from the government, depending on the surplus of the fund.

It was further agreed that the members of the SPP doing police duty in the province of Saskatchewan who were well trained in police work peculiar to that province would be deployed in that province in the interests of efficiency of policing there. However, this policy would not apply to the former APP members possibly because the number of APP members was far beyond the ninety men needed by the RCMP in Alberta. As members of the RCMP, the former APP members might be sent to posts outside Alberta.

As a result of the Saskatchewan agreement, fifty-nine SPP members were actually absorbed into the RCMP in 1928. T.C. Goldsmith was commissioned as superintendent; R.R. Tait, J. Kelly, and J. Taylor were appointed as inspectors. Applications from eight SPP members for joining the RCMP were rejected.[36] Many members of the SPP and the APP did not choose to join the RCMP. If the Mounties were willing, why were the potential recruits turned down? The answer proved to be financial. The scale of pay on the RCMP was much less than on the APP and SPP. The APP and SPP paid their constables about $130 per month on average before the forces were disbanded, while the RCMP constables were paid only $68 per month. This was the key to the RCMP economic advantages: it could police the provinces at half the provincial rate by paying its employees half what the provinces had offered.

Due to the sick leave of SPP Commissioner Mahoney, the assistant commissioner, W.R. Tracey, had taken over routine operation of the SPP in the latter part of 1927. Consequently, Tracey also took charge of matters in connection with the disbandment of the force and liquidation of all equipment. This was revealed in his letter dated April 23, 1928, to Colonel H.J. Martin, Commissioner, Provincial Police of Manitoba, stating that "in view of the fact that the SPP will be disbanded on June 1st next, we have on our hands a certain amount of police equipment for disposal."[37] The police equipment for disposal listed in the letter included 150 .38-calibre Smith & Wesson service revolvers numbered and lettered "S.P.P.," 2,000 rounds of .38-calibre ammunition, slickers, boots, and Kalgan Beaver police coats, etc. Fred Osipoff was able to track down some buyers of SPP's firearms, including the T. Eaton Co. of Regina, the Bank of Commerce, the Province of Manitoba, and the city police of Prince Albert.[38]

APP Commissioner W.C. Bryan, at age sixty-five, retired after fifteen years service in the APP due to serious arthritis. His retirement formally took effect on February 14, 1932. Before his leave, he recommended to the attorney general that Inspector W.F.W. Hancock should become his successor. He stated that "He was a young man, energetic, and had good organizing and administrative ability."[39] Apparently, Attorney General J.F. Lymburn took the former commissioner's advice and appointed Hancock as superintendent and acting commissioner on the day after the commissioner's retirement.[40] The command of the APP men was finally relinquished by Supt. W.F.W. Hancock. However, unlike the assistant commissioner of the SPP, Hancock did not have to take the trouble to liquidate the APP police equipment, as "all arms, equipment, furnishing and supplies of every description of the APP were taken over by the government of the Dominion at a price to be mutually agreed up."[41] According to the respective agreements, the RCMP also took over all suitable APP and SPP buildings.

THE LEGACY OF THE SPP

With the spread of the news that the government intended to replace the SPP with the RCMP, various organizations wrote letters to the premier of Saskatchewan to express their concerns. The letter from the Saskatchewan Retail Merchants' Association indicates that the provincial police had rendered "the splendid service" in the interest of retail merchants as well as in the interest of the Saskatchewan public.[42] A personal letter to the premier from "Kindersled Liberal Association" opposed the forthcoming changes in policing the province by actually attacking the RCMP.[43] The letter said:

> But once again the public of this province is being tickled into parting with money and for sentimental reasons to support the creation of position for the keepers of the Indians, political 'bums,' who are and have been Ottawa Tories out of work. This is the history of the officials of the Mounties.... Present force [the SPP] is nearly by half paying its own way, and lastly they are and have been doing three times the work that was done by the Mounties and they are doing it three times as satisfactory [sic].

At midnight on May 31, 1928, the agreement between the Government of Saskatchewan and the federal government automatically came into effect. At that point, the SPP was disbanded and the RCMP took over the policing of the province without any ceremony. *The Regina Leader* and *The Public Service Monthly* remarked on the police on that occasion. The publications were inclined to regard the SPP as an efficient force that existed through "the most lawless period in the history of western Canada... The Saskatchewan Provincial Police created a record of achievement and efficiency which can compare favourably with that of any other police force in the world confronted with similar difficulties;"[44] The editorial of *The Regina Leader* pointed out that the province would not forget the force soon.

In fact, this province owes much to this force. It has not been a force with the tradition of the Royal Canadian Mounted Police, which supplants it in the policing of the province, but it did build up a record for skill, thoroughness, conscientiousness and fidelity which is one to be proud of.[45]

Indeed, the police did have a difficult job on their hands in combatting "rum-runners" and "bootleggers." Then, they were followed by desperadoes from the United States who robbed Canadian banks, post offices, and trains. These favourable comments on the SPP were further elaborated by the fact that the force not only existed through a difficult and trying time in the history of Saskatchewan, but also had a very humble and difficult beginning. The Public Service Monthly reminisced that

On December 6, 1916, Commissioner Mahoney of the SPP was instructed to take over the policing of Saskatchewan as from January 1, 1917, and authorised to recruit a force of 56 men. The majority of the men eligible for such a force were already in the army, no equipment was available on such short notice, but with characteristic energy and devotion to duty, a partial complement of 40 men was mustered, and the task undertaken. The men were distributed to the strategic points in the province, without uniforms, without a very clear understanding of their powers or the laws they were expected to enforce.... The force reached the apex of its strength in 1920, when it mustered 175 effectives.... It had reached a standard which enabled it to cope effectively with the organised bands of desperadoes engaged in, or attracted by, the illicit liquor traffic on the tempestuous border.[46]

These sentiments were probably what the public liked to remember about the SPP in 1928. Only in 1930 did the Royal Commission Inquiry reveal the SPP's disreputable involvement in civic elections and other political activities, as well as their enforcement of the unpopular liquor laws. In the public mind, the police were probably victims as well, in the sense that they did only what the politicians required them to do.

FAREWELLS TO THE APP: POPULAR REACTION

At the moment of dissolution of the APP, the public brought honour to the APP as well. Before the disbandment, the APP held farewell parties in Edmonton and Calgary. Many eminent people attended the parties, including the members of the judiciary, the bar, military officers, newspaper publishers, and the members of other police forces. On those occasions, the APP were compared favourably with the RCMP. Little was said about the fractious period of prohibition. Colonel G.E. Sanders, police magistrate, said that

> ... the force was formed at a period when vast changes in the province were taking place. Its work was strenuous, and officers had stood the strain and had acquitted with the greatest credit to themselves and have upheld the traditions which the British Constabulary has maintained throughout the world.[47]

Constable Baynes stated that there were difficulties in the beginning when the APP took over the work of the RNWMP in order to keep up the RCMP traditions. He suggested that "these traditions had been maintained and are being handed over intact to the RCMP."[48] Chief Justice Simmons of the Trial Division of the Supreme Court expressed that "it would go down in history as one of the forces which helped to make law and order in Alberta."[49]

The press also presented favourable views on the APP. *The Edmonton Journal* published an article titled "Alberta Provincial Police End 15 years in Control at Midnight; Fine Record" stating that "public opinion was against the APP at first, many openly saying that the force could not take the place of the 'Mounties.' Recent declarations by public men have indicated that the regard for the APP has been as high as for the RCMP."[50] *The Edmonton Bulletin* issued an article with a title, "Fine Tributes Paid A. P. Police Force at Wind-Up Smoker," suggesting that during the fifteen years of its existence, "the APP became friends and advisors of lonely settlers."[51] *The Albertan* remarked that "they had built up a reputation for law enforcement unsurpassed by any police force in the world; they had gained the respect of the citizens of Alberta as fair men and they had followed the hard and sometimes dangerous path of duty without fail."[52]

Many tragic moments in the APP's short history were once more brought forward by the press, and the public recalled the price paid by the APP for enforcing law and maintaining order in Alberta. In the case of the train holdup at Sentinel in the Crow's Nest Pass in 1920, APP constable F.W.E. Baily and RCMP Corporal Usher were killed. Two APP constables, S. Lawson and G.E. Osgood, died in combatting violations of the prohibition law in 1922. In 1931, the murder of Earnest Midwinter, a Calgary taxi-driver was remembered because this was regarded as the cleverest pieces of detective work in the APP history. By following the clue of a stained blackjack left near the scene of the killing, APP members finally captured the three killers.

CONTINUITY IN TRANSITION

Police history in western Canada consisted of the activities of two police forces: the RCMP (and the earlier RNWMP) and the provincial police. Although differences between the two police forces were conspicuous, the organizational continuity remained. Provincial police forces were disbanded. However, many members of the provincial police were not lost to the provinces. In fact, more than 50 per cent of the members of the SPP and APP were absorbed into the RCMP and continued to police the provinces. The press also noticed this continuity between the two different forces. *The Albertan* published an article with a long title expressing such an idea: "Alberta Provincial Police Force Ends Honourable Career, Officers Take Over Duties As *Mounties*: Men Who Built Up Outstanding Organization in This Province are to Continue Work as Members of Dominion Organization."[53] In this sense, Superintendent and Acting Commissioner of the APP Hancock stated at a party that "this is a sort of a sad evening but do not feel too bad – remember, that instead of being the end, it is the start of a new beginning."[54]

In fact, in APP Headquarters the preparation for the change had already begun on March 31, 1932, the day before the RCMP took over policing the province of Alberta. The officers of the APP were cleaning out their desks in preparation for new forms that the RCMP were printing for them. The RCMP would take over the headquarters as well. "Out in those country detachments which are being continued and there APP men are remaining as RCMP men, the constables will retire Thursday night as Provincial Police men and wake up as Mounties."[55] As police forces came and went in the short history of the provinces, the duties would also change in accordance with political and social environments. But policing continued.[56]

Although in the annals of policing, the duties of modern police are multifarious and varied in disparate societies at different points of time, it is nevertheless generally accepted that the most important function of the police is to enforce law and maintain order in society. Law and order have become identified closely with the police. However, it does not follow that law and order were generated by modern police. Arguably, law and order preceded the birth of the police. Modern professional police were created only in the early nineteenth century when traditional law and order were threatened by real and imagined increases in crime and violence due to industrialization and urbanization. The police were created for purposes of more efficiently enforcing law and maintaining order. Law and order were not born because of modern police. Rather the police were born because of the necessity of maintaining law and order. In western Canada, the NWMP began to maintain law and order in 1873. However, the Hudson Bay Company had an earlier history of policing in the Red River settlements starting in 1835.[57] This suggests that law and order had already to some degree been established. Certainly by 1917 they were well entrenched in the prairie societies before the creation of the provincial police. After the disbandment of the provincial forces in 1928 in Saskatchewan and 1932 in Alberta, law and order remained as the RCMP took over policing the provinces.

Although the provincial police arduously and strenuously maintained law and order for more than a decade in the provinces, neither force achieved a long legacy. During the life of the provincial police forces, several crises eroded the legacy of the forces. During the prohibition movement, because the liquor prohibition laws did not possess moral authority, a large segment of the population defied the laws. Police enforcement of the law resulted in a legitimation crisis. Concomitantly, because of continuous financial difficulties, the police were often overstretching their ability to perform various duties. The forces were finally disbanded mainly because of the financial crises resulting from bankruptcy (Saskatchewan, 1928) and the Great Depression (Alberta, 1932). Although the press anticipated that the provinces would remember the police efforts at the time to maintain law and order "for a long time," the population seems to have forgotten the existence of the forces as soon as they were dissolved. Even historians have recorded very little about them.

Unlike their provincial counterparts, the RCMP not only had established and maintained law and order in western Canada since 1873, but they also had established a long legacy. They became a symbol of law and order in the West. This was shown in 1928 in Saskatchewan and 1932 in Alberta when the population greeted the return of the RCMP with open arms, although it must be remembered that they returned without the tarnish of prohibition, petty provincial interference, and financial insolvency, but with a fine tradition in the West and splendid records from World War I and the Boer War.

If the NWMP were created in 1873 to open up and settle the West as part of Canada, the second coming of the federal force probably had a similar symbolic implication for the federal government. The return of the Mounties reflected the political reintegration of the West more fully into the federal sphere of influence. The replacement of provincial institutions with a national institution was not without symbolic importance. Ironically, when they were created in 1873, the NWMP were only a regional police force. Their jurisdiction was limited to the North-West Territories until 1905, when the new provinces were established. Then, the administration of justice fell to the attorneys general of the provinces. Due to financial difficulties, a temporary arrangement was made between the provinces and the federal government, providing that the federal government maintain the NWMP in the West for a small payment by the provinces. In 1917, because of the exigencies of the war, the federal government terminated the agreement. During wartime, the force was employed to patrol the international border with a small number of men, 485 in 1917 including all ranks.[58]

However, right after the war, the federal government amended the RNWMP Act. Contrary to the English tradition that cherishes the idea of locally autonomous police, the 1919 (July) amendment transformed the RNWMP police into a national police force. According to the amendment, the members of the RNWMP were constables in every part of Canada for the purpose of carrying out the criminal and other laws of Canada.[59] This empowered the RNWMP to extend their jurisdiction over and to be employed legally in any part of Canada. In November 1919, the Royal North West Mounted Police were renamed the Royal Canadian Mounted Police in order to reflect their new status.[60]

The establishment of the national police force was an important development in the government's nation-building process. The RCMP were no longer treated simply as a law enforcement agency. They had established a reputation as an important institution carrying Canadian national identity. Peter Newman pointed out that "in Canada's case, the Mountie symbolizes not merely law and order but also Canada itself."[61] Brown and Brown stated that "Canada must be one of the few countries in the world where the main police force is considered a national symbol at home and is used to advertise the country abroad."[62] Up to 1932, the RCMP absorbed or co-opted six provincial police forces in the name of assisting the provinces to solve their financial difficulties. These included the provincial police forces of Alberta, Saskatchewan, Nova Scotia, New Brunswick, Prince Edward Island, and Manitoba.

When the provinces of Alberta and Saskatchewan were created, provincial politicians set out to build the provinces as independent local societies. One step in creating a distinct provincial identity was the creation of local police forces to exercise authority over provincial priorities. The Saskatchewan legislature passed legislation to create provincial police in 1906; Alberta followed in 1908. Alberta in particular recognized the importance of using the police to implement provincial government policies. Due to the financial difficulties, these plans came to fruition only in 1917. By that time, provincial politics were seized by the problems of prohibition and regulating the newly arrived settlers.

We have referred to factors that tended to put the provincial forces in a bad light. By the same token, it can be argued that the federal government in effect avoided performing all of the unpopular tasks initiated by the local governments, including the prohibition and liquor laws, the control of immigrants from central and eastern Europe, and the surveillance of labour unrest during the 1920s. This enabled the RCMP to maintain their popularity in the western provinces.

CONCLUSION

We began this study by highlighting three related elements in the professionalization of the police function in society: the evolution of a professional model of policing, the shift in focus from class control to crime control, and the impact of police on the rates of crime. Following these themes, our study of the development of the provincial police forces in Alberta and Saskatchewan during the period 1905–32 suggests that the professionalization of the provincial police was a result of the interplay between various social factors, including technical innovation, legal framework and government policy of emphasizing police efficiency and impartiality, and continuity between different police forces. Police continuity was very much reflected by continuity in personnel. This was a unique factor that can be attributed largely to the process of professionalization of the provincial police. When the provincial police were created in 1917, 62 out of a total 106 SPP members, including all the inspectors, were ex-RNWMP members. There were almost 100 ex-RNWMP members in the APP (when it was at maximum strength of 150). All APP officers, including the superintendent and inspectors were ex-RNWMP members. Using the RNWMP as a model, these former RNWMP officers organized the provincial police as a professional bureaucratic apparatus and emphasized the efficient and impartial enforcement of law. This professionalization process resulting from the multiple sources lets us revisit the argument by Monkkonen and Lane, whose account of the emergence and development of the professional police focuses on isolated factors such as increasing crimes or the diffusion of ideas about the police. These were certainly relevant, but this study shows that such factors are far from sufficient. There was a professional tradition and a commitment to authority, as well as a belief in law and order, that ran through the successive western police forces. In terms of professionalism, the experience of the SPP with political interference was certainly a setback.[63] The autonomy of the police requires a political culture that restrains politicians from manipulating the police to make it another political arm of government.

At the same time, the professionalization process of policing was also displayed by the shift of police work from controlling a class of people held to be inherently dangerous to controlling a class of behaviour. This shift was highlighted in the transition from the federal police to the provincial police and the heyday of provincial control agendas. The transition was not only a matter of policies and agendas, but a question of changes in the level of serious crime in the West.

However, after the transition in the objects of control from the dangerous classes to serious crime, the police did not focus absolutely on serious criminals as emphasized by some historians. Police in the prairies still devoted a considerable proportion of their resources to the social services required by the lower segments of the population. Police often contended that social service was an important part of order maintenance. The professionalization of police services in favour of law enforcement tended to degrade the social service function of police. In other words, the specialization of the police function on crime control envisaged by police historians appears to have overlooked the importance of the police as a source of assistance – not in respect of the "dangerous classes" as much as in respect of the "vulnerable" classes. Professionalization seems to overshadow this dimension of the police role.

With the evolution of the police function, an association between crime rate and policing was considered as an important outcome of police professionalization. Due to the confounding effect of the changes in police regimes and social movements, there are difficulties in assessing the real effect of the police on crime rates. On the one hand, the police often used *proactive* strategies to suppress public disorder crime, such as drunkenness and disorderly conduct – especially when this was made a priority by prohibition politics. Frequently, the public regarded those caught up in these campaigns as hardly criminals at all. On the other hand, the police employed a *reactive* strategy to control serious crimes and criminals. Police action in these cases was initiated by the public and reflected public demands for protection.

In light of these two strategies, we can argue that the labelling processes governed the trends in control for public order offences. The arrests in these categories were control driven while trends in crimes against persons and property were "crime" driven. The specific tests of crime trends in Alberta and Saskatchewan covering the period before, during, and after the provincial controls suggested some different emphasis arising from the different agenda of the federal and the provincial forces. The provincial police tended to stress the enforcement of provincial statutes, suppress public disorder offences, and provide assistance to other government departments, whereas the federal force emphasized the control of serious crimes and criminals, particularly after 1928 in Saskatchewan and 1932 in Alberta.

The final observation about police professionalization based on this analysis is that the professionalization process was not completely linear. The professionalization of police reflected diffusion from different sources – technological changes, competing political agendas, and a continuity that might be more a matter of personnel than formal policy. At the same time, the public needs for policing were not entirely issues of crime control. Social service and order maintenance continued as elements of a professional police function. The mixed results of the impact of the police on the crime rate reflected the complexities of the services performed by police and complexities in the public's demand for different kinds of law and order.

APPENDICES

APPENDIX A: INTERRUPTED TIME-SERIES ANALYSIS FOR THE ARREST RATES IN PUBLIC ORDER OFFENCES

Variables of public order offences in both provinces are non-stationary processes. Before the ARIMA models were specified, the series were transformed into stationary processes by differencing. As a result, neither series contains long-term trends except for the effect of the intervention term. One can expect that the differences or transformed series will be zero on average. Therefore, the constant was not included in the final equation. In addition, the effect of the intervention terms with both the Alberta and Saskatchewan data was modelled as an abrupt and permanent impact. This is a theoretical decision that was made based on the fact that the transformation in police organization in 1928 in Saskatchewan and 1932 in Alberta represented a dramatic and permanent change in police policy concerning the arrests for public order offences. And the policy remained unchanged afterwards. For a more detailed technical explanation of the interrupted time series analysis, see R. McCleary and R.A. Hay, Jr, with E.E. Meidinger and D. McDowall, *Applied Time Series Analysis for the Social Sciences* (Beverly Hills, CA: Sage, 1980).

With the Alberta data, the model which was specified is ARIMA (0,1,1) and an intervention term was created to represent a transition at 1932. The following equation (Public Order Offences$_t$ = Disturbance$_t$ + θDisturbance$_{t-1}$ + β$_1$Intervention term$_t$) was estimated using the SPSS Trends package.

Table A.1 Interrupted Time-Series Analyses for the Arrest Rates in Public Order Offences

With Alberta Data

	β_t	T-statistics	Probability
MA1	0.35	2.4	0.02*
Intervention term (1932)	−317.13	−2.02	0.049*

With Saskatchewan Data

	β_t	T-statistics	Probability
MA1	0.37	2.57	0.013*
Intervention term (1928)	−455.56	−3.17	0.002*

The * indicates that the population parameters are statistically significant at the 0.05 level.

APPENDIX B: TIME SERIES REGRESSION METHODS: CO-INTEGRATION AND ERROR-CORRECTION MODELS

In the recent years, social scientists and historians have begun to analyze time series data using sophisticated statistical techniques. However, such analyses have often violated an important assumption of regression models – that time series must be stationary processes before they can be adequately analyzed. In this appendix, we will concentrate on the problems of traditional regression methods of time series and their solutions. Because the problems and their solutions are unfamiliar to sociologists and historians, it will be necessary to explain these methods in some detail.

STATIONARITY AND NON-STATIONARITY

Most time series in the social sciences and historical studies are typically non-stationary. The problems of regression analysis with non-stationary time series have been well known to econometricans and are dubbed "spurious regression."[1] Empirical studies of these types of analyses suggest that the presence of non-stationarity invalidates the conventional testing procedures for statistical inference.

A typical social science example of a non-stationary time series is a random walk process with or without a drift, such as homicide rates or police strength rates over the past hundred years. A random walk is a stochastic process that results from an accumulation of successive random shocks. For instance, a random walk process without a drift can be modelled as follows: $y_t = y_{t-1} + e_t$ where e_t represents random shocks. These shocks are normally and independently distributed about zero mean with constant variance $[e_t \approx NID\ (0, \sigma^2)$. For some starting point of the series, $y_0 = 0$, we have $y_t = \sum_{i-1} e_i$. This equation indicates that a random walk process is the sum of all past random shocks. The mean value for y_t becomes meaningless. In the example of police strength, random shocks could be many unspecified factors that cause the changes in police strength. These unspecified factors vary over time and interact in a complex way. None of these unidentified individual factors (called "random shocks") could provide an explanation for the level of police strength. In addition, one expects that police strength might go up and down over a period of time, implying that the random walk might exhibit some drift.

The formal characteristics of a non-stationary series, say y_t, are that the variance of y_t (σ^2) grows infinitely large as time approaches infinity; and the expected value of y_t ($E(y_t)$) or the mean is not constant. In the case of two uncorrelated non-stationary processes, say y_t and x_t, one expects in theory that the coefficient β_1 in the regression of y_t on x_t ($y_t = \beta_0 + \beta_1 x_t + \mu_t$) will be zero. R^2, the coefficient of determination, will also be expected to be close to zero. But this is not always the case in practice. In regression analysis with non-stationary time series, a spurious correlation may exist, particularly with a large sample size. Granger and Newbold reveal that these regression analyses often have low Durbin-Watson (DW) statistics and serially correlated errors.[2] The conventional t statistics used to evaluate regression coefficients are often misleading. This is because in a regression equation with two non-stationary time series, such as $y_t = \beta_0 + \beta_1 x_t + \mu_t$, the conventional inferential statistics for estimates of β_1 no longer have the student's t distribution. For the null hypothesis, $H_0: \beta_1 = 0$, the rejection rate will tend to increase as the sample size increases. This means that a spurious correlation is often statistically acceptable according to the t table, even though the two processes are actually independent.

A common practice to correct these problems is to transform each non-stationary time series into a stationary process through "differencing," and then, to analyze the transformed data using regression methods. A time series is differenced by subtracting the first observation from the second one, the second from the third, and so on. If we use Δ (delta) to denote a differenced series y_t, then,

$$\Delta y_1 = y_0 - y_1$$
$$\Delta y_2 = y_1 - y_2$$
$$\Delta y_3 = y_2 - y_3$$
$$\Delta y_4 = y_3 - y_4$$
$$\dots\dots\dots$$
$$\Delta y_t = y_{t-1} - y_t$$

Through differencing, the mean and variance of a non-stationary series can be stabilized.[3]

The variance of the series becomes constant in the sense that it does not accumulate indefinitely as in a random walk. This series is referred to as an "integrated" process. In other words, an integrated process is a time series that can be transformed into a stationary process by differencing. Most non-stationary time series in the social sciences or historical studies can be transformed into stationary processes after the first differencing. Some series may need differencing more than once before the mean and variance can be stabilized. A time series that is stationary after differencing d times is denoted by $I(d)$. In this case, the series is said to be "integrated of order d." If x_t becomes stationary after differencing once, the series is said to be "integrated of order one," denoted by $I(1)$. In some case, a series may be stationary without differencing. This is said to be integrated of order zero, denoted by $I(0)$.[4]

A CONVENTIONAL SOLUTION TO "SPURIOUS REGRESSION": LONG-RUN VS. SHORT-RUN COMPONENTS

The solution to the problem of "spurious regression" by regressing one differenced and integrated process onto another is problematic for researchers whose primary interests are in the long-run relationships between two time series. This is because the transformed (or "differenced") time series no longer contain the long-run component. The long-run relationship has been described as a state of "equilibrium" between the variables in economics (i.e., supply and demand, short- vs. long-term interest rates, etc.). In a more general sense, the long-run relationship can be defined as an observed relationship between two time series (or among a set of series) that has been maintained for long periods of time.[5] Such series show a systematic long-term co-movement arising from underlying mechanisms that create an equilibrium.

For example, the deterrent theory of punishment in criminology assumes that crime rate and policing should move together over long periods of time. In a regression equation of $y_t = \beta_0 + \beta_1 x_t + \mu_t$, the linear long-run relationship between y_t and x_t can be extracted as follows: $y_t = \beta_1 x_t$. However, a regression equation with differenced y_t and x_t, such as $\Delta y_t = \beta_1 \Delta x_t + v_t$, eliminates such a long-run component. The equation with transformed variables leaves out information about the long-run relationship that the undifferenced time series might contain.

CO-INTEGRATION

Recent studies in econometrics by Granger, Engle, Hendry and others reveal the possibility of establishing a model maintaining both the long-run relationship and short-term effects.[6] These studies show that if both y_t and x_t are integrated of order one, $I(1)$, a new series that results from the linear combination of y_t and x_t will also be integrated of order one.[7] Suppose that y_t is crime rate and x_t is the police strength, then we have a regression equation y_t (crime) $= \beta_0 + \beta_1 x_t$ (police strength) $+ \mu_t$. We rearrange the equation as follows: $\mu_t = y_t - \beta_0 - \beta_1 x_t$ (Error = Crime − Constant − Police Strength). The rearranged equation emphasizes that the disturbance term, μ_t is a linear combination of y_t and x_t. If y_t is integrated of order one and x_t is integrated of order zero, μ_t (the product of y_t and x_t) will also be integrated of order one.

However, there is an important exception to this rule. It is possible that a linear combination of y_t and x_t could be integrated of order zero (i.e., without differencing or "integrated at levels"), that is, μ_t is said to be $I(0)$. If this occurs, y_t and x_t are co-integrated. Substantively, a co-integrated series means that these integrated processes of y_t and x_t move together over the long run. In other words, we can infer that they are related even if each on its own has the property of a random walk. For example, if the deterrence theory holds, crime rates and police strength as integrated processes of order one should be co-integrated and move together over a long period of time. Intuitively, co-integration could occur in the situation where both integrated processes y_t and x_t have the long-run components that offset each other to generate the stationary linear combination detected through the property of the error term. This can be expressed by the following equation:

$$\mu_t = y_t - \beta_1 x_t.$$
$$I(0) \quad\quad I(1) \quad\quad I(1)$$

The importance of the concept of co-integration cannot be understated. It links the relationship between integrated processes and the concept of long-run relationship.[8] The long-run relationship or equilibrium implies that variables that are linked by theory should not diverge from each other over the long run, although they may drift apart over a short period of time. The concept of co-integration allows a researcher to describe the existence of an equilibrium relationship between different time series that are individually non-stationary. Theoretically, empirical evidence of co-integration among a set of variables can be used either to support a theoretical argument about the causal relationship between variables or to lead researchers to search for a "common attractor" that creates the state of equilibrium.[9] Engle and Granger do not give a very concrete definition of this concept. Certainly, the common attractor is not an observable third variable. Rather, it indicates the existence of a mechanism that draws or "attracts" two or a set of variables together over a long period. In other words, the common attractor is like a magnetic force that draws the variables together, providing statistical evidence for the existence of a long-run relationship between the variables. The common attractor can be regarded as the theoretical linkage that regulates the relationship. If co-integration is established, researchers can describe the magnitude of the equilibrium effects caused by the common attractor. This entails analysis of what econometricians call the "error-correction model."

ERROR-CORRECTION MODEL

As mentioned above, in the equation $y_t = \beta_1 x_t + \mu_t$, where the constant is omitted for convenience, we define the equilibrium by the relationship $y_t = \beta_1 x_t$, then, $y_t - \beta_1 x_t = 0$. Therefore, μ_t from the equation $\mu_t = y_t - \beta_1 x_t$ is a measurement of the extent to which the variables y_t and x_t are out of the state of equilibrium. The μ_t is termed "equilibrium error" or disequilibrium. The equilibrium error is stationary since it hardly drifts away from a zero mean. One of the most important results of the concept of co-integration is the error-correction model developed initially by Engle and Granger.[10] The error-correction model provides a solution to the problems resulting from "spurious regression" and regression with differenced time-series that omits the long-run relationship. The error-correction model contains both the long-run relationship and the short-term effects between cointegrated variables without the difficulties in inferential statistics which plague OLS models of time series.

The error-correction model is established through the Granger Representation Theorem. According to the theorem, if one supposes that y_t and x_t are each integrated of order one and possess error terms that prove to stationary, it follows that there is an error-correction representation as follows:

$$\delta(L)\Delta y_t = \Phi(L)\Delta x_{t-1} - \tau Z_{t-1} + \theta(L)e_t.$$

where $\delta(L)$ and $\Phi(L)$ are finite order polynomials, L is a lag operator (or a back shift operator), e_t is a white noise process, and τZ_{t-1} contains the long-run equilibrium.[11] A specific case of the error-correction model is

$\Delta y_t = \beta_0 + \beta_1 \Delta x_t - \tau Z_{t-1} + e_t$.[12] The error-correction term is interpreted as equilibrium error measuring the speed of adjustment of y_t to a deviation or distance from x_t in the previous periods. Banerjee et al. indicate that "error-correction terms are used as a way of capturing adjustments in a dependent variable which depend not on the level of some explanatory variable, but on the extent to which an explanatory variable deviated from the equilibrium relationship with the dependent variable."[13] Error correction estimates the long-term equilibrium, while β_1 is the short-term effect of x_t on y_t. This exposition of integration and error correction has been unavoidably detailed because such approaches have never been employed in published sociological studies of crime trends prior to this investigation.

APPENDIX C: MODELLING THE RELATIONSHIP BETWEEN CRIME RATES AND POLICE STRENGTH

The data analysis involves three discrete steps. First, as a prerequisite, we must establish the properties of individual time series to determine whether they are stationary. If they are not, they can be transformed to achieve stationarity through differencing. Second, we examine if the integrated series are cointegrated with one another. Third, we examine the equilibrium properties of the relationship by calculating the error-correction models where the variables are indeed co-integrated. And finally, we interpret the statistical results from the error-correction models.

TESTING FOR STATIONARITY IN INDIVIDUAL TIME SERIES

To test whether a set of variables is co-integrated, we must determine the order of integration of the series under study. For such purposes, there are two conventional tests: the Dickey-Fuller test (DF) and the Augmented Dickey-Fuller test (ADF). Both tests examine the t statistic for a unit root concerning the parameter β_1 under the null hypothesis: $H_o: \beta_1 = 0$. Each tests non-stationarity in the series.[14] Failure to reject the null hypothesis implies that the time series under test is a random walk possessing a unit root. The Dickey-Fuller test can be performed by conducting the following regression with x_t: $\Delta x_t = \beta_0 + \beta_1 x_{t-1} + v_t$, where v_t is possibly a white noise process and β_0 is a constant. We omitted a trend in this equation for simplicity. With theoretical justification, it can be added into the test equation.[15]

In the Augmented Dickey-Fuller tests, if v_t is not a white noise, then the test for stationarity can be conducted by adding lags (Δx_t). The ADF test can be conducted with the following equation: $\Delta x_t = \beta_1 x_{t-1} + \Sigma \beta_i \Delta x_{t-i} + v_t$ where i denotes the order of lags. In practice, we do not know the order of lags that will best fit the model. Therefore, the number of lags has to be selected empirically. The Akaike Information Criteria (AIC) and/or Schwarz Criteria (SC) can be used to select the optimal number of lags.

The critical value for both the DF test and the ADF test cannot be determined by referring to the critical values from the normal *student-t* statistic. The series under examination for nonstationarity no longer have limiting distributions. For the purpose of the test, Dickey has computed a table of critical values for the nonstationarity test for selected sample sizes.[16] Recently, Mackinnon provided response surface estimations that enable us to calculate critical values of the DF test for any sample sizes.[17] The critical values of the ADF test are the same as those for the DF tests. If the estimated t-statistic for the β_1 coefficient in the test regressions is larger than the tabled critical value provided either by Dickey and Fuller or Mackinnon, we reject the null hypothesis that the series is nonstationary.

Table C.1. Unit Root Tests for Nonstationarity

Variables	$H_o: I(0)$ DF	Variables	$H_o: I(1)$ DF
With Alberta Data			
PSTH	−5.275*	ΔPSTH	−5.300*
POO	−2.123	ΔPOO	−8.517*
SCRI	1.447	ΔSCRI	−7.077*
OPER	−2.890	ΔOPER	−8.758*
OPRO	−1.473	ΔOPRO	−6.619*
With Saskatchewan Data			
PSTH	−2.308	ΔPSTH	−7.802*
POO	−2.887	ΔPOO	−8.527*
SCRI	−2.515	ΔSCRI	−7.711*
OPER	−4.778*	ΔOPER	−10.805*
OPRO	−2.063	ΔOPRO	−6.821*

The * Reject the null hypothesis of nonstationarity. The critical value of Dickey-Fuller statistics for rejecting the null hypotheses of nonstationarity (H_o) is −2.9286 at .05 levels and sample size is 44 with constant in the equation. The critical value is calculated according to Mackinnon's Response Surface Estimates of critical values.[18] PSTH = Police Strength; POO = Public Order Offence; SCRI = Serious Crime; OPER = Offences against Person; OPRO = Offences against Property.

The tests for nonstationarity of the variables for Alberta and Saskatchewan are reported in Table C.1. With the Alberta data, in the first column, the only variable that approaches the critical value ($t = -2.93$) is "police strength" (PSTH). Although the rest of the variables have negative values, they are not statistically significant. These tests suggest that only "police strength" is a stationary process at level $I(0)$; none of the rest of the variables are stationary processes that are $I(0)$. After transforming the series by the first differencing, the other four series yield negative and significant values according to the DF statistics. This enables us to reject the null hypotheses that the series are random walks in the first differencing and conclude that the remaining four series are stationary at $I(1)$.

With the Saskatchewan data, in the first column, only "offences against person" (OPER) has a value that is larger than the critical value (−2.93). This indicates that series "offences against person" is a stationary process at the level $I(0)$. The rest of the series are nonstationary. After first differencing, the remaining four variables yield negative and significant values indicating that they are stationary at $I(1)$.

The results of the tests for stationarity with the Alberta data show that the variable "police strength" and other variables concerning arrest rates in the table do not belong to the same process. The variable "police strength" is integrated of order zero, while serious crime (SCRI) (including crime against person [OPER] and crime against property [OPRO]), and public order offences (POO) are integrated of order one. This result suggests that we do not need to proceed further to test the co-integration between police strength and other arrest variables since co-integration can only be generated between variables that are integrated in the same order. Substantively, this finding tells us that there is no long-run relationship between police strength and any of the arrest rates. This result is inconsistent with Monkkonen's observation that police strength accounted for the variations in both public order offences and serious crime over the long run. However, with the Saskatchewan data, variables "police strength" and "public order offences" (POO) and serious crime (SCRI) are integrated in the same order, $I(1)$.

TESTING FOR CO-INTEGRATION

The conventional method to test for co-integration is to run a cointegrating regression. For instance, with variables x_t and y_t, such a regression is as follows: $y_t = \beta_0 + \beta_1 x_t + \mu_t$

The co-integration test between x_t and y_t is a test for stationarity in the residual (μ_t) from this regression. The null hypothesis (nonstationarity) is that the residual, μ_t, is a nonstationary process with a unit root. The critical value is provided by Engle, Yoo, and Mackinnon.[19] In the case where the estimated t-value associated with β_1 is smaller than the tabled critical value, we would reject the null hypothesis and conclude that the variables under examination are indeed cointegrated.

Another test for co-integration is the Cointegrating Regression Durbin-Watson (CRDW) test. In this case, the Durbin-Watson statistics are referred to in order to determine again if the residual from the cointegrating regression (μ_t) is stationary. Again, the null hypothesis is non-co-integration. If the estimated CRDW statistic from the cointegrating regression is greater than the tabled critical value, we can reject the null hypothesis and conclude that the variables in the equation are cointegrated. The CRDW critical values are available in Sargan and Bhargava.[20]

Following the procedure described above, we test for non-co-integration between the theoretically relevant variables concerning both the Alberta and Saskatchewan data. As Saskatchewan shares many characteristics with Alberta, we suspect there will be co-integration between police strength and public order offences and serious crime for the Saskatchewan data. To test our hypotheses, in cointergration regressions (1) and (2), we regress police strength on serious crime, as well as public order offences. With regard to the relation between public order offences and serious crime, we test to determine if public order offences are cointegrated with serious crime in both provinces. Thus, in testing equation (3), we regress two serious crime variables, namely offences against property (OPRO) and offences against persons (OPER) on public order offences (POO). In equation (4), the variable of offences against property is regressed on public order offences. The results of the tests are presented in Table C.2.

Table C.2. Testing for Non-Cointegration

(1) Cointegration Regression with Saskatchewan Data:
$SCRI_t = \mu_o + \beta_1 PSTH_t + \mu_t$

β_1	T_β	DF	ADF(k=4)
1.614	1.825	−2.672	−0.359

2) Cointegration Regression with Saskatchewan Data:
$POO_t = \beta_o + \beta_1 PSTH_t + \mu_t$

β_1	T_β	DF	ADF(k=1)
−0.384	−0.482	−2.94	−0.186

3) Cointegration Regression with Alberta Data:
$POO_t = \beta_o + \beta_1 OPRO_t + \beta_2 OPER_t + \mu_t$

	T_β	DF	ADF(k=8)
β_1			
−0.823	−6.494	−4.194*	−4.00*
β_2	T_β		
3.3029	8.576		

4) Cointegration Regression with Alberta Data:
$POO_t = \beta_o + \beta_1 PSTH_t + \mu_t$

β_1	T_β	DF	ADF(k=3)
−0.424	−3.16	−4.06*	−3.606*

The critical value of Dickey-Fuller (DF) tests for rejecting the null hypotheses of non-cointegration (H_o) is −3.37 in a two-variable case and −3.93 in a three-variable case at .05 levels with constant and the sample size is 44.[21] The critical values of the Augmented Dickey-Fuller (ADF) tests are −3.17 in two variables case and −3.75 in three variables case.[22] The estimated values are calculated using RATS. PSTH = Police Strength; POO = Public Order Offence; SCRI = Serious Crime; OPER = Offences against Person; OPRO = Offences against Property.

Table C. 2 indicates that serious crime and police strength, as well as public order offences and police strength are not cointegrated since both tests for non-co-integration fail to reject the null hypotheses. These results confirm our hypotheses. However, the values from the DF as well as the ADF tests in the equations (3) and (4) support the argument that public order offences and both offences against property and against persons (Alberta) and public order offences and offences against property (Saskatchewan) are indeed cointegrated.

Furthermore, these findings lead us to reject Monkkonen's argument that changes in police strength explain variations in serious crime and public order offences. At the same time, the results partially confirm our hypothesis that changes in the incidence of serious crime can account for the level of public order offences. With the Alberta data, both categories of serious crime move together with the level of public order offences, while only the category of offences against property varies with the level of public order offences in Saskatchewan. This is because the variable "offences against person" varies little over time.

Theoretically, the co-integration between the increasing trends in the incidence of serious crime and public order offences in Alberta and between property and public order offences in Saskatchewan suggest the existence of a mediating factor or "common attractor," which in this case is policing. Interpreting the attractor is a theoretical issue rather than a statistical one. However, the attractor's capacity to draw the variables together provides statistical evidence indicating a long-run relationship between the variables. In their discussion of co-integration, Pindyck and Rubinfeld emphasize that a co-integration test can be used both as a diagnostic for linear regression and as a test for theory.[23] In our case, the police balanced the tension between the arrest rates for these large and mutually exclusive categories of crime. This allows us to infer that the police behaviour is not concerned exclusively with policing policies and the development of police organization, but also with the amount of criminality. As evidenced by the presence of co-integration, the common attractor is an underlying force that compels the variables to interact causally. Its presence also implies the existence of an error-correction process that can be estimated in the ECM regression equation.

MODELLING THE ERROR-CORRECTION MECHANISM

The error-correction model can capture both the long-run relations and the short-run dynamics between the integrated series. A general error-correction model can be derived from the Granger error-correction representation as follows:

$$\Delta y_t = \beta_0 + \beta_1 \Delta x_t + \beta_2 \Delta x_{t-1} - \beta_3 Z_{t-1} + v_t$$

where $\beta_3 Z_{t-1}$ is the error-correction mechanism that is μ_t in the cointegrating regression ($y_t = \beta_0 + \beta_1 x_t + \mu_t$). The reason we use μ_t as the error-correction representation that reflects the long-run relations between the integrated variables is that, if y_t and x_t are cointegrated, the residual, μ_t, from the regression will have a very small variance. The fact that the μ_t is integrated of order zero proves this point. If μ_t has a large variance, it will be integrated of order one. In that case, the integrated processes of interest will not be cointegrated. Therefore, when μ_t is a stationary process, all series in the general error-correction model, including Δy_t, Δx_t, Δx_{t-1}, and Z_{t-1}, are stationary processes. The long-run equilibrium $(y_{t-1} - \beta_1 x_{t-1})$ can be subsumed within μ_t. We have left out all dynamics in the cointegrating regression. But, we can recapture them using Δy_{t-i} and Δx_{t-i}.[24]

In a model with two or three variables, the error-correction model estimates the changes in an endogenous variable to the past equilibrium error as well as the changes and the past changes in the exogenous variables in the equation. In Tables c.3 and c.4, a number of error-correction models are estimated with public order offences as an endogenous variable.

The variables, "offences against property" and "offences against person," are treated as exogenous variables in both the Alberta and Saskatchewan data. Note that although offences against the person in the Saskatchewan data are not cointegrated with public order offences, we still could estimate their short-term effect on public order offences. In fact, the estimated short-term effect of offences against the person on public order offences was not statistically significant at the .05 level and were left out of the model reported in Table c.4.

We estimate the various error-correction models with the Vector Autoregression (VAR) method recommended by Engle and Granger to allow us to estimate the dynamics of the models.[25] However, theoretically, we do not believe there are causal effects from public order offences on other exogenous variables in this study. Thus, our models estimated using VAR are limited to public order offences as an endogenous variable. Using lags on both endogenous and exogenous variables, the number of potential models is quite large. Akaike's Minimum Information Criterion (AIC) is used to help select the best model.[26]

The results of a vector autoregression of the change in public order offences on an error-correction term (EC_{t-1}), two lagged levels of offences against property, two lags of offences against person as well as two lagged levels of public order offences are reported in Table c.3. The error-correction term is not individually significant at the level of 0.05; but it is significant at the 0.07 level. When the other terms are added, the error-correction terms become statistically significant at 0.05 levels. None of the lagged changes in offences against property and offences against person have significant impact on the level of public order arrests. According to the AIC statistics, the model in the second column is the best one, though it contains many insignificant estimates of the lagged changes of the variables. The R^2 (0.78) implies that the offences against property and offences against the person variables with the error-correction term together explain about 78 per cent of the variance in public order offences.

Table C.3. Error-Correction Model for Variables "Public Order Offences" (POO) and "Offences against Property" (OPRO) and "Offences against Person" (OPER) with Alberta Data

Independent Variables	Dependent Variables		
	Model 1 ΔPOO	Model 2 ΔPOO	Model 3 ΔPOO
EC_{t-1}	−0.299 (−1.83)	−0.336 (−2.144)*	−0.444 (−3.526)*
ΔOPRO		−0.264 (−0.149)	−0.107 (0.595)
$\Delta OPRO_{t-1}$		−0.165 (−0.921)	
$\Delta OPRO_{t-2}$		−0.127 (−0.704)	
ΔOPER		2.411 (7.515)*	2.407 (7.883)*
$\Delta OPER_{t-1}$		0.913 (1.494)	
$\Delta OPER_{t-2}$		−0.221 (−0.534)	
ΔPOO_{t-1}		−0.248 (−1.290)	
ΔPOO_{t-2}		0.258 (1.578)	
Const	−0.159 (−1.97)	−1.143 (−0.665)	−0.542 (−0.310)
AIC	238.1536	208.709	219.639
R^2	0.073	0.78	0.69

The * indicates statistically significant at the .05 level. The values in the bracket are *student-t* statistics and the critical value is 1.96 at .05 levels of significance. All parameters in the table are calculated using Regression Analysis of Time Series (RATS).

In comparing the three models, we prefer the model in the last column since it is the most parsimonious. The squared R (0.69) indicates that the independent variables with the error-correction term together explain about 69 per cent of the total variation in public order offences. The model passes the basic diagnostic tests. The short-term change in offences against persons is significant, while the effect from offence against property is too small to be significant. Assuming that police behaviour is acting as a common attractor, the error-correction mechanism indicates that the police corrected 44 per cent of "public order offences" deviation from its desired path (or equilibrium) per year. It took more than two years for the police to complete the correction on average.

Table C.4: Error Correction Model For "Public Order Offences" (POO) and "Offences Against Property" (OPRO) With Saskatchewan Data
Independent Variables   Dependent Variables

	Model 1 ΔPOO	Model 2 ΔPOO	Model 3 ΔPOO
EC_{t-1}	−0.504 (−4.325)*	−0.457 (−2.777)*	−0.423 (−3.91)*
ΔOPRO		0.498 (2.775)*	0.485 (2.917)*
$\Delta OPRO_{t-1}$		−0.097 (0.469)	
$\Delta OPRO_{t-2}$		0.090 (.441)	
ΔPOO_{t-1}		−0.054 (−0.311)	
ΔPOO_{t-2}		−0.0422 (0.275)	
Const	−0.009 (−0.004)	−0.260 (−0.112)	−0.148 (−0.069)
AIC	271.658	234.012	236.57
R^2	0.302	0.445	0.427

The * indicates statistically significant at .05 level. The values in the bracket are student-t statistics and the critical value is 1.96 at .05 levels of significance. All parameters in the table are calculated using Regression Analysis of Time Series (RATS).

Similar model selection procedures are applied to establish the error-correction models with public order offences and offences against property variables with the Saskatchewan data (Table C.4). The error-correction terms in the models are significant individually and jointly with other variables. Of all the lagged changes in public order offences and offences against property, none of them is statistically significant. According to the AIC statistics, model 2 is the preferable one because of its relatively small value of the AIC. But, it contains many insignificant parameters. We prefer the model in the last column. The police correct 42 per cent of the public order offences deviation from its desired path per year. In effect, it took the police two years and four months to complete the correction. About 45 per cent of the variation in public order offence arrests are accounted for by both the error-correction process and other variables in the equation.

In all models discussed above, the error-correction terms, as explanatory variables, show the relation of changes in public order offences to past equilibrium error as well as to changes in all variables in the equations. More important, they further demonstrate the existence of long-run relationships and short-term effects. Substantively, the significant error-correction terms in the models independently suggest that the police, as an equilibrium force, constantly draw the variables public order offences and serious crime together. The model implies that when other momentous social events, such as the Great War, the Roaring Twenties, the Great Depression, and changing levels of immigration in the provinces, individually pushed an arrest variable away from the systematic relationship with the other variables (which is expressed by the short-term effects), the police as a balancing force tended to draw them back together within a two- or three-year period of time and keep them behaving in an interactive way.

APPENDIX D: STATISTICAL EXAMINATION OF THE RELATIONSHIP BETWEEN IMMIGRATION AND CRIMES

The statistical analysis of the relationship between immigration and crime consists of three steps. First, we establish the properties of the individual time series (testing for nonstationarity). Second, we test for co-integration of these time series. Third, we establish the error-correction models where the variables are co-integrated. The variables analyzed here consisted of annual provincial immigration rates, the rates for serious crime, and the rates for public order offences. Data for the two provinces were examined separately.

UNIVARIANT TIME-SERIES PROPERTIES

In order to conduct a co-integration test, we must establish that the individual time series are integrated in the same order. We test the level of integration of these series using Dickey-Fuller tests.[27] The results of the tests for nonstationarity are presented in Table D.1.

Table D.1. Unit Root Tests for Nonstationarity

Variables	$H_o:I(0)$ DF	Variables	$H_o:I(1)$ DF
With Alberta Data			
IMM	−1.289	ΔIMM	−6.121*
POO	−2.781	ΔPOO	−9.094*
SCRI	−1.447	ΔSCRI	−7.077*
With Saskatchewan Data			
IMM	−1.411	ΔIMM	−5.968*
POO	−2.887	ΔPOO	−8.527*
SCRI	−2.515	ΔSCRI	−7.711*

The * Reject the null hypothesis of nonstationarity. The critical value of Dickey-Fuller statistics for rejecting the null hypotheses of nonstationarity (H_o) is −2.92 at .05 levels and sample size is 44 with constant in the equation. The critical value is calculated according to Mackinnon's response surface estimates of critical values.[28] POO = Public Order Offense Rate; SCRI = Serious Crime Rate; IMMR = Immigrant Rate.

With the Alberta data, in the first column, all variables have negative values; but none of them are significant statistically. These results show that none of the series are stationary processes at $I(0)$. After transforming the series using the first differencing, all series yield negative and significant values. They suggest that all series are stationary at $I(1)$. Similarly, with the Saskatchewan data, in the first column, all series are nonstationary processes at $I(0)$, but the transformed series presented in the second column, all series yield negative and significant values suggesting that they are stationary at $I(1)$. These results indicate that all the series from both data sets of Alberta and Saskatchewan meet the requirement for co-integration tests.

TESTING FOR CO-INTEGRATION

Two formal tests for non-co-integration, DF and ADF tests, are presented in Table D.2.

Table D.2 shows that serious crime and the level of immigration for both Saskatchewan and Alberta data are not cointegrated since both tests for non-co-integration fail to reject the null hypotheses. However, the DF tests suggest that the public order offences and immigrants are cointegrated in both sets of provincial data. We reject the null hypotheses of non-co-integration.

Table D.2. Testing for Non-Cointegration

1) Cointegration Regression with Saskatchewan Data:
$SCRI_t = \beta_0 + \beta_1 IMM_t + \mu_t$

β_1	T_β	DF	ADF(k=4)
−0.004	−3.513	−3.074	−1.913

2) Cointegration Regression with Saskatchewan Data:
$POO_t = \beta_0 + \beta_1 IMM_t + \mu_t$

β_1	T_β	DF	ADF(k=4)
0.004	3.769	−3.417*	−2.24

3) Cointegration Regression with Alberta Data:
$POO_t = \beta_0 + \beta_1 IMM_t + \mu_t$

β_1	T_β	DF	ADF(k=4)
−0.013	−2.53	−1.83	−1.693

4) Cointegration Regression with Alberta Data:
$POO_t = \beta_0 + \beta_1 IMM_t + \mu_t$

β_1	T_β	DF	ADF(k=4)
0.026	5.484	−3.665*	−2.000

The critical value of Dickey-Fuller (DF) tests for rejecting the null hypotheses of non-cointegration (H_o) is −3.37 in a two-variable case with constant and the sample size is 44.[29] The critical values of the Augmented Dickey-Fuller (ADF) tests are −3.17 in two variables case.[30] The * indicates the rejection of null hypothesis of non-cointegration. The estimated values are calculated using RATS.

ERROR-CORRECTION MODELS

We estimated a number of error-correction models with public order offences as a dependent variable and immigration rates as an independent variable for the Alberta and Saskatchewan data respectively. Limited vector autoregressions are used as a means to estimate various models. Again, Akaike's "Minimum Information Criterion" (AIC) is used to help select the best models.[31] Many models were estimated by testing a series of lags, but only a small number are reported here.

The results of a vector autoregression of the change in public order offences on an error-correction term (EC), two lagged levels of immigration rate, as well as two lagged levels of public order offences are reported in Table D.3. The error-correction terms are significant at the level of .05 in all equations.

Table D.3. Error Correction Model for Public Order Offences (POO) and Immigration Rate (IMMR) with Alberta Data

Independent Variables	Dependent Variables		
	Model 1	Model 2	*Model 3*
	ΔPOO	ΔPOO	ΔPOO
EC_{t-1}	−0.534 (−3.566)	−0.426 (−2.131)*	−0.396 (−2.779)*
$\Delta IMMR$		−0.016 (1.301)	−0.006 (0.552)
$\Delta IMMR_{t-1}$		−0.006 (−0.558)	0.008 (0.783)
$\Delta IMMR_{t-2}$		−0.030 (2.715)	0.046 (4.521)*
$\Delta IMMR_{t-3}$			−0.01 (−1.021)
ΔPOO_{t-1}		−0.111 (−0.596)	
ΔPOO_{t-2}		0.006 (0.040)	
Const	−0.288 (−.107)	0.060 (−0.022)	−0.542 (−0.310)
AIC	255.352	242.433	224.805
R^2	0.232	0.44	0.55

The * indicates statistically significant at .05 level. The values in the bracket are *student-t* statistics and the critical value is 1.96 at .05 levels of significance. All parameters in the table are calculated using Regression Analysis of Time Series (RATS).

Table D.3 presents evidence which suggests the existence of a long-run relationship between public order offense arrests and levels of immigration in Alberta. The second lagged changes in immigration levels are significant. According to AIC statistics, the model in the last column is the best one. The R^2 (0.55) implies that the variable "immigration" and the error-correction term together explain about 55 per cent of the variance in public order offences. The error-correction term on its own shows that the police corrected about 40 per cent of the variable Public Order Offences deviation from its desired path per year. It took two and a half years for the police to complete the correction.

A similar model selection procedure is applied to establish the error-correction process with the variable Public Order Offences and the level of immigration variables using the Saskatchewan data. The results are reported in Table D.4.

Table D.4. Error Correction Model for Public Order Offences (POO) and Immigration Rate (IMMR) with Saskatchewan Data

Independent Variables	Dependent Variables		
	Model 1	Model 2	Model 3
	ΔPOO	ΔPOO	ΔPOO
EC_{t-1}	0.455 (−3.534)*	−0.251 (−1.698)	−.267 (−2.32)*
$\Delta IMMR$		0.002 (1.153)	.002 (1.153)
$\Delta IMMR_{t-1}$		−0.002 (−1.163)	−.002 (−0.807)
$\Delta IMMR_{t-2}$		0.008 (3.988)	.009 (4.94)*
$\Delta IMMR_{t-3}$		−0.04 (−2.34)*	
ΔPOO_{t-1}		−0.140 (−0.921)	
ΔPOO_{t-2}		−0.063 (−0.466)	
Const	−0.087 (−0.0345)	−1.110 (−0.49)	1.36 (−0.66)
AIC	247.63	228.99	214.62
R^2	0.229	0.5	0.58

The values in the bracket are student-t statistics and the critical value is 1.96 at 0.05 levels of significance. All parameters in the table are calculated using Regression Analysis of Time Series (RATS).

The error-correction terms are significant individually and jointly with the other variables. Of all the lagged changes in Public Order Offences and the level of immigration, the second and third lagged changes in immigration are statistically significant. According to AIC statistics, the model in the last column is the preferable one because of its relatively small value of the AIC, although it does contain two insignificant estimates.

REFERENCES

ARCHIVAL MATERIALS COLLECTED FROM PROVINCIAL ARCHIVES OF ALBERTA (PAA) AND PROVINCIAL ARCHIVES OF SASKATCHEWAN (PAS)

Annual Reports of the Alberta Provincial Police, 1918–1932

Annual Reports of Saskatchewan Provincial Police, 1917–1928

The files of the Attorney General of the Government of the Province of Saskatchewan

The files of the Attorney General of the Government of the Province of Alberta

GOVERNMENT PUBLICATIONS

British North American Act and Selected Statutes, 1867–1948, Part IV

Provincial Government, A Submission by the Government of Saskatchewan to the Royal Commission on Dominion-Provincial Relations, 1937

Annual Reports of the Royal Northwest Mounted Police, 1905–1919

Annual Reports of the Royal Canadian Mounted Police, 1920–1950

Report of the Royal Commission of Inquiry into Statements Made in Statutory Declarations and Other Matters, 1930, Regina: Government of Saskatchewan

Statutes of Canada

Sessional Papers of Canada

Statutes of Alberta (S.A.)

Statues of Saskatchewan (S.S.)

PERIODICALS

The Albertan

The Calgary Herald

Edmonton Bulletin

The Edmonton Journal

The Journal of the Provincial Legislative Assembly of Alberta

The Lethbridge Herald

The Medicine Hat News

The Morning Alberta

The Public Service Monthly: A Periodical Bulletin on Matters of Public interest in Saskatchewan

The Regina Leader

BOOKS AND ARTICLES

Akaike, Hirotugu. "A New Look at the Statistical Model Identification," *IEEE Transactions on Automatic Control* AC-19, no. 6 (December 1974).

Anderson, David M., and David Killingray. *Policing the Empire: Government, Authority and Control, 1830–1940*. New York: Manchester University Press, 1991.

Anderson, Frank W. *The Rum Runners*. Frontier Book 11. Calgary: Frontier Publishing, 1972.

Anderson, Frank W. *Saskatchewan's Provincial Police*. Frontier Book 28, Calgary: Frontier Publishing, 1972.

Archer, John H. *Saskatchewan: A History*. Saskatoon: Western Producer Prairie Books, 1980.

Avery, Donald. *Dangerous Classes: European Immigrant Workers and Labour Radicalism in Canada, 1896–1932*. Toronto: McClelland and Stewart, 1979.

Banerjee, Anindya, Juan Dolado, J.W. Galbreaith, and D.F. Hendry. *Co-integration, Error-Correction, and the Econometric Analysis of Non-Stationary Data*. New York: Oxford University Press, 1993.

Bayley, D.H. "Police Function, Structure, and Control in Western Europe and North America: Comparative and Historical Studies." *Crime and Justice: An Annual Review of Research* 1 (1979): 109–44.

Bittner, Egon. *The Function of the Police in Modern Society: A Review of Background Factors, Current practices, and Possible Role Models*. Cambridge, MA: Oelgeschlager, Gunn and Hair, 1980.

Blanchard, J., and R.G. Cassidy. *Crime and Criminal Process in Canada: 1880–1970 and Beyond*. Ottawa: Statistics Division, Solicitor General of Canada, (CANJUS Project Report No. 21), 1975.

Boritch, H. "Conflict, Compromise and Administrative Convenience: the Police Organization in Nineteenth-Century Toronto." *Canadian Journal of Law and Society* 3 (1988): 141–74.

Boritch, H., and J. Hagan. "Crime and the Changing Forms of Class Control: Policing Public Order in Toronto The Good 1859–1955." *Social Forces* 66, no. 2 (December 1987): 307–35.

Bottomley, A.K., and C.A. Coleman. "Criminal Statistics: The Police Role in the Discovery and Detection of Crime." *International Journal of Criminology and Penology* 4 (1976): 33–58.

Bradshaw, W., and L. Radbill. "Method and Substance in the Use of Ratio Variables." *American Sociological Review* 52 (1987): 132–34.

Brannigan, Augustine. *Crimes, Courts and Corrections: An Introduction to Crime and Social Control in Canada*. Toronto: Holt, Rinehart and Winston of Canada Ltd., 1984.

Brannigan, Augustine, and Zhiqiu Lin. "Policing Immigration and Drunkenness in Canada, 1913–1943: A Cointegration and Error Correction Approach." Paper presented at the Annual Meeting of the Sociology and Anthropology at the Learned Society Meeting, University of Calgary, June 1994.

———. "'Where East meets West': Police, Immigration and Public Order Crime in the Settlement of Canada from 1896 to 1940." *Canadian Journal of Sociology* 24, no. 1 (1999): 87–107.

Brantingham, Paul, and Patricia Brantingham. *Patterns in Crime*. New York: Macmillan, 1984.

Broeker, Galen. *Rural Disorder and Police Reform in Ireland, 1812–36*. London: Routledge and Kegan Paul, 1970.

Brogden, Michael. *The Police: Autonomy and Consent*. Toronto: Academic Press, 1982.

Brown, Lorne, and Caroline Brown. *An Unauthorized History of the RCMP*. Toronto: J. Lorimer, 1978.

Brown, M.C., and B.D. Warner. "Immigrants, Urban Politics, and Policing in 1900." *American Sociological Review* 57 (June 1992): 293–305.

Cage, R. A. *The Scottish Poor Law 1745–1845*. Edinburgh: Scottish Academic Press, 1981.

Cain, M. E. *Society and the Policeman's Role*. London: Routledge and Kegan Paul, 1973.

Carpenter, J. H. *The Badge and The Blotter: A History of the Lethbridge Police*. Lethbridge: The Whoop-up Country Chapter of Historical Society of Alberta, 1975.

Carson, W.G. "Policing the Periphery: the Development of Scottish Policing 1795–1900." *Australian and New Zealand Journal of Criminology* 17 (December 1984): 207–32 and Vol. 18 (March 1985): 3–16.

Carrigan, D. Owen. *Crime and Punishment in Canada: A History*. Toronto: McClelland and Stewart, 1991.

Cohen, Stanley. *Vision of Social Control: Crime, Punishment and Classification*. Oxford: Polity Press, 1985.

Cooper, Barry, and Koop, Royce. "Policing Alberta: An Analysis of the Alternatives to the Federal Provision of Police Services." In *Public Policy Sources* 72 (November 2003). (A Fraser Institute Occasional Paper).

Corrigan, Philip, and Derek Sayer. *The Great Arch: English State Formation As Cultural Revolution*. London: Basil Blackwell, 1985.

Critchley, T.A. *A History of Police in England and Wales 900–1966*. London: Constable London, 1967.

Cromwell, J., M.J. Hannan, M. Labys, and M. Terraza. *Multivariate Tests for Time series Models*. London: Sage Publications, 1994.

Cromwell, J., M. Labys, and M. Terraza. *Univariate Tests for Time Series Models*. London: Sage, 1994.

Cuthbertson, K., S.G. Hall, and M.P. Taylor. *Applied Econometric Techniques*. New York: Philip Allan, 1992.

Dickey, D., and W. Fuller. "Distribution of Estimators for Autoregressive Time Series with a Unit Root." *Journal of the American Statistical Association* 74 (1979): 1057–72.

Dunham, R.G., and G.P. Alpert. *Critical Issues in Policing: Contemporary Readings*. Illinois: Waveland Press, Inc., 1989.

Durkheim, E. *The Division of Labour in Society*. New York: The Free Press, 1984.

———. *The Rules of Sociological Method*, 8th ed., edited by George Catlin. Glencoe, Illinois: Free Press, 1958.

Emsley, C. *Policing and Its Context 1750–1870*. London: Macmillian, 1983.

Engle, R., and C.W. Granger. "Co-integration and Error Correction: Representation, Estimation, and Testing." *Econometrica* 55, no. 2 (March 1987): 251–76.

Engle, R., and C.W. Granger, eds. *Long-Run Economic Relationships: Readings in Co-integration*. New York: Oxford University Press, 1991.

Engle, R., and B.S. Yoo. "Forecasting and Testing in Co-integrated Systems." *Journal of Econometrics* 35 (1987): 143–59.

Ethington, P. "Vigilantes and the Police: The Creation of A Professional Police Bureaucracy in San Francisco, 1847–1900." *Journal Social History* 21 (1987): 197–227.

Fairburn, M., and S. Haslett. "Violent Crime in Old and New Societies: A Case Study Based on New Zealand 1853–1940." *Journal of Social History* 20 (1986): 89–120.

Ferdinand, T.N. "The Criminal Patterns of Boston Since 1849." *American Journal of Sociology* (July 1967): 84–99.

Field, John. "Police, Power and Communities in a Provincial English Town: Portsmouth 1815–1875." *Policing and Punishment in Nineteenth-Century Britain*, edited by V. Bailey. London: Croom Helm, 1977.

Firebaugh, G., and J. Gibbs. "User's Guide to Ratio variables" *American Sociological Review* 50, no. 5 (1985): 713–22.

Fogelson, R. M. *Big-City Police*. Cambridge, MA: Harvard University Press, 1977.

Fosdick, R. B. *American Police Systems*. Moutclair, NJ: Patterson Smith, 1969.

Foucault, Michael. *Discipline and Punish: The Birth of the Prison*. Translated from the French by Alan Sheridan. New York: Vintage Books, 1979.

Gilkes, M., and Symons, M. *Calgary's Finest: A History of the City Police Force*. Calgary: Century Calgary Publication, No. 2 (September 1975): 307–41.

Gillis, A.R. "Crime and State Surveillance in Nineteenth-Century France." *American Journal of Sociology* 95 (1989): 307–41.

Granger, C.W., and P. Newbold. *Forecasting Economic Time Series*. New York: Academic Press, 1977.

Granger, C. W., and R. Engle. "Co-integration and Error Correction: Representation, Estimation and Testing." *Econometrica* 55 (1986): 251–276.

Gray, James. *Booze: The Impact of Whisky On the Prairie West*. Toronto: Macmillan, 1972.

Gurr, Ted Robert. "Historical Trends in Violent Crime: A Critical Review of the Evidence." In *Crime and Justice: An Annual Review of Research*. Vol. 3. Edited by M. Tonry and N. Morris. Chicago: University of Chicago Press, 1981.

———. "On the History of Violence Crime in Europe and American." In *Violence in America: Historical and Comparative Perspectives*, edited by H.D. Graham and T.R. Gurr. London: Sage Publications, 1979.

———. "Part VI. The Comparative Analysis of Public Order." In *The Politics of Crime and Conflict: A Comparative History of Four Cities*, edited by T.R. Gurr, P. Grabosky and R.C. Hula. London: Sage Publications, 1977.

Gusfield, J.R. *Symbolic Crusade: Status Politics and the American Temperance Movement*. Urbana: University of Illinois Press, 1963.

Habermas, Jürgen. *Legitimation Crisis*, translated by Thomas McCarthy. Boston: Beacon Press, 1975.

Haldance, Robert. *The People's Force: A History of the Victorian Police*. Melbourne: Melbourne University Press, 1986.

Hall, S.G. "An Application of the Granger and Engle Two-Step Estimation Procedure to United Kingdom Aggregated Wage Data." *Oxford Bulletin of Economics and Statistics* 48, no. 3 (1986): 229–39.

Harring, Sidney L. *Policing a Class Society: the Experience of American Cities 1865–1915*. New Brunswick, NJ: Rutgers University Press, 1983.

Hart, Keith. "The Formation of the Alberta Provincial Police, 1917–1919." Unpublished paper, located in the Provincial Archives of Alberta at Edmonton, 1980.

Hawkins, Richard. "The 'Irish Model' and the Empire: a Case for Reassessment." In *Policing the Empire*, edited by Anderson and Killingray. New York: Manchester University Press, 1991.

Hayman, Micheal. "The Volstead Act as a Reflection of Canadian-American Relations." M.A thesis, Department of History, McGill University, 1971.

Hendry, D.F. "Econometric Modelling with Co-integrated Variables: An Overview." *Oxford Bulletin of Economics and Statistics* 48 (1986): 201–12.

Hindus, Michael S. "The Contours of crime and Justice in Massachusetts and South Carolina, 1767–1878." *American Journal of Legal History* 21 (1977): 213–37.

Hogg, P.W. *Constitutional Law of Canada*, 3rd ed. Carswell: Thomson Professional Publishing, 1992.

Hurd, W.B. *Racial Origins and Nativity of the Canadian People, Seventh Census of Canada*. Vol. 12. Ottawa: King's Printer, 1942.

Janowitz, Morris. "Sociological Theory and Social Control." *American Journal of Sociology* 81, no. 1 (1975): 82–108.

Jeffries, Charles. *The Colonial Police*. London: Max Parrish, 1952.

Johnson, Bruce C. "Taking Care of Labour: The Police in American Politics." In *Understanding Policing*, edited by K.R.E. McCormick and L.A. Visano. Toronto: Canadian Scholars' Press, 1976.

Jones, Gareth Stedman. "Class Expression Versus Social Control? A Critique of Recent Trends in the Social History of 'Leisure.'" In *Social Control and the State: Historical and Comparative Essays*, edited by Stanley Cohen and Andrew Scull. Oxford: Marin Robertson, 1983.

Kennedy, P. *A Guide to Econometrics*. Cambridge, MA: MIT Press, 1993.

Kraft, M. "On 'User's Guide to Ratio Variables.'" *American Sociological Review* 52 (1987): 135–56.

Lane, Roger. "Urban Police and Crime in Nineteenth-Century America." *Crime and Justice: An Annual Review of Research*. Vol. 2. Chicago: University Chicago Press, 1980.

———. "Urban Homicide in the Nineteenth Century: Some Lessons for the Twentieth." In *History and Crime*, edited by James A. Inciardi and Charles E. Faupel. London: Sage Publications, 1980.

———. "Crime and Criminal Statistics in Nineteenth-Century Massachusetts." *Journal of Social History* (Winter 1968): 156–163.

Lingard, C. Cecil. *Territorial Government in Canada: The Autonomy Question in the Old North-West Territories*. Toronto: University of Toronto Press, 1946.

Mackintosh, W.A. *Economic Problems of the Prairie Provinces*. Toronto: Macmillian, 1935.

MacKinnon, James. "Critical Values for Co-integration Tests." In *Long-Run Economic Relationships: Readings in Co-integration*, edited by R. Engle and C.W. Granger, 267-76. New York: Oxford University Press, 1991.

Macleod, R.C. *The North-West Mounted Police and Law Enforcement 1873–1905*. Toronto: University of Toronto Press, 1976.

———. "Canadianizing the West: the N.W. Mounted Police as Agents of the National Policy, 1873–1905." In *Essays on Western History in Honour of Lewis Gwynne Thomas*, edited by Lewis H. Thomas, 101–10. Edmonton: University of Alberta Press, 1976.

Marx, K. "Theory of Surplus Value I." In *Marx and Engels On Law*, edited by M. Cain and A. Hunt. London: Academic Press, 1979.

McCleary, R., and R.A. Hay, with D. McDowall and E.E. Meidinger. *Applied Time Series Analysis for the Social Sciences*. Beverly Hills, CA: Sage, 1980.

McCormic, Kevin, R.E. and Livy A. Visano, eds. *Understanding Policing*. Toronto: Canadian Scholars' Press, 1992.

McDonald, Lynn. "Crime and Punishment in Canada: A Statistical Test of *Conventional Wisdom*." In *Crime and Delinquency in Canada*, edited by Edmund W. Vaz and Abdul Q. Lodhi, 57–85. Scarborough, ON: Prentice-Hall of Canada, Ltd., 1979.

McDowall, D., R. McCleary, E.E. Meidinger, and R.A. Hay. *Interrupted Time Series Analysis*. London: Sage Publications, 1980.

Meier, Robert F. "Perspectives on the Concept of Social Control." *Annual Review of Sociology* 8 (1982): 35–55.

Miller, W.R. *Cops and Bobbies: Police Authority in New York and London, 1830–1870*. Chicago: University of Chicago Press, 1973.

Mills, Terence C. *Time Series Techniques for Economists*. Cambridge: Cambridge University Press, 1990.

Moir, Sean I. "The Alberta Provincial Police, 1917–1932." Unpublished M.A. thesis, Department of History, University of Alberta, 1992.

Monkkonen, E.H. *Police in Urban America, 1860–1920*. New York: Cambridge University Press, 1981.

———. "A Disorderly People? Urban Order in the Nineteenth and Twentieth Centuries." *Journal of American History* 68, no. 3 (1981): 539–59.

———. "From Cop History to Social History: The Significance of the Police in American History." *Journal of Social History* (Summer 1982): 575–91.

———. "Toward a Dynamic Theory of Crime and The Police: A Criminal Justice System Perspective." *Historical Methods Newsletter* 10, no. 4 (Fall 1977): 157–65.

Monto, Tom. *The United Farmers of Alberta: A Movement, A Government*. Edmonton: Granh Publishing, 1989.

Muraskin, William A. "The Social-Control Theory in American History: A Critique." *Journal of Social History* 9 (1975–76): 558–69.

Newman, Peter C. "Inside the RCMP: the Conscience of a Good Cop." *Maclean's*. Toronto. (July 1972): 1.

Nye, R. "Crime In Modern Societies: Some Research Strategies For Historians." *Journal of Social History* 11 (1978): 491–507.

Osipoff, Fred. "The S.P.P. 1910–1928." *The Canadian Journal of Arms Collecting* 4, no. 1 (February 1966): 5–11.

Palmer, Howard. *Patterns of Prejudice: A History of Nativism in Alberta.* Toronto: McClelland and Stewart, 1982.

Palmer, Howard, and Tamara Palmer. *Alberta: A New History.* Edmonton: Hurtig, 1990.

Palmer, Stanley H. *Police and Protest in England and Ireland 1780–1850.* New York: Cambridge University Press, 1988.

Parsons, T. *The Social System.* New York: Free Press, 1951.

Pindyck, R.S., and D.L. Rubinfeld. *Econometric Models and Economic Forecasts.* New York: McGraw-Hill Inc., 1991.

Pinno, Erhard. "Temperance and Prohibition in Saskatchewan." Unpublished M.A. thesis, University of Saskatchewan at Regina, 1971.

Porter, John. *The Vertical Mosaic.* Toronto: University of Toronto Press, 1965.

Richardson, J.F. "Police in American: Functions and Control." In *History and Crime*, edited by J.A. Inciardi and C.E. Faupel. London: Sage, 1980.

Robertson, Duncan F. "The Saskatchewan Provincial Police, 1917–1928." Unpublished M.A. thesis, University of Saskatchewan at Saskatoon, 1976.

———. "The Saskatchewan Provincial Police 1917–1928." *Saskatchewan History* 31, no. 3 (Autumn 1978): 1–11.

Robinson, C.D. "Ideology as History: A Look at the Way Some English Police Historians Look at the Police." *Police Studies* 2, no. 2 (1979): 35–49.

Rumbaut, R.G., and E. Bittner. "Changing Conceptions of the Police Role: A Sociological Review." *Crime and Justice: An Annual Review of Research* 1 (1979): 239–289.

Sargan, J.D., and A. Bhargava. "Testing Residuals from Least Squares Regression for Being Generated by the Gaussian Random Walk." *Econometrica* 51 (1983): 153–74.

Siegrist, H. "Professionalization/professions in History." In *International Encyclopaedia of the Social and Behavioral Sciences*, Vol. 18. New York: Elsevier, 2001, p. 12154.

Silver, Allan. "The Demand for Order in Civil Society: A Review of Some Themes in the History of Urban Crime, Police and Riot." In *The Police: Six Sociological Essays*, edited by D.J. Bordau. New York: John Wiley and Sons Inc., 1967.

Skolnick, J.H., and Bayley, D.H. "Theme and Variation in Community Policing." *Crime and Justice: An Annual Review of Research* 10 (1988): 1–37.

Smith, David. *Prairie Liberalism: The Liberal Party in Saskatchewan 1905–1971.* Toronto: University of Toronto Press, 1975.

Smith, George. "The Early Police of Manitoba." Unpublished paper, Historical Society of Manitoba, March 11, 1947.

Steedman, C. *Policing the Victorian Community: The Formation of English Provincial Police Force 1856–80.* London: Routledge and Kegan Paul, 1984.

Stenning, Philip C. "The Role of Police Boards and Commissions as Institutions of Municipal Police Governance." In *Understanding Policing*, edited by K.R.E. McCormick and L.A. Visano. Toronto: Canadian Scholars' Press, 1992.

———. *Police Commissions and Boards in Canada.* Research Report of the Centre of Criminology. Toronto: University of Toronto, 1981.

———. *Legal Status of the Police.* Criminal Law Series, A Study Paper Prepared for the Law Reform Commission of Canada, 1981.

Stewart, Chris, and Lynn Hudson. *Mahoney's Minute Men: Saga of the Saskatchewan Provincial Police 1917–1928.* Saskatoon: Modern Press, 1978.

———. *Murder in Uniform*. Saskatoon: Modern Press, 1978.

Stone, L. *The Past and The Present Revisited*. London: Routledge and Kegal Paul, 1987.

Storch, Robert D. "The Plague of the Blue Locusts: Police Reform and Popular Resistance in Northern England, 1840–57." *International Review of Social History* 20, no. 1 (1975): 61–90.

———. "The Policeman as Domestic Missionary: Urban Discipline and Popular Culture in Northern England, 1850–1880." *Journal of Social History* 9, no. 4 (1976): 481–509.

Thomas, L.G. *The Liberal Party in Alberta: A History of Politics in the Province of Alberta 1905–1921*. Toronto: University of Toronto Press, 1959.

Thompson, E.P. *Whigs and Hunters: The Origin of the Black Act*. New York: Pantheon, 1975.

———. *The Poverty of Theory and Other Essays*. New York: Monthly Review Press, 1978.

Thorner, Thomas. "The Incidence of Crime in Southern Alberta." In *Studies in History*, No. 2. Edited by L.A. Knafla and D.J. Bercuson, 53–88. Calgary: University of Calgary, 1979.

Tobias, J.J. *Crime and Police in England, 1700–1900*. New York: St. Martin's Press, 1979.

Turner, Bryan S. *For Weber: Essays on the Sociology of the Fate*. Boston: Routledge and Kegan Paul, 1981.

Valverde, Mariana. *The Age of Light, Soap, and Water*. Toronto: McClelland and Stewart, 1991.

Villa-Arce, Jose. "Alberta Provincial Police." *Alberta Historical Review* 21, no. 4 (1973): 16–19.

Walker, Samuel. "The Urban Police in American History: A Review of the Literature." *Journal of Police Science and Administration* 4, no. 3 (1976): 252–60.

Watts, E. "Police Response to Crime and Disorder in Twentieth-Century St. Louis." *Journal of American History* 70, no. 2 (1983): 340–58.

Weber, Max. *From Max Weber: Essays in Sociology*. Translated, edited and with an introduction by H.H. Gerth and C. Wright Mills. New York: Oxford University Press, 1946.

———. *The Theory of Social and Economic Organization*. London: The Free Press of Glencoe Collier-Macmillan Limited, 1947.

———. *The Protestant Ethic and the Spirit of Capitalism*. Translated by Talcott Parsons. New York: Charles Scribner's Sons, 1958.

———. *Economy and Society*, Vol. 1–2. Edited by Guenther Roth and Claus Wittich. Berkeley: University of California Press, 1978.

Weinberger, B., and H. Reinke. "A Diminishing Function? A Comparative Historical Account of Policing in the City." *Policing and Society* 1 (1991): 213–23.

Wilson, James. "The Police and the Delinquent in Two Cities." In *Controlling Delinquents*, edited by Stanton Wheeler. New York: John Wiley, 1968.

NOTES

NOTES TO INTRODUCTION

1   E. P. Thompson, *Whigs and Hunters: The Origin of the Black Act* (New York: Pantheon, 1975), 265.

2   R.C. Macleod, "Canadianizing the West: the N.W. Mounted Police as Agents of the National Policy, 1873–1905," in *Essays on Western History in Honour of Lewis Gwynne Thomas*, ed. Lewis H. Thomas (Edmonton: University of Alberta Press, 1976), 103.

3   Jose Villa-Arce, "Alberta Provincial Police," *Alberta Historical Review* 21, no. 4 (Autumn 1973): 16; Macleod, "Canadianizing the West," 102.

4   In 1904, "Royal" was added to the North-West Mounted Police in recognition of distinguished service rendered by members of the NWMP in the Boer War.

5   These materials are compiled in more than a hundred boxes in the Provincial Archives of Alberta in Edmonton and in seventy-four boxes in the Provincial Archives of Saskatchewan in Regina.

6   In a more practical sense, the history of the provincial police forces also provides an opportunity to examine social and political implications of provincial policing in western Canada. Although provincial police existed over three quarters of a century ago, they are still relevant to today's federal and provincial politics. In recent years, the re-establishment of the provincial police force in Alberta has been suggested as part of a larger political "firewall" strategy. Certainly, the implications of previous provincial police forces in the two provinces should be taken into consideration in the current debates on the pros and cons of once again maintaining such a provincial police force.

7   In a broader sense, professionalization refers to "processes affecting the social and symbolic construction of occupation and status." H. Siegrist, "Professionalization/professions in History," in *International Encyclopaedia of the Social and Behavioral Sciences*, vol. 18 (New York: Elsevier, 2001), 12154. The concept of professionalization used in this study, however, is similar to the Weberian concept of "rationalization." By "professionalization," we refer, following Weberian theory, to the process by which traditional custom and habits are increasingly replaced by explicit, intellectually calculable and predictable rules and procedures in various spheres of social life. More specifically, in political and legal domains, the professionalization process entails the promotion and advance of a structure of formal laws, as well as bureaucratic organizations that administer such laws according to calculable and predictable procedures, regardless of political ideology and moral ends (Max Weber, *Economy and Society*, ed. Guenther Roth and Claus Wittich, vol. 1–2 [Berkeley: University of California Press, 1978], 954).

8   E.H. Monkkonen, *Police in Urban America, 1860–1920* (New York: Cambridge University Press, 1981), 39; Roger Lane, "Urban Police and Crime in Nineteenth-Century America," in *Crime and Justice: An Annual Review of Research*, vol. 2 (Chicago: University Chicago Press, 1980); Stanley H: Palmer, *Police and Protest in England and Ireland 1780–1850* (New York: Cambridge University Press, 1988); and Allan Silver, "The Demand for Order in Civil Society: A Review of Some Themes in the History of Urban Crime, Police and Rio," in *The Police: Six Sociological Essays*, ed. D.J. Bordau (New York: John Wiley and Sons, 1967).

9   Silver, "The Demand for Order in Civil Society."

10 Robert D. Storch, "The Plague of the Blue Locusts: Police Reform and Popular Resistance in Northern England, 1840–57," *International Review of Social History* 20, no. 1 (1975): 61–90.

11 According to Stanley H. Palmer in *Police and Protest in England and Ireland*, the widespread collective violence was associated with a series of social movements, such as the "white-boy movements" aiming to occupy land, O'Connell's Movement for Catholic Emancipation, the political struggle for Irish self-rule, and the movements demanding economic rights against payment of tithe.

12 Lane, "Urban Police and Crime in Nineteenth-Century America."

13 According to Macleod, for the Canadian federal government, a federal police force could not only keep the peace and order, but also represent a good government of the North West Territories. The Riel Rebellion in 1869–70 provided evidence supporting the government's reasoning that control of the existing natives and Metis population was a necessary step in developing western Canada. Pressure to create the force, however, was spurred by several immediate crises. One was the constant threat of invasion from Americans seeking to occupy the North West Territories. Another was the growing conflicts between English-speaking Protestants from Ontario and the French-speaking, Roman Catholic Metis in the Red River settlements at the gateway to the territories. The third crisis was a massacre of Indians by American whisky traders on Canadian territory in the spring of 1873. "The Origin of the NWMP," in Macleod, *The North-West Mounted Police and Law Enforcement 1873–1905* (Toronto: University of Toronto Press, 1976).

14 W.G. Carson, "Policing the Periphery: The Development of Scottish Policing 1795–1900," *Australian and New Zealand Journal of Criminology*, part I (December 1984): 224.

15 However, according to R.A. Cage, in urban Scotland, poor relief administration was the responsibility of town councils. *The Scottish Poor Law 1745–1845* (Edinburgh: Scottish Academic Press, 1981), 41.

16 J.J. Tobias, *Crime and Police in England, 1700–1900* (New York: St. Martin's Press, 1979), 74.

17 Monkkonen, *Police in Urban America*.

18 In the early and mid-nineteenth-century America, the vigilance committees were organized not only to bear the national ideals of a more frugal, businesslike administration of municipal government, but also to serve as the instruments to implement the ideals. P.J. Ethington, "Vigilantes and the Police: The Creation of A Professional Police Bureaucracy in San Francisco, 1847–1900," *Journal of Social History* 21 (1987): 219.

19 H. Boritch, "Conflict, Compromise and Administrative Convenience: the Police Organization in Nineteenth-Century Toronto," *Canadian Journal of Law and Society* 3 (1988): 142.

20 Richard Hawkins, "The 'Irish Model' and the Empire: A Case for Reassessment," in *Policing the Empire: Government, Authority and Control, 1830–1940*, ed. David M. Anderson and David Killingray (New York: Manchester University Press, 1991).

21 Palmer, *Police and Protest in England and Ireland*, 297.

22 Ibid., 303.
23 Silver, "The Demand for Order in Civil Society," 15.
24 W.R. Miller, *Cops and Bobbies: Police Authority in New York and London, 1830–1870* (Chicago: University of Chicago Press, 1973), 1.
25 E. Durkheim, *The Division of Labour in Society* (New York: The Free Press, 1984), 39.
26 Samuel Walker, "The Urban Police in American History: A Review of the Literature," *Journal of Police Science and Administration* 4, no. 3 (1976): 252–60; and Lane, "Urban Police and Crime in Nineteenth-Century America."
27 Silver, "The Demand for Order in Civil Society," 14.
28 Miller, *Cops and Bobbies*, 1.
29 For Weber, this consensus can be obtained from different sources: legality, tradition, and the exceptional character of an individual (charisma); see *The Theory of Social and Economic Organization* (London: The Free Press of Glencoe Collier-Macmillan Limited, 1947).
30 Palmer, *Police and Protest in England and Ireland*, 303.
31 Ibid., 45.
32 Sir Charles Jeffries, *The Colonial Police* (London: Max Parrish, 1952); and Palmer, *Police and Protest in England and Ireland*.
33 Jefferies, *The Colonial Police*, 30–31.
34 Anderson and Killingray, eds., *Policing the Empire: Government, Authority and Control, 1830–1940* (New York: Manchester University Press, 1991), 5.
35 Weber, *Economy and Society*, 987.
36 Ibid., 973.
37 Anderson and Killingray, *Policing the Empire*, 2.
38 Sidney L. Harring, *Policing a Class Society: The Experience of American Cities 1865–1915* (New Brunswick, NJ: Rutgers University Press, 1983).
39 Bruce C. Johnson, "Taking Care of Labour: The Police in American Politics," in *Understanding Policing*, ed. K.R.E. McCormick and L.A. Visano (Toronto: Canadian Scholars' Press, 1976), 500.
40 Monkkonen, *Police in Urban America*.
41 William A. Muraskin, "The Social-Control Theory in American History: A Critique," *Journal of Social History* 9 (1975–76): 558–69.
42 Silver, "The Demand for Order in Civil Society," 14; Carson's study of Scottish police function in the period 1795–1900 in "Policing the Periphery" (224) corroborates Silver's argument.
43 Macleod, "Canadianizing the West"; the primary role of the NWMP was to assimilate the Natives and immigrants into Canadian society embodying the value of the middle-class elites; Macleod conceptualizes this role as "Canadianizing Western Canada."
44 Storch, "The Plague of the Blue Locusts," 66.
45 Silver, "The Demand for Order in Civil Society," 13.
46 Ibid., 63.
47 Storch notes "the imposition of the police brought the arm of municipal and state authority directly to bear upon key institutions of daily life in working-class neighbourhoods, touching off a running battle with local custom and popular culture which lasted at least until the end of the century.... In northern industrial towns of England these police functions must be viewed as a direct complement to the attempts of urban middle-class elites – by means of Sabbath, educational, temperance, and recreational reform – to mould

a labouring class amenable to new disciplines of both work and leisure. The other side of the coin of middle-class voluntaristic moral and social reform (even when sheathed) was the policeman's truncheon." Storch, "The Policeman as Domestic Missionary: Urban Discipline an Popular Culture in Northern Englans, 1840–1880," *Journal of Social History* 9, no. 4 (1976): 481.

48   Monkkonen, *Police in Urban America*, 155.
49   Monkkonen, *Police in Urban America*.
50   The first transformation was the bureaucratization of the police organization.
51   H. Boritch and J. Hagan, "Crime and the Changing Forms of Class Control: Policing Public Order in Toronto The Good 1859–1955," *Social Forces* 66, no. 2 (December 1987): 307–35.
52   Ibid., 330.
53   According to Anderson and Killingray in *Policing the Empire* (7), the colonial police also experienced a similar transformation in their duties. But, this change coincided with the transformation of the colonial state toward more responsible government rather than with the adoption of technical innovations by the police.
54   B. Weinberger and H. Reinke, "A Diminishing Function? A Comparative Historical Account of Policing in the City," *Policing and Society* 1 (1991): 213–23.
55   Macleod, *The North-West Mounted Police and Law Enforcement*, 88.
56   J.R. Gusfield, *Symbolic Crusade: Status Politics and the American Temperance Movement* (Urbana: University of Illinois Press, 1963), 11.
57   Ibid., 12.
58   Lane, "Urban Police and Crime in Nineteenth-Century America," 9.
59   Walker, "The Urban Police in American History," 257.
60   Macleod, *The North-West Mounted Police and Law Enforcement*, 133.
61   In Weberian terminology, probably we can say that this shift removed the elements of the "substantive rationality" in bureaucratic police administration. Weber classifies rationality into two classes: "substantive" and "formal" rationality. The substantive rationality of social action refers to the degree to which the action is grounded in ambiguous value-oriented criteria or moral preferences (such as sobriety) but is applied by technically adequate methods – the rule of law. Weber suggests that "it is the tendency of officials to treat their official function from what is substantively a utilitarian point of view in the interest of the welfare of those under their authority. But this utilitarian tendency is generally expressed in the enactment of corresponding regulatory measures which themselves have a formal character and tend to be treated in a formalistic spirit." *Economy and Society*, 226. The formal rationality of action is concerned with conduct organized in accordance with unambiguous, intellectually predicable, and calculable impersonal rules and procedures. For Weber, the direct social consequences of such social action are that "the dominant norms are concepts of straightforward duty without regard to personal considerations. Everyone is subject to formal equality of treatment; that is, everyone is in the same empirical situation" (ibid., 225).
62   Lane, "Urban Police and Crime in Nineteenth-Century America," 36.
63   Ted Robert Gurr, "Historical Trends in Violent Crime: A Critical Review of the Evidence," in *Crime and Justice: An Annual Review of Research*, ed. M. Tonry and N. Morris, vol. 3 (Chicago: University of Chicago Press, 1981).
64   Ibid., 296.
65   Monkkonen, *Police in Urban America*, 130.

66. Ted Robert Gurr, "On the History of Violence Crime in Europe and American," in *Violence in America: Historical and Comparative Perspectives*, ed. H.D. Graham and T.R. Gurr (London: Sage, 1979), 717.
67. A.R. Gillis, "Crime and State Surveillance in Nineteenth-Century France," *American Journal of Sociology* 95 (1989): 313.
68. However, Lynn McDonald suggests a long-term increase in the rates of less serious crime in Canada. "Crime and Punishment in Canada: A Statistical Test of *Conventional Wisdom*," in *Crime and Delinquency in Canada*, ed. Edmund W. Vaz and Abdul Q. Lodhi (Scarborough, ON: Prentice-Hall of Canada, 1979), 57–85.
69. Monkkonen, *Police in Urban America*. James Wilson suggests that the more the police were professionalized, the more the police were likely to make arrests of delinquents. "The Police and the delinquent in two cities," in *Controlling Delinquents*, ed. Stanton Wheeler (New York: John Wiley, 1968).
70. E. Watts, "Police Response to Crime and Disorder in Twentieth-Century St. Louis," *Journal of American History* 70, no. 2 (1983): 340–58.
71. Roger Lane, "Crime and Criminal Statistics in Nineteenth-Century Massachusetts," *Journal of Social History* (Winter 1968).
72. T.N. Ferdinand, "The Criminal Patterns of Boston Since 1849," *American Journal of Sociology* (July 1967): 97.
73. M. Fairburn and S. Haslett, "Violent Crime in Old and New Societies – A Case Study Based on New Zealand 1853–1940," *Journal of Social History* 20 (1986): 89–120.
74. Bryan S. Turner, *For Weber: Essays on the Sociology of the Fate* (Boston: Routledge and Kegan Paul, 1981), 339.
75. Thompson, *Whigs and Hunters* (New York: Pantheon, 1975), 265.
76. E.P. Thompson, *The Poverty of Theory and Other Essays* (New York: Monthly Review Press, 1978).

NOTES TO CHAPTER 1

1. In 1904, the North-West Mounted police were granted the right to use the prefix "royal" for recognition of their services during the Boer War in South African (1899–1902). After that time, the NWMP was changed to the Royal North-West Mounted Police. In *The North-West Mounted Police and Law Enforcement*, Macloed provides more detailed discussions on the police in the war.
2. C. Steedman, *Policing the Victorian Community: The Formation of English Provincial Police Force 1856–80* (London: Routledge and Kegan Paul, 1984); Micheal Brogden, *The Police: Autonomy and Consent* (Toronto: Academic Press, 1982).
3. The British North America Act, 1867. SS. 92(14) and 91(27).
4. P.W. Hogg, *Constitutional Law of Canada*, 3rd ed. (Carswell: Thomson Professional Publishing, 1992), 468.
5. Philip C. Stenning, "The Role of Police Boards and Commissions as Institutions of Municipal Police Governance," in *Understanding Policing*, ed. K.R.E. McCormick and L.A. Visano (Toronto: Canadian Scholars' Press, 1992), 40–60.
6. *Statutes of Canada* (S.C.) 1868, 31 Vict., c. 73.
7. S.C. 1873, 36 Vict., c. 35.
8. Macleod, *The North-West Mounted Police and Law Enforcement*, 6.

9   Howard Palmer and Tamara Palmer elaborate on the North-West Territories' financial difficulties and their badly needed political autonomy. They explain that "at a time when it needed money desperately to supply services to the massive numbers of newcomers, the territorial government was left without the per-capita grants that provinces received. It also lacked the authority to charter railways at a time when settlers were demanding more railways to market their grain." *Alberta: A New History* (Edmonton: Hurtig, 1990), 128.

10 The creation of the provinces of Alberta and Saskatchewan was a significant event in the development of western Canada. The status of a province "established a new relationship between the government of the province and the federal government. The latter retained overriding authority in all matters affecting the national interest. The provincial government had exclusive power to make laws relating to municipal institutions, civil rights, property, marriage, public health, the administration of justice and generally all matters of a local nature." John H. Archer, *Saskatchewan: A History* (Saskatoon: Western Producer Prairie Books, 1980), 133.

11 *British North America Acts and Selected Statutes, 1867–1948*, Part IV; and C. Cecil Lingard, *Territorial Government in Canada: The Autonomy Question in the Old North-West Territories* (Toronto: University of Toronto Press, 1946).

12 Canada, Sessional Papers, no. 28, the Report of the RNWMP Headquarters, 1905, 2.

13 Macleod, *The North-West Mounted Police and Law Enforcement*, 68–70.

14 Canada, Sessional Papers, no. 28, the Report of the RNWMP, 1906, 1.

15 Ibid., 98.

16 According to the Report of the Alberta Provincial Police, the annual expense was $500,511.00 for 1920. PAA, the Attorney General's files, Accession No. 75.370/box 2. 72.270/56; in 1927 the Saskatchewan Government spent $339,664.00 for maintaining their provincial police. PAS. R-997 E6.

17 Canada, Sessional Papers, no. 28, the Report of the RNWMP, 1906, 98.

18 Livestock and Agricultural Associations, banks, and the Council of the Board of Trade in Calgary all submitted petitions to urge the retention of the RNWMP in Alberta. The Petition from the Livestock and Agricultural Associations gave the reasons for the retention of the RNWMP in Alberta as follows: "The RNWMP, by reason of their semi-military organization, by reason of their tradition and standards which they have ever lived up to and by reason of the prestige which they have; and the high esteem in which they are held in the province, afford a feeling of security to the settlers in the rural districts and furnish to them and their property an actual protection which no body of civilian police could render." Printed in *The Medicine Hat News*, 6 January 1917, cited by Keith Hart, "The Formation of the Alberta Provincial Police, 1917–1919," unpublished paper (located in the Provincial Archives of Alberta at Edmonton, 1980).

19 *Statutes of Saskatchewan* (S.S.) 1906, c. 20.

20 P. Stenning, *Legal Status of the Police*, Criminal Law Series, A Study Paper Prepared for the Law Reform Commission of Canada (1981), 46.

21 David Smith, *Prairie Liberalism: The Liberal Party in Saskatchewan 1905–1971* (Toronto: University of Toronto Press, 1975); John H. Archer, *Saskatchewan: A History*.

22 Attorney General File, SPP, Order-in-Council regarding C. A. Mahoney, R-997, Box 1, A (1912–1916), Provincial Archives of Saskatchewan (PAS); Fred Osipoff, in his article "The S.P.P. 1910–192," speculates that the force was established at the time when C.A. Mahoney arrived at Regina on December 29, 1910. But, both the Order-in-Council appointing Mahoney as Chief Constable and the government bulletin suggested that the force was probably formed on the first of December one year after Mahoney's arrival. *The Public Service Monthly: A Periodical Bulletin on Matters of Public Interest in*

Saskatchewan, published by Authority of the Saskatchewan Government, vol. 1, no. 12 (July 1913), 3–4.
23 *Statutes of Alberta* (S.A.) 1908, c. 4.
24 Dennis Ryan, Insp. Commanding Banff Sub-District to the Officer Commanding of the Royal Canadian Mounted Police, Lethbridge, Alberta, June 7th, 1923. Provincial Archives of Alberta (PAA), Accession No. 75.126, 2438a.
25 S.S. 1908, c. 16, sections 72–85.
26 S.A. 1926, c. 41, section 72.
27 S.S. 1908, c. 17, sections 64–70 and S. A. 1911-12, c. 2, sections 64–70.
28 The Village Act, S.S. 1908, c. 18; the Village Act, S.A. 1907, c. 10.
29 The Alberta Police Act, S.A. 1919, c. 26.
30 Macleod, *The North-West Mounted Police and Law Enforcement*, 131.
31 Canada, Sessional Papers, no. 28, the Report of the RWNMP, 1913, 8.
32 Canada, Sessional Papers, no. 28, the Report of the RNWMP, 1907, 2; Canada, Sessional Papers, no. 28, the Report of the RNWMP, 1909, 41.
33 A Divisional Inspector in 1909 RNWMP report noted that "there are very few Towns which have their own constables, and I would strongly recommend that the provincial government do something to make them supply the deficiency. These Towns, if in a province with a provincial police, would be obliged to have their own constables, but here they depend on our force and take up a great deal of our time with trivial matters which often interfere greatly with more important work." Canada, Sessional Papers, no. 28, the Report of the RNWMP, 1909, 41.
34 Canada, Sessional Papers, no. 28, the Report of the RNWMP, 1912, 8.
35 Canada, Sessional Papers, no. 28, the Report of the RNWMP, 1906, 7; and Canada, Sessional Papers, no. 28, the Report of the RNWMP, 1909, 77.
36 Canada, Sessional Papers, no. 28, the Report of the RNWMP, 1914, 52.
37 Canada, Sessional Papers, no. 28, the Report of the RNWMP, 1912, 10.
38 For a description of increased trends in serious crime in the two provinces during 1905–17, see section 2 of chapter 3 of this book.
39 According to English law, the justice of the peace was also considered a chief of police in local communities before 1820s. Since the Metropolitan Police of London were created and operated against strong opposition and under the suspicion that they might develop into an uncontrollable and arbitrary tyranny, the practice where the chief of police was also a justice of the peace was stopped. Egon Bittner, *The Function of the Police in Modern Society: A Review of Background Factors, Current practices, and Possible Role Models* (Cambridge, MA: Oelgeschlager, Gunn and Hair, 1980). However, probably due to the difficulties in finding qualified justices of the peace in western Canada and the undeveloped government administrations, the federal government conferred on the Mounties the same judicial power as the police had before the London Metropolitan Police. This tradition was carried on by the provincial police as well. But, they used their judicial power less frequently than the RNWMP had on the prairies earlier. After 1917, the provincial governments were able to appoint a sufficient number of the justices of the peace, possibly because more qualified people, particularly those who had received education or some legal training, were available to be appointed as justices of the peace than before.
40 Canada, Sessional Papers, no. 28, the Report of the RNWMP, 1905, 96.
41 Canada, Sessional Papers, no. 28, the Report of the RNWMP, 1906–1912.

42   Duncan F. Robertson, "The Saskatchewan Provincial Police, 1917–1928" (Unpublished M.A. thesis, University of Saskatchewan at Saskatoon, 1976), 7; Palmer and Palmer, *Alberta: A New History*, 176; and Sean I. Moir, "The Alberta Provincial Police, 1917–1932," (Unpublished M.A. thesis, Department of History, University of Alberta, 1992), 4.
43   Palmer and Palmer, *Alberta: A New History*, 176.
44   Canada, Sessional Papers, no. 28, the Report of the RNWMP, 1906–1916.
45   The Liquor License Act, S. S. 1909, c. 38.
46   Robertson, "The Saskatchewan Provincial Police," 9.
47   Canada, Sessional Papers, no. 28, the Report of the RNWMP, 1910, 127.
48   Canada, Sessional Papers, no. 28, the Report of the RNWMP, 1915, 9.
49   Canada, Sessional Papers, no. 28, the Report of the RNWMP, 1914, 8.
50   Robertson, "The Saskatchewan Provincial Police," 7.
51   Canada, Sessional Papers, no. 28, the Report of the RNWMP, 1915, 8.
52   For Alberta population statistics, see *Canadian Year Book*, 191; the 1915 Report of the RNWMP indicated that no trouble was anticipated from the Germans and Austrians who became naturalized British subjects. Canada, Sessional Papers, no. 28, the Report of the RNWMP, 1915, 54.
53   Canada, Sessional Papers, no. 28, the Report of the RNWMP, 1914, 101.
54   Ibid., 8.
55   Canada, Sessional Papers, no. 28, the Report of the RNWMP, 1915, 53.
56   Canada, Sessional Papers, no. 28, the Report of the RNWMP, 1914, 18.
57   Palmer and Palmer point out that during the war, growing nationalism had serious consequences for the thousands of immigrants of German and Eastern European background. The frustration, deprivation, and bitterness of war found a convenient scapegoat in the "enemy alien." *Alberta: A New History*, 171.
58   Canada, Sessional Papers, no. 28, the Report of the RNWMP, 1916, 120.
59   Canada, Sessional Papers, no. 28, the Report of the RNWMP, 1917, 59.
60   The Commissioner explained that "this fortunate condition is due to a variety of causes, wise precautions, fair and impartial treatment by the authorities, and an admirable attitude of self-restraint on the part of loyal population towards the enemy aliens, and the recognition by these nationalities that as long as they pursued their ordinary avocations, and refrained from inimical acts, they would not be molested nor interfered with." Canada, Sessional Papers, no. 28, the Report of the RNWMP, 1915, 8.
61   Canada, Sessional Papers, no. 81, 1916.
62   Canada, Sessional Papers, no. 28, the Report of the RNWMP, 1915, 9.
63   Canada, Sessional Papers, no. 28, the Report of the RNWMP, 1916, 8.
64   Ibid., 8.
65   Ibid., 9.
66   Canada, Sessional Papers, no. 28, the Report of the RNWMP, 1917, 8.
67   Ibid., 8.
68   Ibid., 9.
69   Ibid., 9.
70   The Commissioner of the RNWMP, A.B. Perry to the Prime Minister, Sir. Robert Borden, PAA, Accession No. 66.166, 4982; regarding the "enemy alien," Moir notes that "much of the controversy surrounding the 'enemy aliens' stems from the fact that neither Canada's population nor the RNWMP, both predominantly Anglo-Saxon, understand who these

people were. A large percentage of the 17500 'Germans' and 'Austrians' who settled on the prairies were not of German or Austrian descent, rather, many of them were of Ukrainian heritage." "The Alberta Provincial Police," 10.

71 Ibid.
72 "Withdrawal of RNWMP from Alberta, Saskatchewan, and Manitoba," Sessional Papers of Canada, No. 70, 1917.
73 PAS, R-282-No. 49. A Minute of the Executive Council of Saskatchewan, December 19, 1916.
74 This is suggested by a letter to the Deputy Attorney General of the Province of Alberta from the Comptroller of the RNWMP, L. DuPlesses. The letter urged the government of Alberta to pay the fee. PAA, Accession No. 66.166, 4986.
75 Canada, Sessional Papers, no. 28, the Report of the RNWMP, 1917, 9.
76 An Attorney General File, a letter to the Attorney General from John L. Fawcett LLB. April 4th, 1917. PAA, Accession No. 66.166, 4986.
77 Canada, Sessional Papers, no. 28, the Report of the RNWMP, 1918.

NOTES TO CHAPTER 2

1 Correspondence to Mr. Primrose shows that the Alberta Provincial Police closely followed the established rules and regulations of the RNWMP in the process of making their own rules and regulations, see PAA, the Attorney General's files, Accession No. 66.166, 498a.
2 The first Canadian Police Board was created in 1858 under the Upper Canada Statute based on the 1853 New York City precedent. Stenning, "The Role of Police Boards and Commissions."
3 Fosdick, R. B., *American Police Systems* (Moutclair, NJ: Patterson Smith, 1969), 77.
4 Stenning, "The Role of Police Boards and Commissions," 446.
5 Alberta Provincial Police Act, S.A. 1917, c. 4.
6 The Attorney General's Files, Minutes of the Board of the Commissioners, PAA, Accession No. 66.166, 4986.
7 The Attorney General's Files, PAA, Accession No. 66.166, 4986.
8 Alberta Provincial Police Act, S.A. 1917, c. 4, s. 11.
9 Ibid., s. 12.
10 The Attorney General files, the Superintendent to the Board of the Commissioners, PAA, Accession No. 70.414, 243.
11 The Attorney General's files, Nicholson to the Superintendent and the Board, December 1, 1917, PAA, Accession No. 70.414, 243.
12 Ibid., Schurer to the Superintendent, December 1, 1917.
13 Ibid.
14 Journal of the Provincial Legislative Assembly of Alberta, February 28, 1918.
15 Ibid.
16 Another problem with the force in the public mind concerned the enforcement of the provincial Liquor Act. *The Morning Alberta*, February 20, 1919, referred to in Hart "The Formation of the Alberta Provincial Police," 10.

17   The Saskatchewan Provincial Police Act, S.S. 1919–20, c. 19; the Alberta Police Act, S.A. 1919, c. 26.
18   The Alberta Police Act, S.A. 1919, c. 26.
19   Macleod, *The North-West Mounted Police and Law Enforcement*, 113.
20   The Annual Report of the APP, Headquarters, 1918, 43.
21   The Alberta Provincial Police Act, S.A. 1917, c. 4, s. 12(a), the Saskatchewan Provincial Police Act , S.S. 1919–20, c. 19, s. 14(a), and the Royal North-West Mounted Police Act, R.S.C. 1906, c. 91, s. 18(a) had an identical stipulation.
22   The APP Act, 1917, s. 12(b); the SPP Act, 1919–20, s. 14(b).
23   The Annual Reports of the SPP, from Division Headquarters, 1917–1927; the Annual Reports of the APP, from Headquarters 1917–1931.
24   The Annual Report of the APP, "A" Division, 1924, 48.
25   The Annual Report of the APP, Headquarters, 1925, 99.
26   The Annual Report of the APP, Headquarters, 1924, 4.
27   The Annual Report of the APP, Headquarters, 1918, 41.
28   Ibid., 41; the Annual Report of the SPP, Headquarters, 1919, 9.
29   The Annual Report of the APP, Headquarters, 1928, 62.
30   The Annual Report of the APP, Headquarters, 1928, 63.
31   The Annual Report of the APP, Headquarters, 1925, 99.
32   Ibid.
33   The Attorney General's files, a memorandum to officers commanding all Divisions by Superintendent McDonnell, March 20, 1917, PAA, Accession No. 66.166, 4986.
34   Alberta Provincial Police Regulations, s. 3; Saskatchewan Provincial Police Regulations, s. 9; and the Royal North-West Mounted Police Regulations, 1909, s. 24.
35   The Saskatchewan Provincial Police Act, S.S. 1919–20, c. 19; the Alberta Police Act, S.A. 1917, c. 4.
36   The Attorney General's files, a memo for Superintendent McDonnell, June 15, 1917. PAA, Accession No. 66.166, 498a.
37   Government of the Province of Saskatchewan, Canada, *Report of the Royal Commission to Inquire Into Statements Made in Statutory Declarations and Other Matters*, 1930. Regina: Roland S. Garrett, King's Printers, 1931, 21 (hereafter cited as the Royal Commission Report).
38   The Alberta Police Act, S.A. 1919, c. 26; the Saskatchewan Provincial Police Act, S.S. 1919–20, c. 19.
39   Smith, *Prairie Liberalism*, 159.
40   The Royal Commission Report, 69.
41   Ibid.
42   Archer, *Saskatchewan: A History*, 214.
43   Ibid., 14.
44   Ibid., 65.
45   Ibid., 176.
46   Ibid., 176.
47   Ibid., 12.
48   Smith, *Prairie Liberalism*, 35.

49 L.G. Thomas, *The Liberal Party in Alberta: A History of Politics in the Province of Alberta 1905–1921* (Toronto: University of Toronto Press, 1959).

50 Tom Monto, *The United Farmers of Alberta: A Movernent, A Government* (Edmonton: Granh Publishing, 1989), 29.

51 This observation parallels Hawkins' view on the uneasy relationship between police and justices of the peace in nineteenth-century Irish society. "The 'Irish Model' and the Empire," 25.

52 There was the case in the Crow's Nest Pass where a man resisted arrest by a police officer. The man was charged with "resisting a police officer." A police magistrate released him on a nominal fine. The Inspector of "D" Division regarded this sentence as improperly lenient. The Annual Report of the APP, "D" Division, 1924, 28.

53 The Annual Report of the APP, "D" Division, 1922, 39.

54 The Annual Report of the APP, Headquarters, 1921, 60.

55 The Annual Report of the APP, "B" Division, 1924, 5.

56 The Annual Report of the APP, "C" Division, 1925, 4.

57 The Annual Report of the APP, "B" Division, 1922, 20.

58 The Annual Report of the APP, Headquarters, 1924, 77.

59 H. Boritch, "Conflict, Compromise and Administrative Convenience: The Police Organization in Nineteenth-Century Toronto," *Canadian Journal of Law and Society* 3 (1988): 141–74.

NOTES TO CHAPTER 3

1 It has been called "softened labeling theory." Watts, "Police Response to Crime and Disorder," 340.

2 E.H. Monkkonen, *Police in Urban America, 1860–1920*, 22.

3 The arrest statistics for both provinces are compiled based on the return of the numbers of charged offenders in the annual reports of both the RNWMP and the provincial police forces in Alberta and Saskatchewan during the period 1906–50. The constables in the rural detachments usually did not have any legal training. Therefore, their crime estimates were based on arrests as opposed to convictions.

4 For discussions on the use of ratio variables, see G. Firebaugh and J. Gibbs, "User's Guide to Ratio Variables" *American Sociological Review* 50, no. 5 (1985); W. Bradshaw and L. Radbill, "Method and Substance in the Use of Ratio Variables," *American Sociological Review* 52 (1987); and M. Kraft, "On 'User's Guide to Ratio Variables'," *American Sociological Review* 52 (1987). To control for the effect of changes in population over time, all the variables were calculated as rates per 100,000 population.

5 Watts, "Police Response to Crime and Disorder."

6 Monkkonen, *Police in Urban America*.

7 Watts, "Police Response to Crime and Disorder"; and Boritch and Hagan, "Crime and the Changing Forms of Class Control."

8 J. Blanchard and R.G. Cassidy, *Crime and Criminal Process in Canada: 1880–1970 and Beyond* (Ottawa: Statistics Division, Solicitor General Canada, CANJUS Project Report no. 21, 1975).

9 The 1914 crime waves were not unique to the prairie provinces. There was also an escalation in arrest rates in Canada as a whole (ibid.). Paul Brantingham and Patricia Brantingham speculate that such crime waves could be due to changes in law, judi-

cial practices, or policing policies. However, research shows none of these possibilities explain the 1914 crime wave. *Patterns in Crime* (New York: MacMillan Publishing Company, 1984).

10   Owen D. Carrigan, *Crime and Punishment in Canada: A History* (Toronto: McClelland and Stewart, 1991), 61.

11   Thomas Thorner, "The Incidence of Crime in Southern Alberta," in *Studies in History*, no. 2, ed. L.A. Knafla and D.J. Bercuson (Calgary: University of Calgary, 1979), 53–88.

12   This argument is consistent with Monkkonen's explanation for the shift in the function of American urban police in the beginning of this century.

13   For technical discussions related to the data analysis and the results from the analysis, see Appendix A.

14   Watts, "Police Response to Crime and Disorder," 341.

NOTES TO CHAPTER 4

1   In fact, some scholars argue that Sifton dedicated his political career to the western settlement, especially through the settlement by farmers. For more on this topic, see Palmer and Palmer, *Alberta: A New History*, 76–105.

2   Ibid., 78.

3   Census of Canada, 1901, 1911, 1921, 1931.

4   Census of Canada, 1931.

5   Ibid.

6   Palmer and Palmer, *Alberta: A History*, 93.

7   Donald Avery, *Dangerous Classes: European Immigrant Workers and Labour Radicalism in Canada, 1896–1932* (Toronto: McClelland and Stewart, 1979), 14.

8   The term "Canadianization" is used here to conceptualize the various functions of the provincial police during the period 1917–32. This term has been used purposefully by Macleod in "Canadianizing the West" to describe the role of the NWMP during the period 1873–1905. Although the term "Canadianization" is not a conventional sociological term, it is in harmony with the term "social control," which has been applied to sociological research extensively. However, the term "social control" is "so elastic that it fits almost every meaning." Robert F. Meier, "Perspectives on the Concept of Social Control," *Annual Review of Sociology* 8 (1982): 53; Morris Janowitz has the same observation, see Janowitz, "Sociological Theory and Social Control," *American Journal of Sociology* 81, no. 1 (1975): 82–108. For this reason, we deliberately avoid using the concept of social control to describe functions of the provincial police in this study.

Meier points out that the term "social control" has been used in three contexts in the sociological literature: "(a) as a description of a bais social process or condition; (b) as a mechanism to insure compliance with norms; and (c) as a method by which to study (or to interpret data about) social order." "Perspectives on the Concept of Social Control," 35. Among them, the most popular application of the term is as a mechanism to maintain system stability. This functionalist application of the term "social control" was developed and elaborated by Parsons in his studies of deviance. For Parsons, deviance causes a tension in an otherwise stable social system, and social control would return the system to equilibrium. Social control and deviance represent opposing processes: "the theory of social control is the obverse of the theory of the genesis of deviant behavior tendencies. It is the analysis of those processes in the social system which tend to counteract the deviance tendencies, and of the conditions under which such pressures will operate." T. Parsons, *The Social System* (New York: Free Press, 1951), 297; for an application of this perspective, see Stanley Cohen, *Vision of Social Control: Crime, Punishment and Classification* (Oxford: Polity Press, 1985). Parsons suggests using internationalization as a means of social control to prevent most deviance while sanctions are invoked against the rest.

The term "Canadianization" is consistent with Parsons' use of concept of social control. The provincial police, like the NWMP, were important part of the nationwide efforts to realize the national policy of building an ideal Canadian society not only through coercive enforcement of law and moral codes among immigrant populations, but also by providing various social services and assistance to the population. However, it must noted that the police's Canadianization function was not free from bias. In "Canadianizing the West" (110), Macleod explained that "the society they [the NWMP] envisaged was to be orderly and hierarchical; not a lawless frontier democracy but a place where powerful institutions and a responsible and paternalistic upper class would ensure true liberty and justice."

9 The Annual Report of the APP, Headquarters, 1921, 76.

10 A Report by the Inspector of "A" Division on August 10th, 1917, referring to the inquiry of Deputy Attorney General as to Conditions at Andrew, PAA, Accession No: 66.166/498a.

11 Howard Palmer, *Patterns of Prejudice* (Toronto: McClelland and Stewart, 1985), 18–19.

12 Ibid., 7.

13 The Annual Report of the APP, "A" Division, 1929, 97.

14 The Annual Report of the APP, "A" Division, 1928, p. 17. A report from Red Deer showed that the lower crime rate in the area was because the district was composed of a greater proportion of older settlers relative to the foreign-speaking population. The Annual Report of the APP, "B" Division, 1920, 4.

15 The Annual Report of the SPP, Headquarters, 1919, 1.

16 Research indicates that there was no association between immigrant population from central and eastern European countries and the rise in serious crime in Canada. However, immigration waves seemed to be related to public order offences. This is because police in the first part of the twentieth century were inclined to focus their time and resources on immigrant populations. Therefore, the association between immigrants and public order offences was, of course, not an outcome of immigrants' disposition for criminal behaviour as police described, but rather the artefact of policing policy and behaviour. For more discussion of the relationship between immigration and crime in Canada, see G. Brannigan and Zhiqiu Lin, "'Where East Meets West': Police, Immigration and Public Order Crime in the Settlement of Canada from 1896 to 194," *Canadian Journal of Sociology* 24, no. 1 (1999): 87–107; In *Alberta: A History* (158), Palmer and Palmer attribute the apparent association between crime and the immigrant population to the immigrants' difficult living conditions and the large number of single men among them.

17 Palmer and Palmer also tried to explain the reasons why the immigrants in Alberta were interested in radical political activities. They suggest that "in the mines and cities, the central and eastern Europeans held less skilled jobs and made less money than most English speaking workers. Alienated from their fellow Albertans by cultural and linguistic differences and discrimination, some of them turned to radical political and labour groups to try to change their living conditions." *Alberta: A History*, 95.

18 The Annual Report of the APP, Headquarters, 1919, 47.

19 The Annual Report of the APP, "D" Division, 1922, 3; "C" Division, 1920, 53; and the Annual report of the SPP, Regina Division, 1920, 47–50.

20 The Annual Report of the APP, "C" Division, 1918, 9.

21 The Annual Report of the SPP, Regina Division, 1920, 47.
22 Ibid.
23 The Annual Report of the APP, "A" Division, 1918, 2.
24 Palmer and Palmer indicate that the police constantly kept radical union organizers, especially IWW organizers, under surveillance and arrested them on vagrancy charges. *Alberta: A History*, 111.
25 The Annual Report of the APP, Headquarters, 1925, 93.
26 Ibid., 93.
27 Ibid., 94.
28 The Annual Report of the APP, Headquarters, 1923, 76.
29 The Annual Report of the SPP, Regina Division, 1920, 47.
30 The Annual Report of the APP, Headquarters, 1930, 69.
31 The Annual Report of the APP, "A" Division, 1930, 19; Avery also points out that this tactic was strongly supported "by the mine managers of the region, who seized upon the illegitimate status of the [Communist Party of Canada] and [Industrial Workers of the World] to discard all collective bargaining procedures." *Dangerous Classes*, 124.
32 The Annual Report of the APP, "C" Division, 1927, 34; and The Annual Report of the APP, "C" Division, 1925, 39.
33 The Annual Report of the APP, "C" Division, 1926, 41.
34 The Annual Report of the APP, "D" Division, 1924, 12.
35 The Annual Report of the APP, "B" Division, 1923, 19.
36 The Annual Report of the APP, Headquarters, 1926, 74.
37 The Annual Report of the APP, Headquarters, 1927, 34.
38 This large percentage of the unemployed who were refused government relief might also suggest that the police treated the immigrants badly in the allocation of relief.
39 The Annual Report of the APP, Headquarters, 1928, 66.
40 The Annual Report of the APP, "C" Division, 1925, 39.
41 The Annual Report of the APP, Headquarters, 1925, 97.
42 Ibid., 99.
43 The Annual Report of the APP, "C" Division, 1931, 26.
44 The Annual Report of the APP, "A" Division, 1930, 67.
45 The Annual Report of the APP, "C'" Division, 1926, 43.
46 The Annual Report of the APP, "C" Division, 1918, 8.
47 The Annual Report of the SPP, Saskatoon Division, 1918, 6; The Annual Report of the SPP, Headquarters, 1920, 1; and The Annual Report of the APP, "C" Division, 1920, 43.
48 Robertson, "The Saskatchewan Provincial Police," 59.
49 The Annual Report of the SPP, Headquarters, 1917, 1918, 1919.
50 The Annual Report of the SPP, Weyburn Division, 1917, 5.
51 The Annual Report of the SPP, Saskatoon Division, 1919, 13.
52 Meeting of the Board of Commissioners, APP, January 7, 1918. P.A.A., Accession No. 66.166, 1288.
53 The Annual Report of the APP, Headquarters, 1926, 78.
54 The Annual Report of the APP, Headquarters, 1918, 46; The Annual Report of the APP, "D" Division, 1; and The Annual Report of the APP, "A" Division, 1918, 18.

55　The Annual Report of the APP, Headquarters, 43.
56　The Annual Report of the APP, "D" Division, 1926, 28.
57　John H. Archer points out that police Canadianization of immigrants was part of the social gospel movement, which accommodated such ills as prejudice and hatred. World War I actually intensified this effort. *Saskatchewan: A History*, 200.
58　The Annual Report of the APP, "D" Division, 1926, 7.
59　James Gray, *Booze: The Impact of Whisky on the Prairie West* (Toronto: Macmillan, 1972); and Frank W. Anderson, *The Rum Runners*, Frontier Book No. 11 (Aldergrove: Frontier Publishing Ltd., 1972); Carrigan, *Crime, Punishment and Classification*.
60　The Annual Report of the SPP, Regina Division, 1918, 6.
61　The Annual Report of the APP, "A" Division, 1921, 20.
62　The Annual Report of the APP, "A" Division, 1931, 9.
63　The Annual Report of the APP, "A" Division, 1924, 9.
64　The Annual Report of the APP, "A" Division, 1918, 5; The Annual Report of the APP, "A" Division, 1922, 8; and the Annual Report of the SPP, Headquarters, 1920 (the report is unpaged); the case referred to here is "Rex vs. Olkhouck, Kamsack District" in the Regina Division.
65　The Annual Report of the APP, "B" Division, 1924, 9.
66　The Annual Report of the SPP, Prince Albert Division, 1923, 15.
67　The Annual Report of the APP, "A" Division, 1921, 4.
68　The Annual Report of the APP, "A" Division, 1924, 3.
69　The Annual Report of the APP, Headquarters, 1922, 60.
70　The Annual Report of the SPP, Prince Albert Division, 1926, 3; and The Annual report of the APP, "A" Division, 1922, 6 and 13.
71　The Annual Report of the APP, Headquarters, 1919, 14.
72　The Annual Report of the APP, "A" Division, 1926, 5.
73　The Annual Report of the SPP, Saskatoon Division, 1919, 16–17.
74　Ibid., 14–16.
75　The Annual Report of the APP, "B" Division, 1923, 43.
76　The Annual Report of the SPP, Weyburn Division, 1920, 7.
77　The Annual Report of the APP, "A" Division, 1918, 3.
78　Ibid., 7.
79　The Annual Report of the APP, "D" Division, 1920, 9–11.
80　The Annual Report of the APP, Headquarters, 1920, 86.
81　The Annual Report of the SPP, Regina Division, 1923, 17.
82　The Annual Report of the APP, "A" Division, 1921, 7.
83　The Annual Report of the SPP, Weyburn Division, 1922, 22.
84　Ibid., 22.
85　Ibid., 22.
86　The Annual Report of the APP, "A" Division, 1924, 48.
87　Ibid., 47.
88　Ibid., 47.
89　The Annual Report of the APP, "C" Division, 1918, 10; and The Annual Report of the APP, Headquarters, 1919, 33.

90 The Annual Report of the APP, "B" Division, 1924, 4.

91 The Annual Report of the APP, "E" Division, 1927, 16.

92 The Annual Report of the APP, Headquarters, 1926, 77; and The Annual Report of the APP, "D" Division, 1920, 18.

93 The Annual Report of the APP, Headquarters, 1921, 77.

94 W.B. Hurd, *Racial Origins and Nativity of the Canadian People, Seventh Census of Canada*, vol. 12 (Ottawa: King's Printer, 1942), 167.

95 The Annual Report of the APP, "A" Division, 1928, 30.

96 A. Brannigan and Zhiqiu Lin, "'Where East Meets West'," 89–107.

97 The time series data analyzed in this chapter covers the period 1906–1950 as regression analysis of time series requires a minimum of thirty time points.

NOTES TO CHAPTER 5

1 Jürgen Habermas, *Legitimation Crisis*, trans. Thomas McCarthy (Boston: Beacon Press, 1975).

2 The moral and social reform movement in the early twentieth century embodied Canada's "nation-building" process. Mariana Valverde, *The Age of Light, Soap, and Water* (Toronto: McClelland and Stewart, 1991), 14. The purpose of the movement was to preserve and enhance a certain type of human life rather than merely to punish and repress misconduct.

3 Macleod, *The North-West Mounted Police and Law Enforcement*.

4 Chris Stewart and Lynn Hudson, *Mahoney's Minute Men: Saga of the Saskatchewan Provincial Police 1917–1928* (Saskatoon: Modern Press, 1978).

5 Ibid.

6 Gray, *Booze*; and Frank W. Anderson, *The Rum Runners*, Frontier Book No. 11 (Aldergrove: Frontier Publishing Ltd., 1972).

7 Howard Palmer, *Patterns of Prejudice: A History of Nativism in Alberta* (Toronto: McClelland and Stewart, 1982).

8 Gray, *Booze*, 51.

9 Cited from Gray, *Booze*, 46.

10 Gray, *Booze*, 83.

11 Anderson, *The Rum Runners*.

12 World War I helped further the cause of "temperance" immeasurably. Michael Hayman observes that "The advocates of prohibition insisted that the use of the valuable materials in the manufacture of liquor constituted an economic waste the country could not afford. Drunkenness in the face of the need for full mobilization of the nation's manpower was, more than ever, a grievous sin. Sacrifice for the war effort was a slogan upon which prohibitionists could build." See Michael Hayman, "The Volstead Act as a Reflection of Canadian-American Relations," (M.A. thesis, Department of History, McGill University, 1971), 21.

13 The Alberta Liquor Act, S.A. 1916, c. 4; The Saskatchewan Temperance Act, S.S. 1917, c. 23.

14 Section 24 of the Alberta Liquor Act of 1916; and s. 78 of the Saskatchewan Temperance Act of 1917.

15 Section 24 of the Alberta Liquor Act of 1916; and s. 33 of the Saskatchewan Liquor Act of 1917.
16 The Annual Report of the APP, Headquarters, 1918, 21.
17 The Annual Report of the APP, "B" Division, 1918, 9.
18 The Annual Report of the APP, "E" Division, 1921, 29.
19 Sections 26–43 of the Saskatchewan Temperance Act, 1917.
20 Sections 44–46 of the Saskatchewan Temperance Act.
21 The Annual Report of the APP, "D" Division, 1918, 4.
22 The Annual Report of the SPP, Headquarter, 1920, 1.
23 The Annual Report of the APP, Liquor Branch, 1920, 10; and The Annual Report of the SPP, Detective Division, 1917, 3.
24 Report of the Royal Commission of Inquiry into Statements Made in Statutory Declarations and Other Matters, Saskatchewan Government, 1930, 75 (hereafter cited as Report of the Royal Commission, 1930).
25 The Annual Report of the APP, Headquarters, 1918, 21.
26 The Annual Report of the APP, Headquarters, 1921, 62.
27 Gray, *Booze*, 167.
28 The Annual Report of the APP, 1918, 23.
29 The Annual Report of the APP, Liquor Branch, 1920, 6.
30 The Annual Report of the APP, "D" Division, 1922, 18.
31 The Annual Report of the APP, Liquor Branch, 1920, 10.
32 The total expenses by the APP on the enforcement of the liquor law were $55,153.94. PAA, Accession No. 75.370/box, 72.270/56.
33 Stewart and Hudson, *Mahoney's Minute Men*; and Erhard Pinno, "Temperance and Prohibition in Saskatchewan" (Unpublished M.A. thesis, University of Saskatchewan at Regina, 1971).
34 The Annual Report of the SPP, Weyburn Division, 1920, 6.
35 The Annual Report of the APP, Liquor Branch, 1921, 8.
36 The record from the meeting of the Board of Commissioners, APP, on April 1, 1918, Accession no. 66.166, 1288.
37 The record from the meeting of the Board of Commissioners, APP, on May 13, 1918, Accession no. 66.166, 1288.
38 The Annual Report of the APP, Liquor Branch, 1924, 9.
39 The Annual Report of the APP, "C" Division, 1922, 43.
40 The Annual Report of the APP, Headquarters, 1922, 60.
41 Gray, *Booze*, 147.
42 The Annual Report of the APP, Liquor Branch, 1920, 12.
43 Sections 25, 26, the Alberta Liquor Act of 1916; and Section 80 of the Saskatchewan Temperance Act of 1917.
44 Proclamation and Orders of the Governor General in Council Having Force of Law, Statutes of Canada, 1918.
45 See Hayman, *The Volstead Act as a Reflection of Canadian-American Relations*, 24. At the same time, M. Hayman also discussed the profound effects of this change of Canadian legislation on the enforcement of the Volstead Act (1920–1933) in the United States. On January 29, 1919, the United States adopted the Eighteenth Amendment, which made

permanent its wartime legislation outlawing the manufacture, sale, and consumption of liquor. The American enforcement of the Volstead Act effectively stopped American liquor coming to Canada and to some extent, alleviated the SPP and APP's burden in their enforcement of the provincial liquor laws. However, Canada's abandonment of its federal legislation prohibiting the manufacture and sale of liquor in 1919 resulted in a large quantity of Canadian liquor flooding into the United States and created enormous difficulties for Volstead Act enforcement. Michael Hayman recounts that, with the sale of liquor now legal in Canada, thirsty Americans flocked first to Quebec and British Columbia, and then to other provinces. "American tourists entering Canada returned with large quantities of Canadian liquor. They hid this liquor in every receptacle at their disposal, from oversized clothing to egg shells, hot water bottles and baby carriages. They drove cars, boats and airplanes, laden with liquor, across the border." At the same time, a substantial volume of liquor was sent to the United States by "a highly-organised, well-financed, efficient, professional smuggling operation. Canada's distilleries and breweries were eager to exchange their beer and whisky for American money and they capitalised almost immediately on the new opportunities for expansion. They began constructing additional distilleries" (ibid., 26–27). This is the reason why Canadian liquor flowing into the United States was a major issue in Canadian-American relations in the 1920s.

46   S.C. 1919, c. 8.
47   S.A. 1920, c. 7, s. 3.
48   The Annual Report of the APP, Liquor Branch, 1920, 2.
49   S.C. 1922, c. 11.
50   The Annual Report of the APP, Liquor Branch, 1922, 3.
51   Ibid., 4.
52   The Annual Report of the APP, Liquor Branch, 1924, 3.
53   The Annual Report of the APP, Liquor Branch, 1921, 4.
54   John H. Archer also suggests the existence of overlapping jurisdiction between the provincial police and the RNWMP in enforcing liquor laws. *Saskatchewan: A History*, 199.
55   The Annual Report of the APP, Liquor Branch, 1924, 3.
56   The Annual Report of the APP, Liquor Branch, 1921, 14.
57   The Annual Report of the APP, Headquarters, 1919, 15.
58   Pinno suggested that "the Temperance Act of Saskatchewan did not permit veterinarians to keep liquor in their possession for use in their practice. However, the veterinarians felt that they should have the same right as doctors in prescribing alcoholic stimulants for their patients. In 1922 an order-in-council was issued to allow them to keep liquor in their offices." "Temperance and Prohibition in Saskatchewan," 196.
59   The Annual Report of the APP, Liquor Branch, 1920, 5.
60   S.A. 1919, c. 4.
61   S.A. 1921, c. 6.
62   The Annual Report of the APP, Liquor Branch, 1922, 8.
63   The Annual Report of the APP, Liquor Branch, 1920, 1921, 1922, and 1924.
64   The Annual Report of the APP, "A" Division, 1918, 3.
65   The Annual Report of the APP, "C" Division C, 1920, 29.
66   The Annual Report of the APP, "A" Division, 1918, 3.
67   S.A. 1919, c. 4.
68   S.A. 1922, c. 5. According to the Alberta Liquor Act of 1916, a penalty for the first offence was $200. There was no provision for the second offence. According to the 1922

amendment to the Liquor Act, a convicted druggist could face a penalty between $200 and $1,000. For the second offence, the penalty was imprisonment with hard labour for a period of between three and six months, without the option of a fine.

69 S.S. 1920, c. 70.
70 The Annual Report of the APP, Liquor Branch, 1924, 6.
71 The Annual Report of the APP, "C" Division, 1921, 28.
72 The Annual Report of the APP, "B" Division, 1920, the last page of the report. The report is not numbered.
73 The Annual Report of the APP, "C" Division, 1921, 28.
74 The Annual Report of the APP, Liquor Branch, 1921, 10.
75 The Annual Report of the APP, Liquor Branch, 1920, 1.
76 The Annual Report of the APP, Liquor Branch, 1921, 9.
77 Ibid., 10.
78 The Annual Report of the APP, "D" Division, 1924, 13.

NOTES TO CONCLUSION

1 *The Edmonton Journal*, March 31, 1931.
2 The Annual Report of the RCMP, September 30, 1928, 7.
3 *The Lethbridge Herald*, February 1, 1923.
4 *The Regina Leader*, October 19, 1927, 4.
5 Ibid.
6 Ibid.
7 *The Edmonton Journal*, December 9, 1927.
8 The Annual Report of the RCMP, September 30, 1928, 7.
9 *The Public Service Monthly*, June, 1928, 7.
10 *The Calgary Herald*, October 19, 1928.
11 Smith, *Prairie Liberalism*; and Archer, *Saskatchewan: A History*.
12 Archer, *Saskatchewan: A History*, 199.
13 Province of Saskatchewan, *A Submission by the Government of Saskatchewan to the Royal Commission On Dominion-Provincial Relations*, 1937; and W.A. Mackintosh, *Economic Problems of the Prairie Provinces* (Toronto: Macmillan Company of Canada, Ltd., 1935).
14 The Annual Report of the SPP, Headquarters, 1927, 1.
15 *The Calgary Herald*, February 6, 1928.
16 *The Calgary Herald*, March 17, 1928.
17 *The Edmonton Journal*, February 28, 1930.
18 *The Calgary Herald*, February 7, 1929.
19 The Annual Report of the APP, Headquarters, 1929, 16; and *The Calgary Herald*, March 4, 1930.
20 *The Edmonton Journal*, February 28, 1930.
21 Ibid.

22   *The Calgary Herald*, March 4, 1930.

23   The provincial government of Alberta published by order of the executive council, *The Case of Alberta*, addressed to the Sovereign People of Canada and their Government (1938), 346.

24   Circular Memorandum No. A/10/1931, April 21, 1931, PAA, Accession No. 66.1296.

25   Ibid.

26   "The Agreement with Saskatchewan," in the Annual Report of the RCMP, Headquarters, 1928; and "Certified to be a True Copy of a Minute of a Meeting of the Committee of the Privy Council, approved by His Excellency the Governor General on the 3rd February, 1932," in the Annual Report of the RCMP, Headquarters, 1932 (hereafter referred as to "The Agreement with Saskatchewan").

27   The Agreement with Saskatchewan, section 7, in the Report of the RCMP, 1928, 7; and The Agreement with Alberta, section 2, in the Report of the RCMP, 1932, 171.

28   Unlike in Saskatchewan, the agreement allowed Alberta to pay a fixed sum of $50,000 per year for the RCMP to administer prisoners in Alberta. This was a more attractive deal compared to annual expenses paid by the government of Saskatchewan on this item. This was because the payments from Saskatchewan before 1932 were never below $300,000 annually. However, the Saskatchewan agreement on this matter was changed on September 26, 1933, at which time Saskatchewan had the same deal as Alberta on payment of maintaining and transporting prisoners. The Report of the RCMP, Headquarters, 1934, 7.

Expenditure by the Government of Saskatchewan on Transportation and Maintenance of Prisoners:

1926 $327,836.00

1931 $309,588.76

1932 $308,025.55

Source: Provincial Government, A Submission by the Government of Saskatchewan to the Royal Commission on Dominion-Provincial Relations, 1937.

29   Section 9, the Agreement between the Government of the Dominion of Canada and The Government of the Province of Alberta for policing the province, S.A. 1932, c. 13.

30   *The Edmonton Journal*, March 5, 1932.

31   The Annual Report of the SPP, Headquarters, 1927, 16.

32   S.A. 1932, c. 15.

33   The Agreement with Alberta, section 15.

34   *The Regina Leader*, April 14, 1928.

35   *The Edmonton Journal*, March 5, 1932.

36   A Certain Agreement between the Government of the Dominion of Canada and the Province of Saskatchewan, S.S. 1931, c. 86, Schedule and the letter of the Assistant Commissioner of the SPP to the Attorney General of Saskatchewan, T.C. Davis, April 30, 1928. Commissioner's File, PAS, R-997, E3-13.

37   Commissioner's file, PAS, R-997, E3-13.

38   Osipoff, "The S.P.P. 1910–1928," 5–11.

39   Letters to the Attorney General, October 1, 1931 and December 1, 1931, Commissioner's file, PAA, Accession No. 66.166, 1400.

40   The Annual Report of the APP, Headquarters, 1931.

41   Section 14, the Agreement with Alberta.

42   A letter to J.G. Gardiner, Premier of Saskatchewan, from Saskatchewan Retail Merchants' Association, October 17, 1927 in the Commissioner's file, PAS, R-997, E2-13.
43   Letter to J.G. Gardiner, Premier of Saskatchewan, from Kindersley Liberal Association, ibid.
44   Osipoff, "The S.P.P. 1910–1928."
45   *The Regina Leader*, June 1928, 2.
46   *The Public Service Monthly*, June 1928, 8.
47   *The Albertan*, March 28, 1932.
48   *The Edmonton Bulletin*, March 26, 1932.
49   *The Albertan*, March 28, 1932.
50   *The Edmonton Journal*, March 31, 1932.
51   *The Edmonton Bulletin*, March 26, 1932, 9.
52   *The Albertan*, April 1, 1932.
53   Ibid.
54   *The Edmonton Journal*, March 31, 1932.
55   Ibid.
56   In 1932, the RCMP also took over the policing of Manitoba, Nova Scotia, and New Brunswick, in addition to Alberta and Saskatchewan.
57   See George Smith, "The Early Police of Manitoba" (unpublished paper, Historical Society of Manitoba, March 11, 1947).
58   Reports of the RCMP, Headquarters, 1917 and 1920.
59   Section 12, Subsection 3, The RCMP Act in the Report of RCMP, 1920, 7.
60   Ibid.
61   Peter C. Newman, "Inside the RCMP: The Conscience of a Good Cop," *Maclean's* (July 1972), 1.
62   Lorne Brown and Caroline Brown, *An Unauthorized History of the RCMP* (Toronto: J. Lorimer, 1978).
63   In recent years, the creation of a new provincial police force in Alberta has been suggested as part of a larger political "firewall" strategy. Certainly, the implications of previous provincial police forces in the two provinces should be taken into consideration in the current debates on the pros and cons of having once again such a provincial police force. Our examination of the development of the two provincial police forces and their activities leads us to conclude that compared with the federal police, the provincial forces were more likely to be influenced by provincial governments and politics; the provincial statutes, including the controversial prohibition laws, received greater priority. Furthermore, differences in the organizational structures in the two provinces provided less of a check on political interference in Saskatchewan than Alberta, although, in the end, it was provincial finances as opposed to provincial politics that ended the colourful histories of these two organizations. Although the provincial police forces made their best effort to heroically maintain law and order for more than a decade in the provinces, neither force achieved a very memorable legacy. During the life of the provincial police forces, several crises eroded the legacy of the forces. During the prohibition movement, because the liquor prohibition laws had no moral authority, a large segment of the population defied the laws. Police enforcement of the law resulted in a legitimation crisis in public confidence in the impartiality and effectiveness of the law. As a result, the population seems to have forgotten the existence of the forces as soon as they were dissolved. For the recent discussions on the creation of a new provincial police force in Alberta as part of a larger political "firewall" strategy, see Barry Cooper and Royce Koop, "Policing

Alberta: An Analysis of the Alternatives to the Federal Provision of Police Services," in *Public Policy Sources*, no. 72 (November 2003): 3–18 (A Fraser Institute Occasional Paper).

NOTES TO APPENDICES

1   C.W. Granger and P. Newbold, *Forecasting Economic Time Series* (New York: Academic Press, 1977).

2   Ibid.

3   It is often called "weakly stationary." According to Mills, a process is called "strictly stationary" if its properties (such as mean and variance) are unaffected by a change in the time origin of the series. Terence C. Mills, *Time Series Techniques for Economists* (Cambridge: Cambridge University Press, 1990), 64.

4   Informally, a series is said to be integrated if it accumulated some past effects. Such a series is non-stationary because its future path depends upon all such past influences and is not tied to some mean to which it must eventually return. Anindya Banerjee, Juan Dolado, J.W. Galbreaith, and D.F. Hendry, *Co-integration, Error-Correction, and the Econometric Analysis of Non-Stationary Data* (New York: Oxford University Press. 1993), 136.

5   K. Cuthbertson, S.G. Hall, and M.P. Taylor, *Applied Econometric Techniques* (New York: Philip Allan, 1991), 133.

6   R. Engle and C.W. Granger, eds., *Long-Run Economic Relationships: Readings in Co-integration* (New York: Oxford University Press, 1991); D.F. Hendry, "Econometric Modelling with Co-integrated Variables: An Overview," *Oxford Bulletin of Economics and Statistics* 48 (1986): 201–12.

7   This is because of the relative size of the variances associated with y_t and x_t.

8   Engle and Granger, eds., *Long-Run Economic Relationships*.

9   Ibid.

10 R. Engle and C.W. Granger, "Co-integration and Error Correction: Representation, Estimation, and Testing," *Econometrica* 55, no. 2 (March 1987): 251–76.

11 Ibid.

12 This representation is derived from the simple equation as follows: $y_t = \beta_0 + \beta_1 x_t + \beta_2 x_{t-1} + \beta_3 y_{t-1} + e_t$. By subtracting y_{t-1} from both side of the equation, we have:

$$y_t - y_{t-1} = \beta_0 + \beta_1 x_t + \beta_2 x_{t-1} + \beta_3 y_{t-1} - y_{t-1} + e_t$$
$$y_t = \beta_0 + \beta_1 x_t + \beta_2 x_{t-1} + (\beta_3 - 1) y_{t-1} + e_t$$

Then, by adding and subtracting $\beta_1 x_{t-1}$ on the right side of the equation, we have the following:

$$\Delta y_t = \beta_0 + \beta_1 x_t - \beta_1 x_{t-1} + \beta_1 x_{t-1} + \beta_2 x_{t-1} + (\beta_3 - 1) y_{t-1} + e_t$$
$$\Delta y_t = \beta_0 + \beta_1 (\Delta x_{t-1}) + \beta_1 x_{t-1} + \beta_2 x_{t-1} + (\beta_3 - 1) y_{t-1} + e_t$$

Finally, by adding and subtracting $(\beta_3 - 1) x_{t-1}$ on the right side of the equation, we have:

$$\Delta y_t = \beta_0 + \beta_1 \Delta x_{t-1} + \beta_1 x_{t-1} + \beta_2 x_{t-1} + (\beta_3 - 1) y_{t-1} - (\beta_3 - 1) x_{t-1} + (\beta_3 - 1) x_{t-1} + e_t$$
$$\Delta y_t = \beta_0 + \beta_1 \Delta x_{t-1} + \beta_1 x_{t-1} + \beta_2 x_{t-1} + (\beta_3 - 1)(y_{t-1} - x_{t-1}) + (\beta_3 - 1) x_{t-1} + e_t$$
$$\Delta y_t = \beta_0 + \beta_1 \Delta x_{t-1} + (\beta_3 - 1)(y_{t-1} - x_{t-1}) + \beta_1 x_{t-1} + \beta_2 x_{t-1} + \beta_3 x_{t-1} - x_{t-1} + e_t$$

By setting $y_t = y_{t-1}$ and $x_t = x_{t-1}$ to solve for the long-run relationship, this requires that $\beta_1 + \beta_2 + \beta_3 = 1$. Therefore, we have:

$$\Delta y_t = \beta_0 + \beta_1 \Delta x_{t-1} + (\beta_3 - 1)(y_{t-1} - x_{t-1}) + x_{t-1} - x_{t-1} + e_t$$
$$\Delta y_t = \beta_0 + \beta_1 \Delta x_{t-1} + (\beta_3 - 1)(y_{t-1} - x_{t-1}) + e_t$$

This is the Granger Error-Correction Representation for a specific case. $-\tau Z_{t-1} = (\beta_3 - 1)(y_{t-1} - x_{t-1})$ is the error-correction mechanism. Such a derivation of error-correction mechanism allows us to see essential characteristics of the error-correction model.

13. Banerjee, Dolado, Galbreaith, and Hendry, *Co-integration, Error-Correction, and the Econometric Analysis*, 50.
14. A unit root refers to the statistically significant trend component in residual process.
15. J. Cromwell, M.J. Hannan, M. Labys, and M. Terraza, *Multivariate Tests for Time series Models* (London: Sage, 1994), 14.
16. Ibid., 87.
17. James Mackinnon, "Critical Values for Co-integration Tests," in *Long-Run Economic Relationships: Readings in Co-integration*, ed. R. Engle and C.W. Granger (New York: Oxford University Press Mackinnon, 1991).
18. Ibid.
19. R. Engle and B.S. Yoo, "Forecasting and Testing in Co-integrated Systems," *Journal of Econometrics* 35 (1987): 143–59; and Mackinnon, "Critical Values for Co-integration Tests."
20. J.D. Sargan and A. Bhargava, "Testing Residuals from Least Squares Regression for Being Generated by the Gaussian Random Walk," *Econometrica* 51 (1983): 153–74.
21. Mackinnon, "Critical Values for Co-integration Tests."
22. Engle and Yoo, "Forecasting and Testing in Co-integrated Systems."
23. R.S Pindyck and D.L. Rubinfeld, *Econometric Models and Economic Forecasts* (New York: McGraw-Hill, 1991).
24. Mills, *Time Series Techniques for Economists*, 272.
25. Engle and Granger, "Co-integration and Error Correction."
26. Hirotugu Akaike, "A New Look at the Statistical Model Identification," *IEEE Transactions on Automatic Control*, AC-19, no. 6 (December 1974).
27. D. Dickey and W. Fuller, "Distribution of Estimators for Autoregressive Time Series with a Unit Root," *Journal of the American Statistical Association* 74 (1979): 1057–72.
28. Mackinnon, "Critical Values for Co-integration Tests."
29. Ibid.
30. Engle and Yoo, "Forecasting and Testing in Co-integrated Systems."
31. Dickey and Fuller, "Distribution of Estimators for Autoregressive Time Series with a Unit Root."

INDEX

A

Act Respecting the Sale of Intoxicating Liquor, 121
Act to Prevent the Sales of Liquor for Export, 132
Alberta Act, 27
Alberta Liquor Act, 73, 124, 125, 127–31, 136–39, 140
Alberta Liquor Export Act, 132, 133
Alberta Municipal Districts Act, 30
Alberta Police Act, 30, 48–50, 53
Alberta Provincial Police (APP), 2, 29. See also police; provincial police
  absorption into RCMP, 154–57, 164
  Board of Commissioners, 47, 48–50, 98, 129
  creation of, 42, 44, 47, 48
  Criminal Investigation Branch, 57, 95, 149
  duties of, 53–54
  Identification Branch, 57
  influence of RNWMP on, 47, 52–55, 64, 166
  legacy of, 160–61
  pensions, 155
  and politics, 59–63, 64–65, 149
  uniforms, 52–53
Alberta Provincial Police Pension Fund Liquidation Act, 155
Andrew, Alberta, 88
arms, 52
arrest rates. See crime rates
assimilation, 33, 55, 84, 88, 97–99, 119. See also Canadianization; immigrants

B

Baily, F.W.E., 161
Baker, Perren, 150
Banff Springs Hotel, 30
bank robbery. See property crime
Bavin, E.W., 94
Bellevue, Alberta, 105
Boer War, 52, 163
Bolshevik Revolution, 93
Bolter, A.J., 95
bootlegging, 123–24, 125–31, 132–35, 140–43, 144, 159. See also liquor laws
  by doctors, 136–39
Borden, Sir Robert L, 40
Brankley, W., 90–91, 96

Brewster Transportation Company, 30

British Columbia Provincial Police, 57

British Imperial Army, 7

British North America (BNA) Act, 1, 26, 27

Browning, Arthur George, 48

Brownlee, J.E., 146, 151

Bryan, Willoughby Charles, 88, 92, 95, 102–3, 109, 151

C

Calgary, Alberta, 48, 90, 91, 93, 95, 96, 127, 128, 137–38, 149, 160

Calgary City Police, 129

Canada Temperance Act, 132, 133

Canadianization, 85, 88. *See also* assimilation

Canadian National (CN) Train, 106

Canadian Pacific Railway, 29, 41, 105–6

car theft. *See* property crime

Chipman, Alberta, 107

class control, 6, 14

    shift to crime control, 12–17, 21, 83–84, 166, 167

colonial police, 9–10

Communist Party of Canada, 93–96, 117

consensus. *See* legitimation

Conservative Party, 150

Constables Act of Alberta, 29

Constables Act of Saskatchewan, 28–29

County and Borough Police Act, 26

crime, 8

crime control, 14–17, 19, 31, 55

    shift from class control, 12–17, 21, 83–84, 166, 167

crime rates, 18–20, 67–68, 69–70

    and immigrants, 89

    influence of police on, 18–20, 22, 80–81, 166

    serious crime, 108–9

    shift from public order to serious crime offences, 71–84

Criminal Code of Canada, 26, 28, 33, 34, 57, 67–69, 71, 75, 77, 79, 90, 92, 100, 117–18, 145, 152

Cross, James, 59–61, 146, 147, 148, 155

Crow's Nest Pass, 56, 102, 105–6, 127, 161

D

dangerous classes, 68, 75, 85, 116, 117, 167. *See also* class control; immigrants

Department of Neglected Children, 151

domestic violence, 100–102

Dominion Police, 26

Drumheller, Alberta, 90, 92, 94, 96

Duggan, D.W., 150

Dunning, Charles A., 59

E

Edmonton, Alberta, 48, 88, 89, 92, 95, 101, 102, 103, 108, 125, 128, 149, 160

Ewing, A.E., 50
Executive Council of Alberta, 42, 47
Executive Council of Saskatchewan, 42

F

Fawcett, John L., 42

G

Gardiner, James G., 62, 146, 147
Gold Seal Liquor Co., 132–33
Goldsmith, T.C., 156
Grand Prairie, Alberta, 100
Great Depression, 147–48, 150, 163

H

Hancock, W.F.W, 156–57, 162
homicide, 102–3
horse stealing. *See* property crime
Hudson Bay Company, 163
Hughes, John, 41

I

immigrants, 31–33, 44, 52, 68, 84, 85, 86–89, 90, 100–114, 119, 165. *See also* assimilation; Canadianization
and crime rates, 89
and liquor, 120
and public order offences, 89, 115–18
and serious crime offences, 89, 100–114, 115–18

Indian Act, 33, 145
Inland Revenue Act, 134–35, 145, 154
Irish Constabulary (IC), 4–11, 47, 51, 56, 58
comparison with the London Metropolitan Police, 7–11
duties of, 7
and politics, 7–9, 16

K

Kelly, J., 156
Kemmis, J.W.S, 50

L

labour disputes, 90–94, 97
Lake Louise Hotel, 30
Laurier, Sir Wilfrid, 27–28, 32, 86
Lawson, S., 161
legitimation, 3, 8, 17, 21–22, 51, 58, 99
legitimation crisis, 119, 140–43, 144, 145
Lethbridge, Alberta, 94, 100, 102, 106, 109, 121
Liberal Party, 59–62, 147
Liquor Branch (LB), 57, 127–29
Liquor Commission (LC), 127–28, 130
liquor law, 97, 107–8, 152. *See also* Act Respecting the Sale of Intoxicating Liquor; Act to Prevent the Sales of Liquor for Export; Alberta Liquor Act; Alberta Liquor Export Act; Canada Temperance Act; Inland Revenue Act; Liquor Licence Act; Saskatchewan Liquor Licence

Act; Saskatchewan Temperance
Act; War Measures Act

enforcement of, 16–17, 31–32, 35, 72–73, 75–77, 119–22, 125–31, 132–35, 136–39, 140–43, 144, 145, 159, 161, 163, 165

and police corruption, 126–27

and public attitudes, 140–43, 144, 145

punishment of violations of, 123–24

and World War I, 120–21

Liquor Licence Act, 29

Liquor Licence Board of Saskatchewan, 120

London Metropolitan Police (LMP), 4, 6–11, 53

comparison with the Irish Constabulary, 7–11

and politics, 7–9, 16

Lymburn, J.F., 156

M

Macdonald, Sir John A., 1, 26, 47, 86

Macleod Town Police, 43

Mahoney, Charles Augustus, 50, 60–61, 89, 125, 156, 159

Manchester, England, 15

Manitoba Constables Act, 29

Manitoba Provincial Police, 156

Martin, H.J., 156

Martin, W.M., 59, 61–62

McDonald, Lewis, 93–94

McDonnel, Edward Grobst, 49–50, 90

Mounted Police Act, 27

N

New York City Police Force, 47

Nicholson, A.S., 49

Nicholson, John Daniel, 49

North Battleford, Saskatchewan, 106

North-West Mounted Police (NWMP), 1, 6, 22, 25, 54. *See also* Royal North-West Mounted Police (RNWMP)

and class control, 13–14

creation of, 26–27, 163–64

enforcement of liquor law by, 16–17, 35, 119

and politics, 16

and symbolism, 163–64

North-West Territories, 27, 31, 86, 89, 120

North-West Territories Act, 26–27

O

One Big Union, 90

Osgood, G.E., 161

Ottawa, Ontario, 146, 152

P

Peace River, Alberta, 50, 124

Peel, Robert, 6, 9

Perry, A. Bowen, 27–28, 31–32, 35–41, 43

Piper, J.S., 89

police. *See also* provincial police

creation of, 4–6, 162–63

and crime rates, 18–20, 22, 80–81, 166

duties of, 12, 34

officer requirements, 52

and politics, 8–9, 15–16, 23, 48–50, 58–65

Police Act of Canada, 26

police forces. See Alberta Provincial Police (APP); British Columbia Provincial Police; Calgary City Police; Irish Constabulary (IC); London Metropolitan Police (LMP); Macleod Town Police; Manitoba Provincial Police; New York City Police Force; North-West Mounted Police (NWMP); Prince Albert City Police; Royal Canadian Mounted Police (RCMP); Royal North-West Mounted Police (RNWMP); Saskatchewan Provincial Police (SPP); Winnipeg Police

Primrose, Philip Carteret Hill, 48

Prince Albert City Police, 156

Prince Albert, Saskatchewan, 102, 107

professionalization, 3, 9–11, 14–15, 17, 21–23, 25, 44, 57, 64, 83, 166–68

prohibition, 16, 31, 35–37, 44, 89, 101, 120–21, 163, 165

end of, 138

prohibition law. See liquor law

property crime, 103–9

provincial police, 2, 25, 164. See also Alberta Provincial Police (APP); British Columbia Provincial Police; Manitoba Provincial Police; police; Saskatchewan Provincial Police (SPP)

corruption of, 126–27

creation of, 26–30, 35, 42, 44, 166

duties of, 43, 54–55, 97–99

strength in the provinces, 51, 53, 67, 70–71

surveillance activities of, 89, 117

transition to RCMP, 70–71, 75, 79, 83, 145–51, 152–53, 154–55, 156–57, 160, 162–65, 166–67

public order offences. See class control; crime rates

R

Railway Act, 29, 33

Red Deer, Alberta, 123–24, 140, 149

Red Deer Valley Miners Union, 92

Regina, Saskatchewan, 101, 106, 107

Registrars of Alien Enemies, 38

Regulations of the Provincial Police, 58

Riel Rebellion, 5

Royal Canadian Mounted Police (RCMP), 1, 2, 22, 23, 71

absorption of APP and SPP, 154–57, 162, 164

enforcement of the Criminal Code by, 79

enforcement of liquor law by, 135, 152

strength in the provinces, 154

and symbolism, 163–64

transition from the provincial police, 145–51, 152–53, 160, 162–65

Royal Canadian Mounted Police Act, 152

Royal Commission Inquiry (1930), 60–61, 64, 147, 159

Royal Irish Constabulary. *See* Irish Constabulary

Royal North-West Mounted Police (RNWMP), 2, 23, 25, 27–29, 33, 40–41, 58, 71. *See also* North-West Mounted Police (NWMP); Royal Canadian Mounted Police (RCMP)
- duties of, 34, 43, 55, 99
- enforcement of liquor law by, 31–33, 35–36, 120, 121–22
- enforcement of the Criminal Code by, 71
- influence on provincial police, 47, 50, 52–55, 56, 64
- and internal security, 38, 44, 55
- and politics, 34
- renamed RCMP, 164
- strength in the provinces, 39–41, 67
- use of districts by, 51
- withdrawal from the provinces, 28, 35, 37, 41, 42–43, 44, 50, 53, 160

Royal North-West Mounted Police Act, 164

rum-running. *See* bootlegging

Ryan, Dennis, 30

S

Sanders, Gilbert E., 48, 160

San Franciso, California, 6

Saskatchewan Act, 27

Saskatchewan City Act, 30

Saskatchewan Legislative Assembly, 35

Saskatchewan Liquor License Act, 36, 120

Saskatchewan Police Act, 53

Saskatchewan Provincial Police (SPP), 2, 29. *See also* police; provincial police
- absorption into RCMP, 154–57, 164
- creation of, 42, 44
- influence of RNWMP on, 50, 52–55, 64, 166
- legacy of, 156–57
- pensions, 155
- and politics, 59–62, 64–65, 159, 166

Saskatchewan Secret Service, 29, 42, 59, 61
- creation of, 35–36
- enforcement of liquor law by, 29, 35–37, 122

Saskatchewan Temperance Act, 73, 125, 127–28, 130–31, 136–39

Saskatoon, Saskatchewan, 98, 103

School Attendance Act, 97–98

Schurer, A.H., 49

Scott Act of Canada, 120

Scottish Poor Law, 5

Scott, Walter, 59, 61

Sentinel, Alberta, 105

settlers. *See* immigrants

Sifton, Clifford, 86

Spanish influenza epidemic, 98

social control, 55. *See also* class control

social gospel movement, 89

Staines, C.C, 147

strikes. *See* labour disputes

T

T. Eaton Co., 156
Tait, R.R., 156
Taylor, J., 156
Temperance. *See* prohibition
Temperance and Moral Reform Society of Alberta, 120
Toronto, Ontario, 6, 14–15, 64
Total Abstinence League of Saskatchewan, 120
Tracey, William Robert, 50, 156
transportation, 56, 129
Truancy Act, 97–98
Turgeon, W.F.A, 59–60

U

unemployment, 94–96, 109, 117
uniforms, 7, 21, 49, 52–53
Union Bank, 107
United Farmers of Alberta, 62, 121
University of Alberta, 57
University of California, 57
urbanization, 19–20, 162

V

vagrancy laws
　enforcement of, 94–95, 97, 108, 117
Vulcan, Alberta, 59

W

War Measures Act, 132, 134
watch and constable system, 4, 11, 18
weapons, 52
Weyburn, Saskatchewan, 59, 97–98, 104, 107–8, 128–29
Winnipeg Police, 50
women's rights movement, 89
World War I, 33, 41, 98, 145, 163
　impact on crime, 108–9
　and liquor law, 120–21
　as reason for the withdrawal of the RNWMP, 35, 37–38, 44
Wroughton, T.A., 38
Wuppertal, Germany, 15

INDEX | 233